Library of Congress Cataloging-in-Publication Data

Elhammoumi, Mohamed
ocio-historicocultural psychology : Lev Semenovich Vygotsky, 1896-
1934 : Bibliographical notes / Mohamed Elhammoumi.
p.   cm.
Includes bibliographical references and index.
1. Vygotskii, L.S. (Lev Semenovich), 1896-1934-- Bibliography. 2.
Psychology---Soviet Union--History--Bibliography. I. Title.
Z8946.82.V94E44   1997 016.15'0947--dc21   96-49101 CIP
(BF109.V95)

ISBN 0-7618-0648-2 (cloth: alk. ppr.)

SOCIO-HISTORICOC
PSYCHOLOG

Lev Semenovich Vygo.
(1896-1934)

Bibliographical Notes

Mohamed Elhammoumi

University Press of America, Inc.
Lanham • New York • London

This book is dedicated to
my mother Myriam
and
Adam and Cheryl
With deep appreciation for their support during
critical periods of development. This project could not have
been completed without each of them.

Contents

"When I remarked a quarter century ago that Vygotsky's view of development was also a theory of education, I did not realize the half of it. In fact, his educational theory is a theory of cultural transmission as well as a theory of development. For "education" implies for Vygotsky not only the improvement of the individual's potential, but the historical expression and growth of the human culture from which Man springs" (J. Bruner, 1987, p.1-2).

Introduction

The Russian polymath Lev Vygotsky (1896-1934), one of the pioneers of Marxist psychology, was also a philosopher, literary critic and sociologist. He was a prolific thinker, a bibliography compiled towards the end of his life listed more than 296 titles (according to Van Der Veer & Valsiner, 1992), notably of psychological, educational, linguistical and epistemological works which reached a wide public of psychology, education and linguistics. Social scientists are attracted by the logic of his theory, the clarity of his ideas and his methodological approach. Vygotsky seeks to elucidate the laws governing the formation and the development of human higher mental functions. In face of the dangers presented by the rise of irrationality and pragmatism, he proposed as a route to civilized society the creation of a new educational model that elevate the consciousness of the masses, instruct them and having them participate in the construction of Soviet society, in the advance of culture, science and art, in short, in the construction of Soviet civilization.

In recent years there has been a growing interest in the paradigm of sociohistorical approach to mediated action, which derived from the work of philosophers, sociologists and anthropologists like Karl Marx, Frederick Engels, Emile Durkhein, Lévy-Bruhl. The view of Karl Marx, and Frederick Engels, in particular, has been most influential in shaping the Soviet school of sociohistorical approach to mediated action.

During the past two decades, developmental, educational and cognitive psychologists in the United States, as well as in other nations of the world (Elhammoumi, 1994) have turned their attention in growing numbers to the relationship between cognition and culture. Psychologists worldwide have begun to focus on a better understanding of the conceptions of the Soviet school of sociohistorical approach to higher mental functions. The socio-historical research program has helped psychologists to understand the role of variable such as culture, social, history, signs, tools and social institutions on coconstruction of cognition and culture.

Sociohistorical approach to mind is an interdisciplinary theory dedicated to promoting a philosohpy of dialectical historical materialism that stresses the material basis of reality and cognition are constantly changing in a dialectical process.

Intellectual roots of Vygotsky's thought

Vygotsky's training in the social sciences was from Marx-Engels writings, German philosophy and French sociology. The impact of

Marx-Engels is particularly powerful: concepts like 'mediated action', 'historical evolution', 'cultural development', 'speech', 'language', 'activity', 'individual decisions', 'labor', 'tools', 'sign and symbol', 'consciousness', 'intelligence', 'social cooperation', 'struggle at the scientific front', 'freeing of the hands', 'phylogeny', 'ontogeny', 'unit of analysis', and 'dialectic' preponderate Vygotsky's thought processes. Since the psychological thought of Vygotsky is so deeply Marxist-dialectical in its foundation and its conceptions, the allusions to Marxism philosophy forms an important apparatus. Marx's work, is notorious for two things. Firstly, its erudition, Marx's writings provide psychologists and social scientists with a detailed comparative analyses of every kind of social structure mankind has experienced. Secondly, its methodological approach, Marx analyzes a "single living "cell" of capitalist society-for example, the nature of value. Within this cell he discovers the structure of the entire system and all of its economic institutions." (1978, p.8).

Thought in action

The young Vygotsky was deeply involved in the process of social change that shaked the foundations of social structure of Russian society in the beginning of this century. He combines his theoretical thought processes with revolutionary practice, consistently pursue and develop the principle of Soviet psychology, implement the principle of commitment to Marxism theory and metatheory, and procced from the principles of dialectical-historical materialist philosophy. Accordingly, Vygotsky, as a great figure of Soviet psychology, was in the Stalinist psychologists view, a defender of bourgeois psychology, classical idealism and the charges of betrayl Soviet political, economical and social organization. Vygotsky was an ardent defender of the ideal of Russian revolution. He was a lifelong opponent of bigotry, dogmatism and irrationalism that haunted Soviet society after Lenin's death. Vygotsky the Titan of 20th century Marxist psychology, never ceased to fight against the degradation of Marxism-Leninism thought, evolutionist determinism which descended from the Second International, and mechanistic approach of thinking. He defended the intellectual values of communism thretened by the rise of Stalinism philosophy. He was firmly convinced that the rise of irrationality and dogmatism in a Russia delivred to Stalinism philosophy is a disaster of immense proportions. Readers of Vygotsky's writings may find some of the ideas he puts forward are still strikingly topical.

Classical philosophy and the crisis of psychology

Vygotsky did not need to read classical German philosophy (i.e. the idealist tradition from Kant to Hegel), because he had already understood classical German philosophy, having closely read and understood the whole of Marx's theory and methodology.

In the 1920s the theoretical crisis of psychology involves a recognition of the need to break with elements of the classical tradition of competing schools in order to develop and elaborate theory that meets the needs of the new Soviet society. Vygotsky lived with a deep conflict, torn between classical psychology, mechanical materialist psychology, and the quest for a new psychology based on the revolutionary idealism of the Russian revolution. He found in marxism the solution to this conflict. For Vygotsky, the core of Marx's thought is his view of history and his analysis of social consciousness. In this respect, Vygotsky placed a high premium on the origin and the real life-functions of consciousness. For the first time in Marxist philosophy consciousness is treated as something subjective, progressively formed, and culturally bounded rather than determined mechanically by objective economic existence. In this connection Vygotsky wrote: "I don't want to discover the nature of mind by patching together a lot of quotations. I want [...] to approach the study of the mind having learned the whole of Marx's method. .... The whole of Capital is written according to the following method: Marx analyzes a single living "cell" of capitalist society-for example, the nature of value. Within this cell he discovers the structure of the entire system and all of its economic institutions. .. Anyone who could discover what a "psychological" cell is-the mechanism producing even a single response-would thereby find the key to psychology as a whole." (1978, p.8).

Vygotsky and the zeitgeist of the 1920s

Why do theories advanced so long ago in developmental psychology continue to have such powerful force and influence? No current theoretical approach has been offered as an alternative to the Piagetian and the Vygotskian research programs. These two paradigms were conceptualized during the course of the 1920s and 1930s in intense theoretical, methodological and philosophical conflict within Western psychology as well as Soviet psychology. During the 1920s and 1930s, there was a worldwide concern and interest in child development and education. Liberal progressive pedagogy was institutionalized in the public school system in Britain guided by the activities of the New

Education Fellowship Group (NEF). Vienna after World War I emerged as a mecca of psychology (K and C. Bühler, Freud, Vienna circle of epistemology, among others). The Prague linguistic circle in the 1920s had developed a body of doctrine in structural linguistics. Piaget in Geneva had made a breakthrough in the study of child development. After the aftermath of the first war, an International Committee on Intellectual Cooperation was created in 1922 focussing its attention on the "future of culture", "education of moden man", "future of the European mind"; the committee consisted of an interdisciplinary thinkers, among them Henri Bergson president, Paul Valéry, Albert Einstein, Gilbert Murray, Marie Curie. Soviet psychology enjoyed a brief, remarkable two decades of creativity and scientific innovation. The greatest beneficiary of the 1920s intellectual zeitgeist worldwide was Lev S. Vygotsky. A closer look at Vygotsky's research program indicates that Vygotsky's thought was based on an ongoing dialogue with worldwide leading theories in human sciences. Vygotsky integrated a wide range of theories and empirical findings in his unified scientific project. In this connection, Vygotsky's ten year career as a psychologist coincided with the most intensive period of development of psychological science in the Soviet Union and worldwide.

Vygostky's fame

Vygostky's fame could be viewed in term of five stages:
1) notoriety of the 1920s, 2) total eclipse after his death (1934-1956), 3) resurrection in the end of the1950s, 4) rehabilitation in the 1980s, 5) celebrity in the whole world in the1990s. At universities, department of psychology, education, linguistics and anthropology around the world, Vygotsky's theories of sociocultural approach to mediated action is being stretched and refined by social scientists today. A series of new books are heralding a new age in psychological sciences, which could be termed Vygotsky's new paradigm shift (Blanck,1984; Daniels,1993; Joravsky,1989; Kozulin,1990; Mecacci,1983; Moll,1990; Newman & Holzman,1993; Ratner,1991; Rivière,1990; Schneuwly & Bronckart,1985; Siguan,1987; Van Der Veer & Valsiner,1991; Van Der Veer, Valsiner & Cole, 1994; Wertsch,1985; Wertsch,1991; Yaroshevsky, 1989). In spite of ideological and political differences, language difficulties and scientific traditions, Soviet psychology has affected and influenced in many ways Western psychology in the last decade. In his foreword to "Thought and language" Lucien Sève (1985) admitted that Vygotsky is a true initiator of a Marxist way of thinking in psychology. To conclude, Alexander Luria qualified Vygotsky a 'genius', Karl Levitin said Vygotsky is an 'Outsdanding psychologist',

Stephan toulman viewed him as 'the Mozart of psychology', Benjamin Lee said he was a 'polymath and polyphonic thinker', Fred Newman and Lois Holzman claimed their Vygotsky is a 'revolutionary scientist', and Guillermo Blanck characterizes Vygotsky's theory as an 'habitable building'.

Why Vygotsky?

Few developmental psychologists have influenced as many readers as Lev S. Vygotsky. Yet no comprehensive study of his ideas existed-until the mid 80s. Eighty four of his major writings are available in English language, and over 2000 published studies on his key concepts. These published studies examine Vygotsky's theoretical framework over ten years of scientific activities. Destined to show to what extent Vygotsky's ideas shed light on the complex issues of mind, culture and human activity. Reviving Vygotsky's thought both enriches our understanding of Soviet school of sociohistorical approach to human mind and provides powerful interpretive tools for bridging Soviet psychology and Western psychological traditions. Most recently in the United States, psychologists (Cole, Kozulin, Rogoff, Valsiner, Wertsch) have brought Vygotsky's theory into focus with rigorous methodological, theoretical and philosophical interpretation. Vygotsky and his school have enjoyed an enormous popularity in recent years in North American psychology.

Why this growing interest in Vygotsky's work? How has Vygotsky's thought been interpreted? Vygotskian psychology was conceptualized and developed in the tradition of dialectical historical materialism, with emphasis on qualities rather than quantities, on processes rather than products. During the 1920s and early 1930s, Soviet psychology was conceptualized on the basis of the heuristic value of dialectics. By the late 1920s Soviet psychology had produced a new paradigm shift and integrated theories and formed psychologists at the calibre of Basov, Blonsky, Luria, Leontiev, Vygotsky, Kornilov, among others. What characterized the 1920s and early 1930s is that, no current theoretical approach had a monopoly on truth, there was room for all psychological ideas in the vast field of psychology. Over one decade, Soviet psychology achieved a remarkable rapid development which could be characterized as the golden age of Soviet psychology.

Vygotsky and Lenin

Reviewing the achievement of the five years of the Russian revolution, Lenin noted, moreover, that the most important thing for comrades to do was to sit down, and study. Vygotsky did just that and the result was Psychology of art (1925), Educational psychology (1926), Historical meaning of the crisis in psycholgoy (1926/27), Pedology of the school child (1928), Behavior of animals and man, Tools and signs, History of the development of the higher psychological functions. Lenin placed greater emphasis on the need to continue the class struggle. He characterized socialism as the continuation of class struggle in new forms. This statement became the kernel of Vygotsky's scientific activities. Vygotsky insisted that the struggle at the scientifc front reflect the magnitude of the class struggle in the society as a whole. His struggle at the scientific front was reflected in his writings, critics and theoretical reflection. He opposed the idea that the class struggle had ceased to exist in the USSR. He refuted vulgar marxism and the slogan of the 1930s that labor tools and technology decide everything.

Vygotsky's political views

Vygotsky was a committed Marxist, who lived in an age of collapsing empires and rising revolutions. His life (under Stalin era) as a leading Marxist intellectual was textured with suffering, humiliations, drama, and intellectual exile. As a committed thinker, by writing and practice, Vygotsky became a representative social type an active revolutionary Marxist.

Marxist psychology: Forces of production and the relations of production

Marx argued that the motor of historical transformations was the contradiction between the forces of production and the relations of production. Relations of production are viewed by Vygotsky as social and forces of production conceived as pure technology. Vygotsky defends the ideas that the relations of production constitute the basis of human mental functioning. In the last analysis the development of the forces of production prepare the ground for new relations of production and new social relations. In this connection, the development of technology and tools of labor facilitate-not determine-the changes in these forces. This point has been clarified by Lukàcs (1925) in his critical review of Bukharin's book (Historical materialism: A system of sociology) in which he argued that "technique is a part, a moment, naturally of great importance, of the social productive forces, but it is neither simply identical with them, nor ... the final or absolute moment of the changes in these forces (p.29). This view has been discussed in depth in Vygotsky's writings. For Vygotsky and Lukàcs, technology is only a moment of the forces of production which are in themselves social phenomena. Vygotsky extends his analysis by relying upon the contradiction between forces and relations of production to resolve the individual-society problem. In this connection, human intellectual processes were grounded in social relations, social forces of production and change in the direction of technical development which is based on a "change in the economic structure of society: the change in labor potentialities and conditions" (Lukàcs, 1925, p.30). Vygotsky claims that cultural development is governed by two driving forces: social evolution and technological evolution. These driving forces have been discussed in depth in Marxist literature. Whatever the results and achievement of such technological development and socio-political system, two questions must be asked, why the development of mentality of man/woman lags behind his/her actual condition? why the development of mentality of man/woman lags behind the development of technology? These questions have not received considerable attention in Marxist psychology. In his study of human consciousness Vygotsky has tried several times to include human alienation in his theoretical conceptions. Human alienation has been analyzed and discussed in depth from the point of view of dialectical-historical materialism by Marx, Engels and Lukàcs. Vygotsky is the only psychologist who has given it considerable attention.

Vygotsky's writings continue to provide new insights into complex issues of human mental functioning. Three main ideas can be outlined:
1) The use of genetic or developmental analysis, but so did Piaget.
2) Higher mental functions in the individual are grounded in social processes, but so did Janet, Mead, Piaget, Politzer and Wallon.
3) Human thought processes are fundamentally shaped by cultural tools-signs and tools-or mediational means, but so did Blonsky, Basov, and the Russian formalists.

Vygotsky is an investigator of "Hot cognition"

Piaget was introduced into American psychology in the early 1960s as an investigator of "cold psychology" who viewed the child as a scientist thinker inside his isolated universe controling his physical reality through logical means. As Youniss pointed out, Piaget's work "had been transformed to fit the methodology on which American psychologists had built their identity"(p.120). Vygotskian scholars, however, have made the case that Vygotsky's approach to human cognition "stands alone among developmental approaches in its capacity to explain how quality of particular social experience influences the nature of the ideas and values that arise from that experience" (Youniss & Damon, 1992, p.284) Authors inspired by the Soviet school of sociohistorical approach to mind have directed their effort to understand the theory properly, texts must be scholarly translated, managed and exploited to their full potential.

What can we learn about psychological science from Vygotsky and his school. How can such a research program developed in 1920s helps psychologists and allied disciplines understand human psychological functioning? In my view, Vygotsky's research program can be used to bridge the wide division between different systems of psychology.

The collected works of L. S. Vygotsky

Vygotsky, L. S. (1925). The principles of social education of deaf and dumb children in Russia. *Proceedings of the International Conference on the Education of the Deaf,* (pp. 227-237). London. Also, In R. Van Der Veer & J. Valsiner (Eds.), *The Vygotsky reader* (pp. 19-26). Oxford: Basil Blackwell. 1994. Also, In L. S. Vygotsky, *The collected works of L. Vygotsky. The fundamentals of defectology: Abnormal psychology and learning disabilities* (Vol. 2, pp. 110-121). New York: Plenum Press. 1993

Vygotsky, L. S. (1926). The methods of reflexological and psychological investigation. In R. Van Der Veer & J. Valsiner (Eds.), *The Vygotsky reader* (pp. 27-45). Oxford: Basil Blackwell. 1994.

Vygotsky, L. S. (1929). II. The problem of the cultural development of the child. *Journal of Genetic Psychology, 36,* 414-434. Also, In R. Van Der Veer & J. Valsiner (Eds.), *The Vygotsky reader* (pp. 57-72). Oxford: Basil Blackwell. 1994.

Vygotsky, L. S. (1929). Die genetischen wurzen des sprechens und denkens.*Unter dem Banner des Marxismus, 3,* 450-469, *4,* 607-623.

Vygotsky, L. S. (1930). The socialist alteration of man. In R. Van Der Veer & J. Valsiner (Eds.), *The Vygotsky reader* (pp. 175-184). Oxford: Basil Blackwell. 1994.

Vygotsky, L. S. (1930). Le problème des fonctions intellectuelles supé-rieures dans le système des recherches psychotechniques. *Anals d'Orientacio Professional,* 323-341.

Vygotsky, L. S. (1931). The development of thinking and concept formation in adolescence. In R. Van Der Veer & J. Valsiner (Eds.), *The Vygotsky reader* (pp. 183-265). Oxford: Basil Blackwell. 1994.

Vygotsky, L. S. (1931). Imagination and creativity in the adolescent. *Soviet Psychology, 28* (1), 73-88, 1990. Also, In R. Van Der Veer & J. Valsiner (Eds.), *The Vygotsky reader* (pp. 266-288). Oxford: Basil Blackwell. 1994.

Vygotsky, L. S. (1934). Thought in schizophrenia. *Archives of Neurology & Psychiatry, 31,* 1063-1077. Also, In R. Van Der Veer & J. Valsiner (Eds.), *The Vygotsky reader* (pp. 313-326). Oxford: Basil Blackwell. 1994.

Vygotsky, L. S. (1934). The development of academic concepts in school aged children. In R. Van Der Veer & J. Valsiner (Eds.), *The Vygotsky reader* (pp. 355-370). Oxford: Basil Blackwell. 1994.

Vygotsky, L. S. (1935). Fascism in psychoneurology. In R. Van Der Veer & J. Valsiner (Eds.), *The Vygotsky reader* (pp. 327-337). Oxford: Basil Blackwell. 1994.

Vygotsky, L. S. (1934). The problem of the environment. In R. Van Der Veer & J. Valsiner (Eds.), *The Vygotsky reader* (pp. 338-354). Oxford: Basil Blackwell. 1994.

Vygotsky, L. S. (1939). Thought and speech. *Psychiatry, 2,* 29-54. Reprinted in S. Saporta (Ed.), *Psycholinguistics: A book of readings* (pp. 509-537). New York: Holt, Rinehart & Winston, 1961.

Vygotsky, L. S. (1962). *Thought and language* (Translated by E. Hanfmann & G. Vakar). Cambridge, Mass.: MIT Presss.

Vygotsky, L. S. (1966). *Pensiere e linguaggio.* Firenze: Giunti Barbara.

Vygotsky, L. S. (1969). *Denken und sprechen.* Frankfurt/ Main: Fischer.

Vygotsky, L. S. (.......). *Selected papers of L. S. Vygotskii.* Submitted for publication since 1968 to Pergamon Press, London. Cancelled.

Vygotsky, L. S. (1971-1974). *Sprog og toenkning* [Language and thought]. Copenhagen: Reitzel.

Vygotsky, L. S. (1976). *Tafkir wa lugha.* Egypt, Cairo: Anglo-Egyptian Press.

Vygotsky, L. S. (1992). *Tafkir wa Alkhytab* (Translated into Arabic by Mohamed ELhammoumi from the version 1987 Plenum Press included Vygotsky's six lectures).

Vygotsky, L. S. (1977). *Pensiamento y lenguaje.* Buenos Aires: La Pléyade.

Vygotsky, L. S. (1985). *Pensée et langage* (Traduit par: F. Sève). Paris: Messidor/Editions Sociales.

Vygotsky, L. S. (1986). *Thought and language* (Translated by A. Kozulin). Cambridge, Mass.: MIT Press.

Vygotsky, L. S. (1987). Thinking and speech. In L. S. Vygotsky, *The collected works of L. Vygotsky. Problems of general psychology* (Vol. 1, 37-285). (translated by N. Minick). New York: Plenum Press.

Vygotsky, L. S. (1963). The problem of learning and mental development at school age. In B. Simon & J. Simon (Eds.), *Educational psychology in the USSR* (pp. 21-34). London: Routlege & Kegan Paul. Also in French: In B. Schneuwly, & J. P. Bronckart (Eds.), *Vygotski aujourd'hui* (pp. 95-117). Neuchâtel-Paris: Delachaux & Niestlé (Collection Textes de Base en Psychologie).

Vygotsky, L. S. (1965). Psychology and localization of functions. *Neuropsychologia, 3,* 381-386.

Vygotsky, L. S. (1967). Play and its role in the psychological development of the child. *Soviet Psychology and Psychiatry, 5* (3), 6-18. Also reprinted in: J. Bruner, A. Jollyand, & K. Sylva (Eds.),

Play: Its role in development and evolution (pp. 537-544). New York: Penguin Books.

Vygotsky, L. S. (1967). Memorial Issue. *Soviet Psychology, 5*(3).

Vygotsky, L. S. (1970). Thought and language (A retranslation of the concluding pages of). In E. E. Berg, *L. S. Vygotsky's theory of the social and historical origins of consciousness* (pp. 533-535). PhD thesis. University of Wisconsin.

Vygotsky, L. S. (1971). *The psychology of art.* Cambridge, Mass.: MIT Presss.

Vygotsky, L. S. (1972). *La tragedia di Amleto.* Roma: Editori Riuniti.

Vygotsky, L. S. (1972). Spinoza's theory of emotions in light of contemporary psychoneurology. *Soviet Studies in Philosophy, 10,* 362-382.

Vygotsky, L. S.. (1974). Problem of age periodization of child development. *Human Development, 17,* 27-40.

Vygotsky, L. S. (1977). The development of higher psychological functions. *Soviet Psychology, 15*(3), 60-73. Also in *Soviet Review, 18*(3), 38-51, fall 1977. Also in A. Leontiev, A. Luria & A. Smirnov (Eds.), *Psychological research in the USSR* (Vol. 1, pp. 11-46). Moscow: Progress Publishers, 1966.

Vygotsky, L. S. (1978). *Mind in society: The development of higher psychological processes.* Edited by M. Cole, V. John-Steiner, S. Scribner & E. Souberman. Cambridge, MA: Harvard University Press.

Vygotsky, L. S. (1978). Tool and symbol in child development. In M. Cole, V. John-Steiner, S. Scribner, & E. Souberman (Eds.), *Mind in society: the development of higher psychological processes* (pp. 19-30). Cambridge, MA: Harvard University Press.

Vygotsky, L. S. (1978). The development of perception and attention. In M. Cole, V. John-Steiner, S. Scribner, & E. Souberman (Eds.), *Mind in society: The development of higher psychological processes* (pp. 31-37). Cambridge, MA: Harvard University Press.

Vygotsky, L. S. (1978). Mastery of memory and thinking. In M. Cole, V. John-Steiner, S. Scribner, & E. Souberman (Eds.), *Mind in society: The development of higher psychological processes* (pp. 38-51). Cambridge: Harvard University Press.

Vygotsky, L. S. (1978). Internalization of higher psychological functions. In M. Cole, V. John-Steiner, S. Scribner, & E. Souberman (Eds.), *Mind in society: the development of higher psychological processes* (pp. 52-57). Cambridge: Harvard University Press.

Vygotsky, L. S. (1978). Problems of method. In M. Cole, V. John-Steiner, S. Scribner, & E. Souberman (Eds.), *Mind in society: the development of higher psychological processes* (pp. 58-75). Cambridge MA: Harvard University Press.

Vygotsky, L. S. (1978). Interaction between learning and development. In M. Cole, V. John-Steiner, S. Scribner, & E. Souberman (Eds.), *Mind in society: the development of higherpsychological processes* (pp. 79-91). Cambridge: Harvard University Press.

Vygotsky, L. S. (1978). The role of play in development. In M. Cole, V. John-Steiner, S. Scribner, & E. Souberman (Eds.), *Mind in society: the development of higher psychological processes* (pp. 92-104). Cambridge, MA: Harvard University Press.

Vygotsky, L. S. (1978). The prehistory of written language. In M. Cole, V. John-Steiner, S. Scribner & E. Souberman (Eds.), *Mind in society: the development of higher psychological processes* (pp. 105-119). Cambridge, MA: Harvard University Press. (French translation. La préhistoire du discours écrit. *Social Science Information, 17* (1), 1-17. 1978.

Vygotsky, L. S. (1979). Consciousness as a problem in the psychology of behavior. *Soviet Psychology, 17*(4), 3-35.

Vygotsky, L. S. (1979). On the development of higher forms of attention in childhood. *Soviet Psychology, 18*(1), 67-115.

Vygotsky, L. S. (1981). The genesis of higher mental functions. In J. V. Wertsch (Ed.), *The concept of activity in Soviet psychology* (pp. 144-188). Armonk, N.Y: M. E Sharpe. Also: In P. Light, S. Sheldon, & M. Woodhead (Eds.), *Learning to think. Child development in social context* (Vol. 2, pp. 32-41). Routledge, 1991. Also: In K. Richardson, & S. Sheldon, (Eds.), *Cognitive develo-pment to adolescence: A reader* (pp. 61-79). NJ: Lawrence Erlbaum Associates, 1988.

Vygotsky, L. S. (1981). The instrumental method in psychology. In J. V. Wertsch (Ed.), *The concept of activity in Soviet psychology* (pp. 134-143). Armonk, N.Y: M. E Sharpe. Also in French: B. Schneuwly, & J. P. Bronckart (Eds.), *Vygotski aujourd'hui* (pp. 39-47). Neuchâtel-Paris: Delachaux & Niestlé (Collection Textes de base en psychologie).

Vygotsky, L. S. (1981). The development of higher forms of attention in childhood. In J. V. Wertsch (Ed.), *The concept of activity in Soviet psychology* (pp. 189-240). Armonk, N.Y: M.E Sharpe.

Vygotsky, L. S. (1983). From the notebooks of L. S Vygotsky. *Soviet Psychology, 21*(3), 3-17.

Vygotsky, L. S. (1983). School instruction and mental development. In M. Donaldson, R. Grieve, & C. Pratt (Eds.), *Early childhood development and education.* New York: Guilford Press.

Vygotsky, L. S. (1985). Le problème des fonctions intellectuelles supé-rieures dans le système des recherches psychotechniques.

Anuario de Psicologia, 33(2), 7-16.

Vygotsky, L. S. (1985). Les bases épistémologiques de la psychologie. In B. Schneuwly & J. P. Bronckart (Eds.), *Vygotski aujourd'hui* (pp. 23-38). Neuchâtel-Paris: Delachaux & Niestlé (Collection Textes de Base en Psychologie).

Vygotsky, L. S. (1985). La méthode instrumentale en psychologie. In B. Schneuwly & J. P. Bronckart (Eds.), *Vygotski aujourd'hui* (pp. 39-47). Neuchâtel-Paris: Delachaux & Niestlé (Collection Textes de Base en Psychologie).

Vygotsky, L. S. (1985). Les racines génétiques du langage et de la pensée. In B. Schneuwly & J. P. Bronckart (Eds.), *Vygotski aujourd'hui* (pp. 49-65). Neuchâtel-Paris: Delachaux & Niestlé (Collection Textes de Base en Psychologie).

Vygotsky, L. S. (1985). La pensée et le mot. In B. Schneuwly & J. P. Bronckart (Eds.), *Vygotski aujourd'hui* (pp. 67-94). Neuchâtel-Paris: Delachaux & Niestlé (Collection Textes de Base en Psychologie).

Vygotsky, L. S. (1985). Le problème de l'enseignement et du développement mental à l'âge scholaire. In B. Schneuwly & J. P. Bronckart (Eds.), *Vygotski aujourd'hui* (pp. 49-65). Neuchâtel-Paris: Delachaux & Niestlé (Collection Textes de Base en Psychologie).

Vygotsky, L. S. (1985-1987). *Ausgewalte schriften* [Selected texts]. Cologne: Pahl Rugenstein.

Vygotsky, L. S. (1987). The problem of mental retardation: A tentative working hypothesis. *Soviet Psychology, 26*(1), 78-85

Vygotsky, L. S. (1987). Diagnosis of the development and pedological clinical care of difficult children. *Soviet Psychology, 26*(1), 86-101.

Vygotsky, L. S. (1987). *The collected works of L. S. Vygotsky. Problems of general psychology (*Vol. 1). *New York: Plenum Press.* Translated into Arabic by Mohamed ELhammoumi).

Vygotsky, L. S. (1987). Thought and speech. In *The collected works of L. S. Vygotsky: Problems of general psychology* (Vol. 1, pp. 39-285). New York: Plenum Press. (Translated into Arabic by Mohamed ELhammoumi)

Vygotsky, L. S. (1987). The problem of speech and thinking in Piaget's theory. In *The collected works of L. S. Vygotsky: Problems of general psychology* (Vol. 1, pp. 53-91). New York: Plenum Press. (Translated into Arabic by Mohamed ELhammoumi)

Vygotsky, L. S. (1987). Lecture 1. Perception and its development. In *The collected works of L. S. Vygotsky: Problems of general psychology* (Vol. 1, pp. 289-300). New York: Plenum Press. (Transl into Arabic by Mohamed ELhammoumi)

Vygotsky, L. S. (1987). Lecture 2. Memory and its development. In *The collected works of L. S. Vygotsky: Problems of general psychology* (Vol. 1, pp. 301-310). New York: Plenum Press. (Trans. into Arabic by Mohamed ELhammoumi)

Vygotsky, L. S. (1987). Lecture 3. Thinking and its development in childhood. In *The collected works of L. S. Vygotsky: Problems of general psychology* (Vol. 1, pp. 311-324). New York: Plenum Press. (Translated into Arabic by Mohamed ELhammoumi)

Vygotsky, L. S. (1987). Lecture 4. Emotions and their development in childhood. In*The collected works of L. S. Vygotsky: Problems of general psychology* (Vol. 1, pp. 325-337). NY: Plenum Press. (Translated into Arabic by Mohamed ELhammoumi)

Vygotsky, L. S. (1987). Lecture 5. Imagination and its development in childhood. In *The collected works of L. S. Vygotsky: Problems of general psychology* (Vol. 1, pp. 339-349). New York: Plenum Press. (Translated into Arabic by Mohamed ELhammoumi)

Vygotsky, L. S. (1987). Lecture 6. The problem of will and its development in childhood. In *The collected works of L. S. Vygotsky: Problems of general psychology* (Vol. 1, pp. 351-358). New York: Plenum Press. (Translated into Arabic by Mohamed ELhammoumi)

Vygotsky, L. S. (1988). On inner speech. In M. B. Franklin, & S. S. Barten (Eds.), *Child language: A reader* (pp. 181-187). NY: Oxford University Press.

Vygotsky, L. S. (1989). Concrete human psychology. *Soviet Psychology, 27*(2), 53-77.

Vygotsky, L. S. (1989). La signification historique de la crise de la psychologie. *Enfance,42*(1-2), 13-16. (Originally published in 1926).

Vygotsky, L. S. (1990). Imagination and creativity in childhood. *Soviet Psychology, 28*, 84-96 (Originally published in 1930).

Vygotsky, L. S. (1990). Language and thought. In J. Pickering & M. Skinner (Eds.), *From sentience to symbols: Readings on consciousness* (pp. 240-247). Toronto: University of Toronto Press.

Vygotsky, L. S. (1991). *L. S. Vygotski obras escogidas 1*. Edited by A. Alvarez & P. del Rio. Madrid: Visor.

Vygotsky, L. S. (1991). El significado historico de la crisis de la psicologia. In A. Alvarez & P. del Rio (Eds.), *L. S. Vygotski obras escogidas* (Vol.1, pp. 259-407). Madrid: Visor.

Vygotsky, L. S. (1993). *L. S. Vygotski obras escogidas 2*. Edited by A. Alvarez & P. del Rio. Madrid: Visor.

Vygotsky, L. S. (1992). *Educational psychology.* (Translated by Robert Silverman). Oxford: Basil Blackwell. Cancelled.

Vygotsky, L. S. (1992). *Educational psychology* (Translated by Robert Silverman). Orlando, FL: Paul M. Deutsch Press (Classic Soviet Psychology Series). Cancelled.

Vygotsky, L. S. (1992). *Childhood, imagination and creativity.* Orlando, FL: Paul M. Deutsch Press (Classic Soviet Psychology Series). Cancelled.

Vygotsky, L. S. (1993). *The collected works of L. S. Vygotsky. The fundamentals of defectology: Abnormal psychology and learning disabilities.* (Vol. 2). New York: Plenum Press.

Vygotsky, L. S. (1993). Fundamental problems of defectology. In *The collected works of L. S. Vygotsky. The fundamentals of defectology: Abnormal psychology and learning disabilities* (Vol. 2, pp. 29-51). New York: Plenum Press. Also in French: In K. Barisnikov & G. Petipierre (Eds.), *Vygotsky: Défectologie et déficience mentale* (pp. 31-83). Neuchâtel-Paris: Delachaux & Niestlé (Collection Textes de Base en Psychologie).

Vygotsky, L. S. (1993). Defect and compensation. In *The collected works of L. S. Vygotsky. The fundamentals of defectology: Abnormal psychology and learning disabilities* (Vol. 2, pp. 51-64). New York: Plenum Press. In K. Barisnikov & G. Petipierre (Eds.), *Vygotsky: Défectologie et déficience mentale* (pp. 85115). Neuchâtel-Paris: Delachaux & Niestlé (Collection Textes de Base en Psychologie).

Vygotsky, L. S. (1993). Principles of education for physically handicapped children. In *The collected works of L. S. Vygotsky. The fundamentals of defectology: Abnormal psychology and learning disabilities* (Vol. 2, pp. 65-75). N.Y: Plenum Press.

Vygotsky, L. S. (1993). The psychology and pedagogy of children's handicaps. In *The collected works of L. S. Vygotsky. The fundamentals of defectology: Abnormal psychology and learning disabilities* (Vol. 2, pp. 76-93). New York: Plenum Press.

Vygotsky, L. S. (1993). The blind child. In *The collected works of L. S. Vygotsky. The fundamentals of defectology: Abnormal psychology and learning disabilities* (Vol. 2, pp. 97-109). NY: Plenum Press.

Vygotsky, L. S. (1993). Compensatory processes in the development of retarded child. In *The collected works of L. S. Vygotsky. The fundamentals of defectology: Abnormal psychology and learning disabilities* (Vol. 2, pp. 122-238). New York: Plenum Press. In K. Barisnikov & G. Petipierre (Eds.), *Vygotsky: Défectologie et déficience mentale* (pp. 117154). Neuchâtel-Paris: Delachaux & Niestlé (Collection Textes de Base en Psychologie).

Vygotsky, L. S. (1993). The difficult child. In *The collected works of L. S. Vygotsky. The fundamentals of defectology: Abnormal psychology and learning disabilities* (Vol. 2, pp. 139-149). New York: Plenum Press.

Vygotsky, L. S. (1993). Moral insanity. In The collected works of L. S. Vygotsky. *The collected works of L. S. Vygotsky. The fundamentals of defectology: Abnormal psychology and learning disabilities* (Vol. 2, pp. 150-152). NY: Plenum Press.

Vygotsky, L. S. (1993). The dynamics of child character. In *The collected works of L. S. Vygotsky. The fundamentals of defectology: Abnormal psychology and learning disabilities* (Vol. 2, pp. 153-163). New York: Plenum Press. In K. Barisnikov & G. Petipierre (Eds.), *Vygotsky: Défectologie et déficience mentale* (pp. 237-258). Neuchâtel-Paris: Delachaux & Niestlé (Collection Textes de Base en Psychologie).

Vygotsky, L. S. (1993). Defectology and the study of the development and education of abnormal children. In *The collected works of L. S. Vygotsky. The fundamentals of defectology: Abnormal psychology and learning disabilities* (Vol. 2, pp. 164-170). NY: PlenumPress.

Vygotsky, L. S. (1993). The study of the development of the child. In *The collected works of L. S. Vygotsky. The fundamentals of defectology: Abnormal psychology and learning disabilities* (Vol. 2, pp. 173177). New York: Plenum Press.

Vygotsky, L. S. (1993). Bases for working with mentally retarded and physically handicapped children. In *The collected works of L. S. Vygotsky. The fundamentals of defectology: Abnormal psychology and learning disabilities* (Vol. 2, pp. 178-183). NY: Plenum Press.

Vygotsky, L. S. (1993). Fundamental principles in a plan of pedological research in the field of "difficult children. In *The collected works of L. S. Vygotsky. The fundamentals of defectology: Abnormal psychology and learning disabilities* (Vol. 2, pp. 184-190). New York: Plenum Press.

Vygotsky, L. S. (1993). The collective as a factor in the development of the abnormal child. In *he collected works of L. S. Vygotsky. The fundamentals of defectology: Abnormal psychology and learning disabilities* (Vol. 2, pp. 191-208). New York: Plenum Press. In K. Barisnikov & G. Petipierre (Eds.), *Vygotsky: Défectologie et déficience mentale* (pp. 155-194). Neuchâtel-Paris: Delachaux & Niestlé (Collection Textes de Base en Psychologie).

Vygotsky, L. S. (1993). Introduction to Ia. K. Tsveifel's book, Essay on the behavioral characteristics and education of the deaf-mute. In *he collected works of L. S. Vygotsky. The fundamentals of defectology: Abnormal psychology and learning disabilities* (Vol. 2, pp. 209-211). New York: Plenum Press.

Vygotsky, L. S. (1993). Introduction to E. K. Gracheva's book, The education and instruction of severely retarded children. In *he collected works of L. S. Vygotsky. The fundamentals of defectology:*

Abnormal psychology and learning disabilities (Vol. 2, pp. 212-219). New York: Plenum Press.

Vygotsky, L. S. (1993). The problem of mental retardation. In *he collected works of L. S. Vygotsky. The fundamentals of defectology: Abnormal psychology and learning disabilities* (Vol. 2, pp. 220-240). New York: Plenum Press. In K. Barisnikov & G. Petipierre (Eds.), *Vygotsky: Défectologie et déficience mentale* (pp. 195-236). Neuchâtel-Paris: Delachaux & Niestlé (Collection Textes de Base en Psychologie).

Vygotsky, L. S. (1993). The diagnostics of the development and the pedological clinic for difficult children. In *The collected works of L. S. Vygotsky. The fundamentals of defectology: Abnormal psychology and learning disabilities* (Vol. 2, pp. 241-291). NY: Plenum Press.

Vygotsky, L. S. (1993). Experimental verification of new methods for teaching speech to deaf-mute children. In *he collected works of L. S. Vygotsky. The fundamentals of defectology: Abnormal psychology and learning disabilities* (Vol. 2, pp. 292-295). NY: Plenum Press.

Vygotsky, L. S. (1993). Methods for studying mentally retarded children: Thesis of an address. In *he collected works of L. S. Vygotsky. The fundamentals of defectology: Abnormal psychology and learning disabilities* (Vol. 2, pp. 295-296). New York: Plenum Press.

Vygotsky, L. S. (1993). Anomalies in the cultural development of the child. In *he collected works of L. S. Vygotsky. The fundamentals of defectology: Abnormal psychology and learning disabilities* (Vol. 2, pp. 296). New York: Plenum Press.

Vygotsky, L. S. (1993). From the article "conference results". In *he collected works of L. S. Vygotsky. The fundamentals of defectology: Abnormal psychology and learning disabilities* (Vol. 2, pp. 296-297). New York: Plenum Press.

Vygotsky, L. S. (1993). On the length of childhood for mentally retarded children. In *he collected works of L. S. Vygotsky. The fundamentals of defectology: Abnormal psychology and learning disabilities* (Vol. 2, pp. 298). New York: Plenum Press.

Vygotsky, L. S. (1993). On the question of speech development and educational training for deaf-mute children: Theses and address. In *he collected works of L. S. Vygotsky. The fundamentals of defectology: Abnormal psychology and learning disabilities* (Vol. 2, pp. 298-299). New York: Plenum Press.

Vygotsky, L. S. (1993). Cultural development of anomalous and difficult to educate children: Theses of lecture. In *he collected works of*

L. S. Vygotsky. The fundamentals of defectology: Abnormal psychology and learning disabilities (Vol. 2, pp. 299). NY: Plenum Press.

Vygotsky, L. S. (1993). Comments on lecture by P. D. Mernenko, P. O. Efrussi, and A. M. Scherbina. In *he collected works of L. S. Vygotsky. The fundamentals of defectology: Abnormal psychology and learning disabilities* (Vol. 2, pp. 299-301). NY: Plenum Press.

Vygotsky, L. S. (1993). Behavior of the anthropoid age. In L. S. Vygotsky & A. R. Luria, *Studies on the history of behavior: Ape, primitive and child* (pp. 40-78). (Translated and edited by V. Golod & J. Knox). New Jersey: Lawrence Erlbaum Associates.

Vygotsky, L. S. (1993). Primitive and his behavior. In L. S. Vygotsky & A. R. Luria, *Studies on the history of behavior: Ape, primitive and child* (pp.79-139). (Translated and edited by V. Golod & J. Knox). New Jersey: Lawrence Erlbaum Associates.

Vygotsky, L. S. (1994). *Défectologie et déficience mentale.* Neuchâtel-Paris: Delachaux & Niestlé (Collection Textes de Base en Psychologie).

Vygotsky, L. S. (Forthcoming). *The collected works of L. S. Vygotsky. Questions in the theory and history of psychology* (Vol. 3). New York: Plenum Press.

Vygotsky, L. S., & Luria, A. R. (1930). The function and fate of egocentric speech. *Proceedings of the 9th International Congress of Psychology,* (pp. 464-465). Princeton: The Psychological Review.

Vygotsky, L. S., & Luria, A. R. (1925). Introduction to the Russian translation of Freud's Beyond the pleasure principle. In R. Van Der Veer & J. Valsiner (Eds.), *The Vygotsky reader* (pp.10-18). Oxford: Basil Blackwell. 1994

Vygotsky, L. S., & Luria, A. R. (1930). Tool and symbol in child development. (Unpublished manuscript submitted for publication in C. Murchison's *Handbook of child development,* 2nd edn. Cancelled). Recently published in R. Van Der Veer & J. Valsiner (Eds.), *The Vygotsky reader* (pp. 99-174). Oxford: Basil Blackwell. 1994

Vygotsky, L. S., & Warshava, B. (1930). A dictionary of psychology. Moscow.

Vygotsky, L. S., & Luria, A. R. (1992). *Ape, primitive man and child: Essays in the history of behavior* (Translated by Evelyn. Rossiter). London: Harvester Wheatsheaf. Popular Translation.

Vygotsky, L. S., & Luria, A. R. (1993). *Studies on the history of behavior: Ape, primitive and child.* (Translated and edited by V. Golod & J. Knox). New Jersey: Lawrence Erlbaum Associates. Scholarly Translation.

Vygotsky's collected work was finally completed in 1982 in USSR, some important manuscripts are still unpublished (see Yaroshevsky, M. G.). In 1987 Vygotsky's writings began to be published in USA by Plenum Press.

Vygotsky, L. S. (1982a). *Sobranie sochinenij. Tom 1. Voprosy teorii i istorii psikhologii* [collected works: Vol.1. Problems in the theory and history of psychology]. Moscow: Pedagogika. (Translated into Spanish)

Vygotsky, L. S. (1982b). *Sobranie sochinenij. Tom 2. Problemy obshchej psikhologii* [collected works: Vol.2. Problems of general psychology]. Moscow: Pedagogika. (Translated into English & Spanish)

Vygotsky, L. S. (1982c). *Sobranie sochinenij. Tom 3. Problemy razvitija psikhiki* [collected works: Vol.3. Problems in the deveolopment of mind]. Moscow: Pedagogika.

Vygotsky, L. S. (1982d). *Sobranie sochinenij. Tom 4. Osnovy defekto-logii* (collected works: Vol.4. Foundations of defectology). Moscow: Pedagogika. [Translated into English & French]

Vygotsky, L. S. (1982e). *Sobranie sochinenij. Tom 5. Detskaja psikhologija* (collected works: Vol.5. Child psychology). Moscow: Pedagogika.

Vygotsky, L. S. (1982f). *Sobranie sochinenij. Tom 6. Nauchnoe nasledstvo* [collected works: Vol.6. Scientific legacy]. Moscow: Pedagogika.

Reviews of:
Thought and language, L. S. Vygotsky (1962). (Trans. by E. Hanfmann & G. Vakar). Cambridge, Mass: MIT Presss.
Adelman, G. (1962, April). *Library Journal, 87*(8), 1619.
Bernstein, R. J. (1962). *Review of Metaphysics, 16*(2), 400.
Bettinghaus, E. (1962). *Journalism Quarterly, 39*(3), 378.
Carroll, J. B. (1963). *Harvard Educational Review, 33*(2), 246-251.
Ervin, S. M. (1962). *Contemporary Psychology, 7*, 406-407.
Gratch, I. (1963). *ETC, 20*, 356-360.
Hinshaw,V. (1964). *Philosophy of Science, 31*(2), 190-191.
James, H. E. (1964). *British Journal of Psychology, 55*, 103-104.
Jensen, P, J. (1964). *Journal of Speech Disorder, 29*, 504-506.
Jonckheere, A. (1964). *British Journal of Social & Clinical Psychology, 3*, 71-73.
Line, W. (1962-1963).*American Journal of Psychiatry, 119*, 1111.
McLeon, R. B. (1963). *American Journal of Psychology, 76*, 532.
Miller, G. (1962). *Science, 136*, 36.

12 Socio-historicocultural Psychology

Newman, S. (1963). *Romance Philosophy, 27*(2), 442-444.
Nicholson, S. J. (1964). *Main Currents in Modern Thought, 45.*
Oldfield, R. C. (1964). *Quarterly Journal of Experimental Psychology, 16,* 77-78.
Paul, I. H. (1964). *Journal of Nervous & Mental Disease, 139,* 202-203.
Shands, H. (1964). *Psychosomatic Medicine, 26,* 191-192.
Weinreich, U. (1963). *American Anthropologist, 65*(6), 1401-1404.
Wilkes, A. L. (1964). *Philosophical Quarterly, 14*(5), 178-179.
Wright, M. J. (1965). *Canadian Psychiatric Association Journal, 10,* 68-69.

Vygotsky's writings in Psychological Abstracts:
American Psychological Association: From 1930 to 1969.

Vygotsky, L. S. (1930). II. The problem of the cultural development of the child. *4,* 48. [387].
Vygotsky, L. S. (1932). The pedology of adolescence. *6,* 197. [1602].
Vygotsky, L. S. (1934). Development of active attention in a preschool child. *8,* 97. [925].
Vygotsky, L. S. (1934). Imagination and creative ability of the school. *4,* 200. [1887].
Vygotsky, L. S. (1935). Thought and speech. *9,* 435-436. [3861].
Vygotsky, L. S. (1935). Pedology of the school child. *9,* 448. [3967].
Vygotsky, L. S. (1935). The problem of learning and mental development in school age: The mental development of children. *9,* 503. [4431].
Vygotsky, L. S. (1935). The problem of learning and mental development in the preschool age: The mental development of children. *9,* 503. [4429].
Vygotsky, L. S. (1935). The mental development of children in the process of learning. *9,* 503. [4430].
Vygotsky, L. S. (1935). Thought in schizophrenia. *9,* 533. [4668].
Vygotsky, L. S., & Daniusheveski, I. I. (1935). The mentally defective child. *9,* 598. [5195].
Vygotsky, L. S. (1959). The problem of emotion. *33,* 558. [5534].
Vygotsky, L. S. (1962). The development of higher psychic functions. *36,* 584. [4AI00V].
Vygotsky, L. S. (1963). Thought and language. *37,* 46. [464].
Vygotsky, L. S. (1968). Two directions in the conceptualization of the nature of emotions in non-Russian psychology at the beginning of the 20th century. *42*(7), 1135. [11323].
Vygotsky, L. S. (1968). Imagination and creativity in childhood (2ed

Ed.). *42* (11), 1700. [17004].

Vygotsky, L. S. (1969). Play and its role in the mental development of the child. *43*(7), 945. [9514].

International Symposium on Vygotsky's Thought.

Vygotsky and social sciences: Congress held in Rome, Italy, June, 1979.

Soviet pedagogical psychology: Theory and practice. Symposium at the American Psychological Association Meeting: New York, September 1979.

Ideas of the Soviet psychologist and semiotician Lev Semenovich Vygotsky. Conference held in Chicago: Center for Psychological Studies, October, 1980.

Theory of activity. The Joint US-USSR Conference. Institute of Psychology, USSR, Academy of Sciences, Moscow, 1980.

Scientific Creativity of L. S. Vygotsky and Modern Psychology (All-Union Conference on the), Moscow, 22-24 December 1981.

Vygotsky and cultural Anthropology. Congress held in Buenos Aires, Argentina, 1984.

Soviet psychology and the social construction of cognition. 84th Annual Meeting of the American Anthropological Association: Session of the society for psychological anthropology. Washington DC, December, 1985.

Activity theory. First International Congress for Research on Activity Theory. Berlin, Germany, 1986.

Vygotsky's thought. France: Paris, december, 1987.

Vygotsky: Proceedings of the 7th European CHEIRON Conference sponsored by Society for History of Behavioral & Social Sciences, Hungary, Budapest, 4-8 September 1988.

Vygotsky and education. Annual Meeting of the American Educational Research Association, San Francisco, CA, March, 1989.

Vygotsky's theory of creative imagination. Symposium conducted at the Biennial Meeting of the Society for Research in Child Development. Kansas: Kansas City, 1989.

Activity theory. Second International Congress for Research on Activity Theory, Lahti, Finland, May 21-25,1990.

Learning, development and zone of proximal development. Workshop, France, Bordeaux: 11-12 December, 1992.

Perspectives in socio-cultural research. International Conference, Madrid, Spain, September, 1992.

The social genesis of thought: Piaget and Vygotsky. 14th Advanced Course of the Jean Piaget Archives University of Geneva, Switze-

rland, Geneva: 19th-22nd September 1994.
Lev S. Vygotsky an contemporary human sciences. International
Conference. Golitsyno, Moscow, Russia.

Special Issues of Journals Devoted to Vygotsky's Thought

Soviet Psychology, 1967, *5*(3): Vygotsky
Soviet Psychology, 1979-1980, *18*(2): The Karkhov school of developmental psychology.
Contemporary Educational Psychology, 1980, *5*(2): Soviet pedagogical psychology: Theory and practice.
Eta Evolutiva, 1981, *8,* Vygotskij e la psicologia evolutiva contemporanea.
Infancia y Aprendizaje, 1984, (27-28): Vygotski, Cincuenta anos después.
New directions for child development, 1984, (23): Children's learning in the "zone of proximal development".
Anuario de Psycologia, 1985, *33*(2): Vygotsky's thought.
Quarterly Newsletter of the Laboratory of Comparative Human Cognition, 1987, *9*(3): Reading Vygotsky at CUNY.
Quarterly Newsletter of the Laboratory of Comparative Human Cognition, 1988, *10* (4): Special issue on Vygotsky.
Cultural Dynamics, 1989, *2*(2): Sociocultural approaches to mind.
Studies in Soviet Thought, 1989, *37*(3): The changing face of Soviet psychology.
Enfance, 1989, *42*(1&2): L. Vygotski (1896-1934).
Contemporary Psychoanalysis, 1990, *26*(1): Vygotsky and psychoanalysis.
Studies in Soviet Thought, 1991, *42*(2): Lev Vygotsky and contemporary social thought.
Infancia y Aprendizaje, 1991, (53): Spanish historical-cultural psychology: Language and development.
Comenius, 1992, *12*(4): Vygotsky's thought.
Creativity Research Journal, 1992, *5*(1): Play, Vygotsky, and imagination.
Cognition & Instruction, 1993, *11*(3-4): Discourse and shared reasoning.
Journal of the Society of Accelerative Learning & Teaching, 1993, *18,* (1-2): A cultural-historical approache to learning and teaching: New perspectives on advancing development.
Child & Youth Care Forum, 1993, *22*(5): A new perspective for child and youth care practice: Vygotsky's theory in action.

Discussion of the works of L. S. Vygotsky in Russia & Former USSR

Aidarova, L. (1982). *Child development and education*. Moscow: Progress.

Aidman, E. V. (1988). Development of means activity control: Today's vision of Lev S. Vygotsky. *Proceedings of the 7th European CHEIRON Conference* (150-153). Budapest: Hungarian Psychological Association.

Aidman, E. V., & Leontiev, D. A. (1991). From being to motivated to motivating oneself: A Vygotskian perspective. *Studies in Soviet Thought, 42*(2), 137-151.

Akutina, T. V. (1978). The role of inner speech in the construction of utterance. *Soviet Psychology, 16*(3), 3-31.

Ananev, B. G. (1948). Achievements of Soviet psychologits. *Journal of General Psychology, 38*, 257-262.

Ananev, B. G. (1959). *Psychological science in the USSR* (Vol. 1). Washington, DC: American Psychological Association.

Ananev, B. G. (1960). *Psychological science in the USSR* (Vol. 2). Washington, DC: American Psychological Association.

Ananev, B. G. (1988). Some psychological problems of the primer period in the initial teaching of literacy. In J. Downing (Ed.), *Cognitive psychology and reading in the USSR* (pp. 257-274). Amsterdam: North-Holland.

Andreyev, I. (1977). The origins of man and society. *Social Science, USSR, 8*(3), 101-112.

Arutiunova, N. (1975). Signs. In*The great Soviet encyclopedia* (Vol. 9, pp. 431-432). NY: Macmillan.

Asmolov, A. G. (1987). Basic principles of a psychological analysis in the theory of activity. *Soviet Psychology, 25*(2), 78-102.

Asmolov, A. G. (1988). Premises of a socioevolutinary concept of the personality. *Soviet Psychology,* 51-63.

Averintsev, S. S. (1975). Dialectical materialism. In *The Great Soviet encyclopedia* (Vol. 8, pp. 187-192). NY: Macmillan.

Bagaturiia, G. A. (1975). Dialectic of nature. in *The Great Soviet encyclopedia* (Vol. 8 , pp. 192-194). NY: Macmillan.

Bassin, F. V. (1960). A debate on Freudism: A critical analysis of Freudism. *Soviet Review, 1*, 3-14.

Bassin, F. V. (1960). A debate on Freudism: A rejoinder to Pr. Musatti. *Soviet Review, 1*, 27-44.

Bassin, F. V. (1969). Consciousness and unconscious. In M. Cole & I. Maltzman (Eds.), *Handbook of contemporary Soviet psychology* (pp. 399-420). New York: Basic Books.

Focus on Learning Problems in Mathematics, 1993, *15*(2-3): Implica tions of Vygotsky's psychology for mathematics education educa tion.

Journal of Russian & East European Psychology, 1994, *32*(2): The Kharkov school of psychology.

Human Development, 1994, *37*(6): New directions in interpreting Vygotsky.

Modern Language Journal, 1994, *78*(4): Sociocultural theory and second language learning.

European Journal of Psychology of Education, 1994, *9*(4): Learning and development: Contributions from Vygotsky's theory.

Educational Psychologist, 1995, *30*(2).
Lev S. Vygotsky and contemporary educational psychology.

School Psychology International, 1995, *16*(2): Lev S. Vygotsky and contemporary school psychology.

Anthropology & Education Quarterly, 1995, *26*(4): Vygotsky's cultural-historical theory of human development: An international perspective.

Journal of Russian & East European Psychology, 1996, *34*(1): Papers from the international conference on "*Lev S. Vygotsky an the contemporary human sciences*" -1.

Journal of Russian & East European Psychology, 1996, *34*(2): Papers from the international conference on "*Lev S. Vygotsky an the contemporary human sciences*" -2 (pp. 54-96).

Oxford Review of Education,, 1996, *21*(1): Vygotsky and education.

Bein, E. S., Vlasova, T. A., Levina, R. E., Morozova, N. G., & Shif, Zh. I. (1993). Afterword. In L. S. Vygotsky, *The collected works of L. S. Vygotsky. The fundamentals of defectology: Abnormal psychology and learning disabilities* (Vol. 2, pp. 302-314). New York: Plenum Press.

Beliakova, G. P. (1988). The segmentation of speech into words by the oldest preschool children. In J. Downing (Ed.), *Cognitive psychology and reading in the USSR* (pp. 347-352). Amsterdam: North-Holand.

Bibler, V. (1984). Thinking as creation (Introduction to the logic of mental dialogue). *Soviet Psychology, 22*(2), 29-54.

Biriukov, B. (1975). Sign. In *The Great Soviet Encyclopedia* (Vol. 9, pp. 430-433). NY: Macmillan.

Blonski, P. (1928). The subject of psychology and psychopathology from a genetic standpoint. *Journal of Genetic Psychology, 35*, 356-373.

Bochenski, J. M. (1963). *Soviet Russian dialectical materialism (Diamat)*. Dordrecht: Reidel.

Bogojavlenskij, A. A. (1957). The psychology of understanding. In B. Simon (Ed.), *Psychology in the Soviet Union* (pp. 69-83). Stanford: Stanford University Prsess.

Bogojavlenskij, A. A. (1963). The relation between learning and mental development in school children. In B & J. Simon (Eds.), *Educatio-nal psychology in the USSR* (pp. 101-161). London: Routlege & Kegan Paul.

Boguslavsky, G. W. (1957). Psychological research in Soviet education. *Science, 125*(3254), 915-918.

Bojko, E. I. (1957). A contribution towards the definition of "skill" and "habit". In B. Simon (Ed.), *Psychology in the Soviet Union* (pp. 233-245). Stanford: Stanford University Prsess.

Borovskij, V. M. (1929). Psychology in the USSR. *Journal of General Psychology*, (2), 177-186.

Bozhovich, L. J. (1977). The concept of the cultural-historical development of mind and its prospects. *Soviet Psychology, 16*, 5-22. Also in *Soviet Review, 19*(1), 31-48, spring 1980.

Bozhovich, L. J. (1979). Stages in the formation of the personality in ontegeny. *Soviet Psychology, 17*, 3-24.

Bozhovich, L. J. (1980). Stages in the formation of the personality in ontegeny. *Soviet Psychology, 18*, 36-52.

Bozhovich, L. J. (1981). Stages in the formation of the personality in ontegeny. *Soviet Psychology, 19*, 61-79.

Brushlinskij, A. V. (1979). The interrelationship of the natural and the social in human development. *Soviet Psychology, 17*, 36-52.

Brushlinsky, A. V. (1987). Activity, action, and mind as process. *Soviet Psychology, 25*(4), 59-81.

Bugrimenko, E. A., & Smirnova, E. (1992). Paradoxes of children's play in Vygotsky's theory. In G. C. Cupchik, & J. Laszlo (Eds.), *Emerging visions of the aesthetic process: Psychology, semiology, and philosophy* (pp. 286-299). NY: Cambridge University Press.

Bulanov, I. (1993). Findings from a study of the behavior of the Tungus child. *Journal of Russian & East European Psychology, 31*(1), 45-60. (Original work published in 1930).

Burmenskaya, G. V., & Raku, Z. P. (1989). Speech for oneself in preschoolers.*Vestnik Moskovskogo Universiteta Seriya 14 Psikhologiya* (1), 3-15

Bustamante de, M. (1978). Child development in Soviet psychology. *Revista Latinoamericana de Psicologia, 10*(3), 411-421.

Christensen, A. (1992). *Luria's neuropsychological investigations.* [Film], Video Series. Orlando, FL: Paul M. Deutsch Press (Classic Soviet Psychology Series).

Davydov, V. V. (1967). The problem of generalization in the works of L. S. Vygotsky. *Soviet Psychology, 5*(3), 42-52.

Davydov, V. V. (1981). The category of activity and mental reflection in the theory of A. N. Leont'ev. *Soviet Psychology, 19*, 3-29.

Davydov, V. V. (1985). Leont'ev's theory of the relationship between activity and mental reflection. *Soviet Psychology, 23*(3), 28-45

Davydov, V. V. (1988). Learning activity: The main problems needing further research. *Multidisciplinary Newsletter for Activity Theory, 1* (1-2), 29-36.

Davydov, V. V. (1988). Problem of the child's mental development. Part 1. *Soviet Education, 30*(8), 44-97.

Davydov, V. V. (1988). Problem of developmental teaching: The experience of theoretical and experimental psychological research. Part 2. *Soviet Education, 30*(9), 1-81

Davydov, V. V. (1988). Problem of developmental teaching: The experience of theoretical and experimental psychological research. Part 3. *Soviet Education, 30*(10).

Davydov, V. V. (1988). The concept of theoretical generalization and problems of educational psychology. *Studies in Soviet Thought, 38*, 169-202.

Davydov, V. V. (1990). *Types of generalization in instruction.* Reston, VA: National Council of Teachers of Mathematics.

Davydov, V. V. (1995). The influence of L. S. Vygotsky on education theory, research, and practice. *Educational Researcher, 24*(3), 12-21.

Davydov, V. V. (1995). The state of research on learning activity. *Journal of Russian & East European Psychology, 33*(4), 55-70.

Davydov, V. V., & Markova, I. (1983). A concept of educational activity in school-children. *Soviet Psychology, 21*, 50-76.

Davydov, V. V., & Zinchenko, V. P. (1989). Vygotsky's contribution to the development of psychology. *Soviet Review, 30*(1), 77-89.

Davydov, V. V., & Zinchenko, V. P. (1993). Vygotsky's contribution to the development of psychology. In H. Daniels (Ed.), *Charting the agenda: Educational activity after Vygotsky* (pp. 93-106). London: Routledge. Also in *Soviet Psychology*, Vol.27 (2).

Deborin, A. M. (1935). Karl Marx and the present. In A. M. Deborin, *Marxism and modern thought* (pp. 91-189). London: George Routledge and Sons.

Dobkin, S. (1982). Ages and days. In K. Levitin (Ed.), *One is not born a personality: Profile of Soviet educational psychologists* (pp. 23-38). Moscow: Progress Publishers.

Denisov, V. (1981). The category of activity and mental reflection in human life activity. In *Philosophy in the USSR: Problems of dialectical materialism (Collective authors)* (pp. 165-182). Moscow: Progress Publishers.

Dobzhansky, T. (1963). Cultural direction of human evolution. *Human Biology, 35*(3), 311-316.

Dobzhansky, T. (1969). *The biology of ultimate concern*. London: Rapp & Whiting.

Egorov, T. G. (1988). Reading comprehension in skilled and unskilled readers. In J. Downing (Ed.), *Cognitive psychology and reading in the USSR* (pp. 189-215). Amsterdam: North-Holland.

Egorov, T. G. (1988). Children's mastery of representations of speech-sounds. In J. Downing (Ed.), *Cognitive psychology and reading in the USSR* (pp. 217-256). Amsterdam: North-Holland.

Elkonin, D. B. (1967). The problem of instruction and development in the works of L. S. Vygotsky. *Soviet Psychology, 5*(3), 34-41.

Elkonin, D. B. (1972). La psychologie de l'enfant.*Recherches Internationales à la Lumière du Marxisme*, (71-72), 157-190.

Elkonin, D. B. (1988). Further remarks on the psychological bases of the initial teaching of literacy. In J. Downing (Ed.), *Cognitive psychology and reading in the USSR* (pp. 365-377). Amsterdam: North-Holland.

Elkonin, D. B. (1988). How to teach children to read. In J. Downing (Ed.), *Cognitive psychology and reading in the USSR* (pp. 387-426). Amsterdam: North-Holland.

Elkonin, D. B. (1995). Problems in the psychology of action. *Journal of Russian & East European Psychology, 33*(4), 32-34.

Etkind, A. M. (1994). More on L. S. Vygotsky: Forgotten texts and undiscovered contexts. *Journal of Russian & East European*

Psychology, 32(6), 6-34.

Feigenberg, Ye. I., & Asmolov, A. G. (1989). Some aspects of the study of nonverbal communication: Beyond the threshold of rationality. *Soviet Journal of Psychology, 10*(6), 62-71.

Frumkina, R. M., & Mikhejev, A. V. (1995). Categorization and concept formation: From Vygotsky-Sacharov and further. In R. M. Frumkina & A. V. Mikhejev, *Meaning and categorization.* NY: Nova Science Publishers.

Furman, A. V. (1989). Levels of problem solving in students. *Voprosy Psikhologii,* (3), 43-53

Heaman I. (1988). Notes on Russian orthography and pronunciation. In J. Downing (Ed.), *Cognitive psychology and reading in the USSR* (pp. 29-35). Amsterdam: North-Holand.

Galperin, P. Ya. (1966). Essai sur la formation par étapes des actions et des concepts. In A. Leontiev, A. Luria & A. Smirnov (Eds.), *Recherches psychologiques en USSR* (pp. 114-132). Moscou: Editions du Progrès.

Galperin, P. Ya. (1967). On the notion of internalization. *Soviet Psychology, 5*(3), 28-33.

Galperin, P. Ya. (1995). Problems in the psychology of action. *Journal of Russian & East European Psychology, 33*(4), 18-31.

Golubeva, A. P. (1993). Study of the Oirot child in the Altai region. *Journal of Russian & East European Psychology, 31*(1), 61-77. (Original work published in 1930).

Goretsky, V. G., Kiriushkin, V. A., & Shanko, A. F. (1988). The quest must continue. In J. Downing (Ed.), *Cognitive psychology and reading in the USSR* (pp. 353-363). Amsterdam: North-Holand.

Gurova, R. (1977). A study of the influence of sociohistorical conditions on child development (comparative investigation, 1929 and 1966). In M. Cole (Ed.), *Soviet developmental psychology* (pp. 369-392). New York: M. E. Sharpe.

Ilyenkov, E. V. (1975). The ideal. In *The Great Soviet Encyclopedia* (Vol.9, pp.115-116). NY: Macmillan.

Ilyenkov, E. V. (1977). The concept of the ideal. In *Philosophy in the USSR: Problems of dialectical materialism (Collective authors)* (pp.71-99). Moscow: Progress Publishers.

Ilyenkov, E. V. (1982). *The dialectics of the abstract and the concrete in Marx's capital.* Moscow: Progress Publishers.

Ilyenkov, E. V. (1982). *Leninist dialectics and the metaphysics of positivism.* London: New Park.

Ilyenkov, E. V. (1989). *Dialectical logic: Essays on its history and theory.* Moscow: Progress Publishers.

Ivanov, V. V. (1971). Commentary. In L. S. Vygotsky, *The psycho-*

logy of art (pp. 265-295). Cambridge, Mass: MIT. Presss.

Ivanov, V. V. (1974). The significance of M. M. Bakhtin's ideas of sign, utterance, and dialogue for modern semiotics. In H. Baran (Ed.), *Semiotics and structuralism: Readings from the Soviet Union*. White Plains, NY: International Arts and Science Press.

Ivanov, V. V., Lotman, I., Ouspenski, B., & Piatigorski, A. (1974). Thèses pour l'étude sémiotique des cultures. *Recherches Internationales à la Lumière du Marxisme*, (81-84), 125-156.

Kapustin, M. (1988). Dialectics by command: Revolutionism in philosophy and the philosophy of revolutionism. *Studies in Soviet Thought, 28(2)*, 6-29.

Karlsen, E. G. (1988). The process of mastering literacy. In J. Downing (Ed.), *Cognitive psychology and reading in the USSR* (pp. 275-293). Amsterdam: North-Holand.

Karpov, Y.V. (1994). *'Vygotskian approach to instruction: The problem of learning and transfer'*. Unpublished manuscript, Vanderbilt University, Department of Psychology and Human Development, Nashville, TN.

Karpov, Y.V. (1995). L.S. Vygotsky as the founder of a new approach to instruction. *School Psychology International, 16(2)*, 131-142.

Karpov, Y. V., & Bransford, J. D. (1995). L. S. Vygotsky and the doctrine of empirical and theoretical learning. *Educational Psychologist, 30(2)*, 61-66.

Kelle, V., & Kovalzon, M. (1981). The social history of people as the history their individual development. In *Philosophy in the USSR: Problems of dialectical materialism (Collective authors)* (pp. 104-133). Trans. by S. Syrovatkin. Moscow: Progress Publishers.

Kharin, F. (1981). *Fundamentals of dialectics*. Moscow: Progress Publishers.

Khrustov, G. F. (1970). The problem of the origin of man. *Soviet Psychology, 9*, 6-31.

Koczanowicz, L. (1994). G. H. Mead and L. S. Vygotsky on meaning and the self. *Journal of Speculative Philosophy, 8(4)*, 262-276.

Kornilov, K. N. (1930). Psychology in the light of dialectic materialism. In C. Murchison (Ed.), *Psychologies of 1930* (pp. 243-278). Clark University Press.

Lebedeva, G. M. (1976). Historical materialism. In *The Great Soviet encyclopedia* (Vol. 10, pp. 76-80). NY: Macmillam.

Lektorsky, V. (1984). *Subject, object, cognition*. Moscow: Progress Publishers.

Lektorsky, V. (Ed.). (1990). *Activity: The theory, methodology and problems*. Olando, FL: Paul M. Deutsch Press.

Leontiev, A. A. (1969). Inner speech and the processes of the grammatical generation of utterances. *Soviet Psychology, 7,* 12.

Leontiev, A. A. (1971). Social and natural semiotics. In J. Morton (Ed.), *Biological and social factors in psycholinguistics* (pp. 122-130). London: Logos Press.

Leontiev, A. A. (1976). Some new trends in Soviet psycholinguistics. *Soviet Psychology, 15(2),* 15-25.

Leontiev, A. A. (1984). The productive career of Aleksei Nikolaevich Leont'ev. *Soviet Psychology, 23(1),* 6-56.

Leontiev, A. A. (1995). Ecce homo: 'Summit' psychology and the prospects of investigating activity. *Journal of Russian & East European Psychology, 33(4),* 35-46.

Leontiev, A. N. (1930). Studies of the cultural development of the child: III. The development of voluntary attention of the child. *Journal of genetic Psychology, 37,* 52-83. Also, In R. Van Der Veer & J. Valsiner (Eds.), *The Vygotsky reader* (pp. 289-312). Oxford: Basil Blackwell. 1994.

Leontiev, A. N. (1957). L'individu et les oeuvres humaines. *Les Etudes Philosophiques,* (3), 186-188.

Leontiev, A. N. (1963). Principles of mental development and the problem of intellectual backwardness. In B and J. Simon (Eds.), *Educational psychology in the USSR* (pp. 68-82). London: Routlege & Kegan Paul.

Leontiev, A. N. (1966). Le concept du reflet: Son importance pour la psychologie scientifique. *Bulletin de Psychologie,* 236-241.

Leontiev, A. N. (1967). Quelques problèmes du développement du psychisme. *Bulletin de Psychologie, 21(267),* 513-520.

Leontiev, A. N. (1974). On the reduction and unfolding of sign systems. In H. Baran (Ed.), *Semiotics and structuralism: Readings from the Soviet Union.* White Plains, NY: International Arts and Science Press.

Leontiev, A. N. (1975). Education and upbringing must be oriented toward the future. *Soviet Education, 17(3),* 74-80.

Leontiev, A. N. (1976). *Le développement du psychisme.* Paris: Editions Sociales.

Leontiev, A. N. (1976). L'homme et la culture. In A. N. Leontiev, *Le développement du psychisme* (pp. 251-275). Paris: Editions Sociales.

Leontiev, A. N. (1976). Le développement du psychisme chez l'enfant. in A. N. Leontiev, *Le développement du psychisme* (pp. 277-305). Paris: Editions Sociales. Also in *La Raison. Psychologie, Psychopathologie, Psychiatrie,* (19), 85-96, 1957.

Leontiev, A. N. (1976). Essai sur le développement du psychisme. In A. N. Leontiev, *Le développement du psychisme* (pp. 11-132).

Paris:Editions Sociales.
Leontiev, A. N. (1976). Le biologique et le social dans le psychisme de l'homme. In A. N. Leontiev, Le développement du psychisme (pp. 223-249). Paris: Editions Sociales. Also in Acta Psychologica, 19, 65-77, 1961. Bulletin de Psychologie, 15(201), 297-306, 1962.
Leontiev, A. N. (1976). La démarche historique dans l'étude du psychisme humain. In A. N. Leontiev, Le développement du psychisme (pp. 133-190). Paris: Editions Sociales.
Leontiev, A. N. (1978). The psycholinguistic aspect of liguistic meaning. In J. Wertsch (Ed.), Recent trends in Soviet psycholinguistics (pp. 21-64). White Plains, New York: Sharpe.
Leontiev, A. N. (1977). Activity and consciousness. In Philosophy in the USSR: Problems of dialectical materialism (Collective authors) (pp. 180-202). Moscow: Progress Publishers.
Leontiev, A. N. (1978). Activity, consciousness, and personality. New Jersey: Prentice-Hall.
Leontiev, A. N. (1981). The problem of activity in psychology. In J. V. Wertsch (Ed.), The concept of activity in Soviet psychology. Armonk, N.Y: M. E Sharpe.
Leontiev, A. N. (1982). Problems of the development of mind. Moscow: Progress Publishers.
Leontiev, A. N. (1983). Karl Marx ja psykologia. [Karl Marx and psychology]. Psykologia 18(6), 403-411.
Leontiev, A. N., & Leontiev, A. A. (1959). The social and the individual in language. Language & Speech, 2(4), 193-204.
Leontiev, A. N., & Luria, A. R., Rubenstein, S. L., Smirnov, A., & Teplov, B. M. (1957). Les problèmes actuels de la psychologie en USSR. La Raison: Psychologie, Psychopathologie, Psychiatrie, (19), 97-100.
Leontiev, A. N., & Luria, A. R., & Smirnov, A. (Eds.). (1966). Psychological research in the USSR. Moscow: Progress Publishers.
Leontiev, A. N., & Luria, A. R., & Smirnov, A. (Eds.). (1966). Recherches psychologiques en USSR. Moscou: Editions du Progrès.
Leontiev, A. N., & Luria, A. R. (1968). The psychological ideas of L. S. Vygotskii. In B. B. Wolman (Ed.), Historical roots of contemporary psychology (pp. 338-367). Harper & Row.
Leontiev, A. N., & Luria, A. R. (1972). Some notes concerning Dr. Fodor's 'Reflections on L. S. Vygotsky's thought and language'. Cognition, 1, 311-316.
Levina, R. E. (1981). L. S. Vygotsky's ideas about the planning function of speech in children. In J. V. Wertsch (Ed.), The concept of activity in Soviet psychology (pp. 279-299. Armonk, New York: Sharpe.

Levitin, K. (1979). The best path to man. *Soviet Psychology, 18*(1), 85-143.

Levitin, K. (Ed.). (1982). *One is not born a personality: Profile of Soviet educational psychologists.* Moscow: Progress Publishers.

Levitin, K. (1982). Lev Vygotsky: A bibliographical profile. In K. Levitin (Ed.), *One is not born a personality: Profile of Soviet educational psychologists* (pp. 18-38). Moscow: Progress Publishers.

Levitin, K. (1982). The Mozart of psychology: An imaginary exchange of views between: A. Petrovsky, R. Jackobson, S. Toulman, L. Vygotsky, V. Zinchenko, G. Schedrovisky, M. Yaroshevsky, M. Cole, V. Davydov, J. Wertsch, A. Luria, and A. Leontiev. In K. Levitin (Ed.), *One is not born a personality: Profile of Soviet educational psychologists* (pp. 39-101). Moscow: Progress Publishers.

Lisina, M. (1985). *Child-adults-peers.* Moscow: Progress Publishers.

Lomov, B. F. (1971). Lenin's theory of reflection and psychology. *Studia Psychologia 13*(3), 173-179.

Lomov, B. F. (1977). Bio' and socio': An untenable contrast. *Social Sciences, 8,* 38-51.

Lomov, B. F. (1982-83). The personality in a system of social relations. *Soviet Psychology, 21,* 55-91.

Lomov, B. F. (1983) The problem of activity in psychology. *Soviet Psychology, 21,* 22-49.

Lomov, B. F. (1983). The study of the laws of the psyche. *Social Sciences, 14,* 115-130.

Lomov, B. F. (1984). A system of the sciences of man. *Social Sciences, 15,* 22-33.

Lotman, Yu. M. (1973, October, 12). Different cultures, differnt codes. *Times Literary Supplement,* 1213-1215.

Lotman, Yu. M. (1974). On the relation and unfolding of sign systems: The problem of Freudian and semiotic culturology. In H. Baran (Ed.), *Semiotics and structuralism: Readings from the Soviet Union.* White Plains, NY: International Arts and Science Press.

Lotman, Yu. M. (1988). Text within a text. *Soviet Psychology, 26,* 32-51.

Lotman, Yu. M. (1988). The semiotics of culture and the concept of a text. *Soviet Psychology, 26,* 52-58.

Lotman, Yu. M. (1990). *Universe of the mind: A semiotic theory of culture.* Blomington: Indiana Universiy Press.

Lotman, Yu. M., & Uspensky, B. A. (1978). On the semiotic mechanism of culture. *New Literary History, 9,* 211-232.

Luria, A. R. (1928). The problem of the cultural behavior of the child.

Journal of Genetic Psychology, 35, 493-506. Also, In R. Van Der Veer & J. Valsiner (Eds.), *The Vygotsky reader* (pp. 46-56). Oxford: Basil Blackwell. 1994.

Luria, A. R. (1928). Psychology in Russia. *Journal of Genetic Psychology, 35,* 347-348.

Luria, A. R. (1931). Psychological expedition to central Asia. *Science, 74,* 383-384.

Luria, A. R. (1932). Psychological expedition to central Asia. *Journal of Genetic Psychology, 40,* 241-242.

Luria, A. R. (1933). The second psychological expedition to central Asia. *Science, 78,* 191-192.

Luria, A. R. (1934). The second psychological expedition to central Asia. *Journal of Genetic Psychology, 44,* 255-257.

Luria, A. R. (1935). L. S. Vygotsky. *Character & Personality, 3,* 238-240.

Luria, A. R. (1935). Professor L. S. Vygotsky (1896-1934). *Journal of Genetic Psychology, 46,* 224-226.

Luria, A. R. (1959). The directive function of speech in development and dissolution: Part 1: Development of directive function of speech in early childhood. *Word, 51*(2), 341-352. And Part2: Dissolution of the regulative function of speech in pathological states of the brain. *Word, 51*(3), 453-464.

Luria, A. R. (1961). *The role of speech in the regulation of normal and abnormal behavior.* New York: Irvington

Luria, A. R. (1963). *The mentally retarded child.* New York: Pergamon Press.

Luria, A. R. (1966). *Higher cortical functions in man.* New York: Basic Books.

Luria, A. R. (1966). *Human brain and psychological processes.* New York: Harper & Row.

Luria, A. R. (1966). Vygotski et l'étude des fonctions psychiques supérieures. *Recherches Internationales à la Lumière du Marxisme,* (51), 93-103.

Luria, A. R. (1967). L. S. Vygotsky and the problem of functional lateralization. *Soviet Psychology, 5*(3), 53-57.

Luria, A. R. (1971). Towards the problem of the historical nature of psychological processes. *International Journal of Psychology, 6*(4), 259-272.

Luria, A. R. (1974). A child's speech responses and the social environment. *Soviet Psychology,* 7-39.

Luria, A. R. (1974). Scientific perspectives and philosophical dead ends in modern linguistics. *Cognition, 3*(4), 377-385. (See Chomsky's reply, 1976 below)

Luria, A. R. (1976). *The nature of human conflicts.* New York: Liveright.

Luria, A. R. (1976). *Cognitive development: Its cultural and social foundations.* Cambridge: Cambridge University Press.

Luria, A. R. (1976). *Basic prolems of neurolinguistics.* The Hague: Mouton.

Luria, A. R. (1976). *The neuropsychology of memory.* Whashington: Winston.

Luria, A. R. (1976-77). The development of writing in the child. *Soviet Psychology, 12*(2), 65-114.

Luria, A. R. (1978). *The selected writings of A. R. Luria.* Ed. by. M. Cole. White Plains: Merle Sharpe.

Luria, A. R. (1978). Bibliographical note on L. S. Vygotsky. In L. S. Vygotsky, *Mind in society* (pp. 15-16). Cambridge, MA: Harvard University Press.

Luria, A. R. (1978). Vygotsky's works. In L. S. Vygotsky, *Mind in society* (pp. 141-151). Cambridge, MA: Harvard University Press.

Luria, A. R. (1979). Soviet psychology. II. In H. J. Eysenck, W. A. Würzburg, & R. M. Berne (Eds.), *Ecyclopedia of psychology* (pp. 1037-1039). The Seabury Press.

Luria, A. R. (1979). *The making mind: A personal account of Soviet psychology.* Cambridge, MA: Harvard University Press.

Luria, A. R. (1979). Vygotsky. In R. A. Luria, *The making mind: A personal account of Soviet psychology* (pp. 38-57). Cambridge, MA: Harvard University Press.

Luria, A. R. (1987). *The mind of a mnemonist: A little book about a vast memory.* Cambridge, MA: Harvard University Press.

Luria, A. R. (1987). *The man with a shatterd world: The history of a brain wound.* Cambridge, MA: Harvard University Press.

Luria, A. R. (1987). Afterword to the Russian edition. In L. S. Vygotskt, *The collected works of L. S. Vygotsky: Problems of general psychology* (Vol. 1, pp. 359-373). NY: Plenum Press.

Luria, A. R. (1988). The pathology of grammatical operations. In J. Downing (Ed.), *Cognitive psychology and reading in the USSR* (pp. 95-141). Amsterdam: North-Holand.

Luria, A. R.. (1993). The child and its behavior. In L. S. Vygotsky & A. R. Luria, *Studies on the history of behavior: Ape, primitive and child* (pp. 140-231). (Translated and edited by V. Golod & J. Knox). New Jersey: Lawrence Erlbaum Associates.

Luria, A. R., & Leontiev, A. N. (1970). The formation of consciousness: A translation of Luria and Leontiev's criticism of Vygotsky. In E. E. Berg, *L. S. Vygotsky's theory of the social and historical origins of consciousness* (pp. 536-542). PhD thesis. University of

Wisconsin.

Luria, A. R., & Majovski, L. V. (1977). Basic approaches used in American and Soviet clinical neuropsychology. *American Psychologist, 32,* 959-968.

Luria, A. R., & Tsvetkova, L. S. (1992). *The neuropsychological analysis of problem solving.* Orlando, FL: Paul M. Deutsch Press (Classic Soviet Psychology Series).

Luria, A. R., Yudovich, F. A. (1959). *Speech and development of the mental processes of the child.* London: Staples Press.

Luria, E. (1992). *Soviet neuropsychology: Historical and current perspectives.* [Film] Video Series by Luria's daughter Elena Luria. Orlando, FL: Paul M. Deutsch Press (Classic Soviet Psychology Series).

Maksimov, L. K. (1993). The principle of the order of mathematical actions and its mastery by elemnetary school pupils. *Focus on Learning Problems in Mathematics, 15*(2-3), 40-47.

Markova, A. (1979). *The teaching and mastery of language.* White Plains, NY: M.E. Sharpe.

Matejka, L., & Pomorska, K. (Eds.). (1971). *Readings in Russian poetics: Formalist and struturalist view.* Cambridge: MIT Press.

Mikailov, E. T. (1980). *The riddle of the self.* Moscow: Progress Publishers.

Morozova, N. G. (1988). The psychological prerequisites for reading comprehension in young school children. In J. Downing (Ed.), *Cognitive psychology and reading in the USSR* (pp. 295-312). Amsterdam: North-Holand.

Nazarova, L. K. (1988). An outline of the history of methods of teaching literacy in Soviet Russia, 1917-1947. In J. Downing (Ed.), *Cognitive psychology and reading in the USSR* (pp. 37-65). Amsterdam: North-Holand.

Meshcheryakov, A. (1979). *Awakening to life.* Moscow: Progress Publishers.

Mikhalevich, A. (1993, March). Russia: The revenge of subjectivity. *The Courier of UNESCO,* 36-39.

Monjam, K. (1980). *Landmarks in history.* Moscow: Progress Publishers.

Mukhina, V. (1982). The social development of the child. *Soviet Psychology, 20,* 60-79.

Mukhina, V. (1984). *Growing up human.* Moscow: Progress Publishers.

Nakhimovsky, A., Stone, A. (Eds.). (1985). *The semiotics of Russian cultural history: Essays by Lurii M, Lotman, Lidiia Ia. Ginsburg, and Boris A. Uspenskii.* Ithaca: Cornell University Press.

Ochanine, D. (1980). Image opérative. In *Actes du Séminaire du 1 au 5 Juin 1981*, Université de Paris 1, (pp. 165-315).

Ochanine, D. (1980). *Hommage à Ochanine*. Actes du Séminaire du 1 au 5 Juin 1981, Université de Paris 1. Paris, France.

Orlova, A. M. (1988). Developing syntactical concepts in primary school students. In J. Downing (Ed.), *Cognitive psychology and reading in the USSR* (pp. 333-345). Amsterdam: North-Holand.

Petrovsky, A. (1984). *Age-group and pedagogical psychology*. Moscow: Progress Publishers.

Petrovsky, A. (1988). *The collective and the individual.* Moscow: Progress Publishers.

Petrovsky, A. (1990). *Psychology in the Soviet Union: a historical outline.* Moscow: Progress Publishers.

Pavlenko, V. N. (1994). Prospects for using the theory of activity in enthnopsychology. *Journal of Russian & East European Psychology, 32(2)*, 75-84.

Pedagogika Editorial Staff. (1983). L. S. Vygotsky and contemporary defectology. *Soviet Psychology, 21(4)*, 79-90

Philipov, A. P. (1952). *Logic and dialectic in the Soviet Union.* New York: Research Program on the USSR.

Philosophy in the USSR: Problems of dialectical materialism (Collective author). Trans. by R. Dalgish. Moscow: Progress Publishers, 1977.

Philosophy in the USSR: Problems of dialectical materialism (Collective authors). Trans. by S. Syrovatkin. Moscow: Progress Publishers, 1981.

Pletnikov, Y. (1981). Social relations. In *Philosophy in the USSR: Problems of dialectical materialism (Collective author)* (pp. 52-71). Trans. by S. Syrovatkin. Moscow: Progress Publishers.

Porshnev, B. (1965). Echolalia as a stage in the formation of the second signal system. *Soviet Psychology, 3*, 3-9.

Psychologie. (1966). *Recherches Internationales à la Lumière du Marxisme*, (51).

Puzyrei, A. (1983). From the notebooks of L. S. Vygotsky. *Soviet Psychology, 21(3)*, 3-17

Puzyrei, A. A. (1986). *Cultural-historical theory of L. S. Vygotsky and contemporary psychology* (in Russian). Moscow: Moscow Universi-ty.

Radzikhovskii, L. A. (1986-1987, winter). The dialogic quantity of consciousness in the works of M. M. Bakhtin. *Soviet psychology, 6*, 103-116.

Radzikhovskii, L. A. (1987). L. S. Vygotsky: In commemoration of 90th birthday. *Psikologicheskii Zhurnal, 8(1)*, 157-161.

Radzikhovskii, L. A. (1990). The language of description of holism and L. S Vygotsky's notion of "units". *Soviet psychology, 28*(3), 5-22.

Radzikhovskii, L. A. (1991). The historical meaning of the crisis of psychology. *Soviet psychology, 29*(4), 73-96.

Radzikhovskii, L. A., & Khomskaya, E. D. (1981). A. R. Luria and L. S. Vygotsky: Early years of their collaboration. *Soviet psychology, 20* (1), 3-21. Also in *Soviet Review, 23*(1), Spring 1982.

Rahmani, L. (1973). S*oviet psychology: Philosophical, theoretical, and experimental issues.* NY: International Universities Press.

Rahmani, L. (1973). Vygotskii's cultural-historical theory. In L. Rahmani, *Soviet psychology: Philosophical, theoretical, and experimental issues* (pp.38-48). New York: International Universities Press.

Razran, G. (1971). *Mind in evolution.* Boston: Houghyon-Mufflin.

Redozubov, S. P. (1988). The innovation and development of teaching reading by the phonetic method. In J. Downing (Ed.), *Cognitive psychology and reading in the USSR* (pp. 143-153). Amsterdam: North-Holland.

Redozubov, S. P. (1988). The scientific basis of methods of classroom instruction in reading at primary level. In J. Downing (Ed.), *Cognitive psychology and reading in the USSR* (pp. 155-158). Amsterdam: North-Holland.

Redozubov, S. P. (1988). Teaching literacy in the light of contemporary phonetics and experimental data. In J. Downing (Ed.), *Cognitive psychology and reading in the USSR* (pp. 159-160). Amsterdam: North-Holland.

Redozubov, S. P. (1988). Research method of teaching literacy. In J. Downing (Ed.), *Cognitive psychology and reading in the USSR* (pp. 161-178). Amsterdam: North-Holland.

Redozubov, S. P. (1988). Problems of teaching to children at the age of six. In J. Downing (Ed.), *Cognitive psychology and reading in the USSR* (pp. 179-187). Amsterdam: North-Holland.

Rudnev, P. (1963). Party and public education. *Soviet Education, 6*, 14-33.

Rubinstein, S. (1944). Soviet psychology in wartime. *Philosophy and Phenomenological Research,* (5), 181-198.

Rubinstein, S. (1946). Consciousness in the light of dialectical materialism. *Science & Society, 10*, 252-261.

Rubinstein, S. (1948). Psychological science and education. *Harvard Educational Review,* (18), 158-170.

Rubinstein, S. (1971-72). L. S. Vygotsky on the psychological development of mentality retarded children. *Soviet Education, 14* (1-2-3), 6-19.

Rubinstein, S. (1987). Problems of psychology in the works of Karl Marx. *Studies in Soviet Thought, 33,* 111-130.

Rubenstein, R. (1992). *Soviet psychology.* Orlando, FL: Paul M. Deutsch Press (Classic Soviet Psychology Series).

Rubtsov, V. V. (1981). The role of cooperation in the development of intelligence. *Soviet Psychology, 19,* 41-62. (Translated into Arabic by Mohamed ELhammoumi)

Rubtsov, V. V. (1989). Organization of joint actions as a factor of child psychological development. *International Journal of Educational Research, 13*(6), 623-636.

Rubtsov, V. V. (1991). *Learning in children: Organization and development of cooperation actions.* Commack, NY: Nova.

Sakharnyi, L. (1978). The structure of word meaning and situation. In J. Wertsch (Ed.), *Recent trends in Soviet psycholinguistics.* White Plains, New York: Sharpe.

Sakharov, L. (1930). Methods for investigating concepts. In R. Van Der Veer & J. Valsiner (Eds.), *The Vygotsky reader* (pp. 73-98). Oxford: Basil Blackwell. 1994.

Samarin, V. D. (1957). TheSoviet school 1936-1942. In G. L. Kline (Ed.), *Soviet education* (pp. 25-52). London: Routledge & Kegan Paul.

Sapogova, Y. Y. (1986). Characteristics of the transitory period in 6-7 yr old children. *Voprosy Psikhologii,* (4), 36-43.

Semenov, Yu. I. (1965). The doctrine of Morgan, marxism and contemporary ethnography. *Soviet Anthropology & Archaeology, 4* (2), 3-15.

Sémiotique. (1974). *Recherches Internationales à la Lumière du Marxisme,* (81-84).

Sereda, G. K. (1994). The Kharkov school of psychology. *Journal of Russian & East European Psychology, 32*(2), 7-8.

Sereda, G. K. (1994). What is memory? *Journal of Russian & East European Psychology, 32*(2), 8-21.

Sevastyanov, O. F. (1989). A dialogue that never was: Jean Piaget and Lev Vygotsky on the nature of egocentric speech. *Soviet Journal of Psychology, 10*(1), 71-76.

Shakhlevich-Lifanova, T. M. (1978). Vygotsky's works. In L. S. Vygotsky, *Mind in society.* Cambridge, MA: Harvard University Press.

Shchedrovitskii, L. P. (1994). L. S. Vygotsky's "tragedy of hamlet prince of Denmark". *Journal of Russian & East European Psychology, 32*(2), 49-65.

Shepovalova, A. (1993). The everyday social environment of Tungus children in the northern Baikal region. *Journal of Russian & East*

European Psychology, 31(1), 19-36. (Original work published in 1930).

Shubert, A. M. (1993). The experience of pedological-pedagogical expeditions to study the peoples of far-off regions. *Journal of Russian & East European Psychology, 31*(1), 13-18. (Original work published in 1930).

Shvarts, L. M. (1988). Psychological analysis of the process of reading in beginners and a methods of teaching literacy. In J. Downing (Ed.), *Cognitive psychology and reading in the USSR* (pp. 67-94). Amsterdam: North-Holland.

Smirnov, G. (1973). *Soviet man.* Moscow: Progress Publishers.

Sobkin, V. S., & Leontiev, D. A. (1992). The beginning of a new psychology: Vygotsky's psychology of art. In G. C. Cupchik, & J. Laszlo (Eds.), *Emerging visions of the aesthetic process: Psychology, semiology, and philosophy* (pp. 185-193). NY: Cambridge University Press.

Sokhin, F. A. (1988). Preschoolers's awareness of speech and readiness for learning literacy. In J. Downing (Ed.), *Cognitive psychology and reading in the USSR* (pp. 379-386). Amsterdam: North-Holland.

Sokolov, A. (1968). Brain mechanisms of thought. *Soviet Psychology, 6*, 10-20.

Sokolov, A. (1972). *Inner speech and thought.* London: Routledge & Kegan Paul.

Spirkin, A. (1983). *Dialectical materialism.* Moscow: Progress Publishers.

Stepanov, Y. S. (1974). Qu'est-ce la sémiotique? *Recherches Internationales à la Lumière du Marxisme,* (81-84), 26-37.

Suvorov, A. V. (1983). The formation of representation in blind-deaf children. *Soviet Psychology, 22*(2), 3-28.

Taglin, S. A. (1994). Piaget's tests in contemporary animal psychology: An assessment on their philosophical significance. *Journal of Russian & East European Psychology, 32*(4), 79-88.

Talyzina, N. (1980). *De l'enseignement programmé à la programmation de la connaisssance.* Lille: Presses Universitaires de Lille.

Talyzina, N. (1981). *The psychology of learning.* Moscow: Progress Publishers.

Tikhomirov, O. K. (1959). Review of B. F. Skinner, Verbal behavior. *Word, 15*, 362-367.

Tkachenko, A. N. (1983). Methodology of elaboration of analysis of mind in the history of the Soviet psychology. *Psikologicheskii Zhurnal, 4*(2), 3-14

Todorov, T. (1984). *Mikhail Bakhtin: The dialogical principles.* Manchester: Manchester University Press.

Tolstykh, A. (1987). *Man and his stages of life*. Moscow: Progress Publishers
Toutoundzhian, O. M. (1989). The psychological heritage of L. S. Vygotsky in Western Europe. *Voprosy Psikhologii*, (1), 156-161
Toutoundzhian, O. M. (1983). Works of L. S. Vygotsky in North America. *Voprosy Psikhologii, 21*, 39-142.
Tulviste, P. (1978). L. Lévy-Bruhl and problems of the historical development of thought. *soviet Psychology, 25*(3), 3-21.
Tulviste, P. (1979). On the origins of theoretic syllogistic reasoning in culture and the child. *Quarterly Newsletter of the Laboratory of Comparative Human Cognition*, (1), 73-80.
Tulviste, P. (1982). Is there a form of verbal thought specific to childhood. *Soviet Psychology, 21*, 3-17.
Tulviste, P. (1989). Education and the development of concepts: Interpreting results of experiments with adults with and without schooling. *Soviet Psychology, 27*(1), 5-21
Tulviste, P. (1989). Discussion of the works of L. S. Vygotsky in the USA. *Soviet Psychology, 27*(2), 37-52.
Tulviste, P. (1991). *Cultural-historical development of verbal thinking: A psychological study*. Commack, NY: Nova.
Tutundjian, O. (1966). La psychologie de Georges Politzer. *Recherches Internationales à la Lumière du Marxisme*, (51), 104-129.
Ushakova, T. N. (1986). Inner speech. *Soviet Psychology, 24*, 3-25.
Ushakova, T. N. (1994). Inner speech and second language aquisition: An experimental-theoretical approach. In J. P. Lantolf & G. Appel (Eds.), *Vygotskian approaches to second language research* (pp. 135-156). New Jersey: Ablex.
Usova, K. I. (1993). The Tungus child in school. *Journal of Russian & East European Psychology, 31*(1), 37-44. (Original work published in 1930).
Vari-Szilagi, I. (1989). G. H. Mead and L. S. Vygotsky: A comparative analysis. *Activity Theory*, (3-4), 39-42.
Vasilyuk, F. (1988). *The psychology of experiencing*. Moscow: Progress Publishers.
Vlasova, T. A. (1972). New advances in Soviet defectology. *Soviet Education, 14*(2-3), 20-39.
Vlasova, T. A. (1987). *Marxist-Leninist philosophy*. Moscow: Progress Publishers.
Velichkovsky, B. (1988). Commentary on Cole's article: Cross-cultural research in the sociohistorical tradition. *Human Development, 31*, 153-155.
Vorobyeva, L. I., & Snegiryeva, T. V. (1990). Psychological experience of the individual: Concerning the substantiation of the

approach. *Voprosy Psikhologii,* 25-13.

Vygodskaja, G. L. (1988). *Lev Semenovich Vigotskii (1896-1934 gg).* Unpublished manuscript.

Vygodskaja, G. L. (1988). L. S. Vygotsky. Life and work. *Proceedings of the 7th European CHEIRON Conference* (pp. 733-739. Budapest: Hungarian Psychological Association.

Vygodskaja, G. L. (1993). Remembering father. *Focus on Learning Problems in Mathematics, 15*(2-3), 57-59.

Vygodskaja, G. L. (1995). His life. *School Psychology International, 16*(2), 105-116.

Yaroshevsky, M. G. (1985). On the role of L. S. Vygotsky's defectology studies for the development of his general psychology conception. *Defektologiya,* (6), 78-84

Yaroshevsky, M. G. (1986). L. S. Vygotsky: Search for principles of constructing the theory of psychology. *Voprosy Psikhologii,* (6), 95-107.

Yaroshevsky, M. G. (1987). The psychology of creativity and creativity in psychology. *Soviet Psychology, 25*(2), 22-44

Yarochevsky, M. G. (1989). L. Vygotsky: A la recherche d'une nouvelle psychologie. *Enfance, 42*(1-2), 119-125.

Yarochevsky, M. G. (1989). *Lev Vygotsky.* Moscow: Progress Publishers.

Yarochevsky, M. G. (1990). *A history of psychology.* Moscow: Progress Publishers.

Yaroshevsky, M. G. (1992). *Vygotsky and his position on psychological sciences.* Orlando, FL: Paul M. Deutsch Press (Classic Soviet Psychology Series). Cancelled.

Yaroshevsky, M. G. (1994). L. S. Vygotsky -- victim of an "optical illusion". *Journal of Russian & East European Psychology, 32*(6), 35-43.

Yoo, Y. (1980). *Soviet education: An annotated bibliography and readers's guide to works in English.* Westport, Conn., & London: Greenwood Press.

Zaitseva, G. L. (1979). Intercenter interactions in the neocortex in three-year-old children under the influence of verbal stimuli. *Soviet Psychology, 17,* 23-36.

Zaitseva, G. L. (1990). L. S. Vygotsky and studies of sign language in Soviet psycholinguistics. In S. Prillwitz & T. Vollhaber (Eds.), *Sign language research and application.* (pp. 271-290). Hamburg, Gremany: Signum.

Zalkind, A. B. (1993). Psychoneurological study of national minorities. *Journal of Russian & East European Psychology, 31*(1), 11-12. (Original work published in 1930).

Zaporozhets, A. V. (1967). L. S. Vygotsky's role in the study of problems of perception. *Soviet Psychology, 5*(3), 19-27.

Zaporozhets, A. V. (1993). The mental development and psychological characteristics of Oirot children. *Journal of Russian & East European Psychology, 31*(1), 78-91. (Original work published in 1930).

Zaporozhets, A. V. (1995). Problems in the psychology of action. *Journal of Russian & East European Psychology, 33*(4), 12-17.

Zaporozhets, A. V., & Elkonin, D. (1971). *The psychology of pre-school children.* Cambridge, MA: MIT Press.

Zavadskii, K. M., Georgievskii, A. M., & Mozelov. A. P. (1971). Engels and darwinism. *Soviet Studies in Philosophy, 10*(1), 63-80.

Zeigarnik, B. V. (1986). Comment. In M. Golder (Ed.), *Reportajes contemporaneos a la psicologia sovietica* [Contemporary reports on Soviet psychology]. Buenos Aires: Cartago.

Zhiukov, S. F. (1988). The development of morphological concepts in the youngest school children. In J. Downing (Ed.), *Cognitive psychology and reading in the USSR* (pp. 313-331). Amsterdam: North-Holland.

Zinchenko, V. (1982). Preface. In K. Levitin, One is not born a personality: Profile of Soviet educational psychologists (pp. 7-12). Moscow: Progress Publishers.

Zinchenko, V. (1985). Vygotsky's ideas about units for the analysis of mind. In J. V. Wertsch (Ed.), *Culture, communication and cognition: Vygotskian perspectives.* Cambridge University Press.

Zinchenko, V. (1987). Artificial intelligence and paradoxes of psycholo-gy. *Social Sciences, 18*, 15-29.

Zinchenko, V. (1994). *The zone of proximal development and beyond.* Paper presented at the International Conference on L. S. Vygotsky an contemporary human sciences, Golitsyno, Moscow, Russia.

Zinchenko, V. (1995). Cultural-historical psychology and the psycholo-gical theory of activity: Retrospect and prospect. In J. Wertsch, P. del Rio & A. Alvarez (Eds.), *Sociocultural studies of mind* (pp. 37-55). NY: Cambridge University Press.

Zinchenko, V. (1995). The psychological theory of activity and the psychology of action. *Journal of Russian & East European Psychology, 33*(4), 47-54.

Zinchenko, V., Van Chzhi-Tsin,., & Tarakanov, A. V. (1963). The formation and development of perceptual activity. *Soviet Psychology and Psychiatry, 2*(1), 3-12.

Zinchenko, V., & Gordon, V. M. (1981). Methodological problems in the psychological analysis of activity. In J. V. Wertsch (Ed.), *The concept of activity in Soviet psychology.* Armonk, NY: Sharpe.

Zinchenko, V., & Davydov, V. V. (1985). Foreword. In J. V. Wertsch. *Vygotsky and the social formation of mind.* Harvard University Press.

Zinchenko, V., & Leontiev, D. A (1995). Discussions of problems of activiy. *Journal of Russian & East European Psychology, 33*(4), 8-11.

Zinkin, N. I. (1968). *Mechanisms of speech.* Holland: The Hague.

Zinkin, N. I. (1971). Semiotic aspects of communication in animal and man. *Semiotics,* (4), 75-93.

Zinkin, N. I. (1976). Thought and speech. J. Prucha (Ed.), *Soviet studies in language and language behavior.* NY: North-Holland.

Zotov, V. D. (1985). *The Marxist-Leninist theory of society.* Moscow: Progress Publishers.

Zuckerman, G. A. (1985). *Why children should learn together?* Moscow: Novaya Shkola (in Russian).

Zuckerman, G. A. (1994). A pilot study of a ten-day course incooperative learning for beginning Russian first graders. *Elementary School Journal, 94*(4), 405-420.

Discussion of the works of L. S. Vygotsky in the USA

Aber, J. (1986). *Toward reconceptualizing teacher training in composition: An ethnographic account and theoretical appraisal.* Unpublished doctoral dissertation, The Ohio State University, USA.

Adachi, M. (1994). The role of the adult in the child's early musical socialization: A Vygotskian perspective. *Quarterly Journal of Music Teaching and Learning, 5*(3), 26-36.

Adams, A. (1987). *Vygotskian approaches to semantic development: Implications for design and analysis.* Paper presented at the Fourth International Congress for the Study of Child Language, Lund, Sweden.

Adams, A., Scortino-Brudzynsky, A., Bjorn, K., & Tharp, R. (1987). *Forbidden colors: Vygotsky's experiment revisited.* Paper presented at the Meeting of the Society for research in Child Development, Baltimore, April 1987.

Ado, A. (1978). The ecology of man and the problem of the mediation of the biological by the social. *Social Sciences, 9,* 49-59.

Agre, P. H. (1992). Scribner on the history of work. *Quarterly Newsletter of the Laboratory of Comparative Human Cognition., 14*(4), 110-111.

Aljaafreh, A. A. (1992). *Negative feedback in second language learning and the zone of proximal development.* Unpublished doctoral dissertation, University of Delaware, USA.

Ames, G & Murray, F. (1982). When two wrongs make a right: Promoting cognitive change by social conflict. *Developmental Psychology, 18,* 894-897.

Anastopoulos, A. D. (1983). *Therapeutic component considerations in the use of cognitive self-instructional training programs with impulsive children.* Unpublished doctoral dissertation, Perdue University, USA.

Anderman, E. M., & al. (1995). *The zone of proximal development as the context for motivation.* (ERIC Document Reproduction Service No. ED 374 631)

Andrade, R., & Moll, L. (1993). Children's social worlds: An emic view. *J of the Society of Accelerative Learning & Teaching, 18*(1-2)

Appel. G. (1986). *L1 and L2 narrative and expository discourse production: A Vygotskian analysis.* Unpublished doctoral dissertation, University of Delaware, USA.

Appel, G. (1986). L1 and L2 narrative and expository discourse production: A Vygotskian analysis. *Dissertation Abstracts International, 47,,* 4373.

Applebee, A. N., & Langer, J. A. (1983). Instructional scaffolding: Reading and writing as natural language activities. *Language Arts,* *60,* 168-175.

Arns, F. J. (1981). *Joint problem-solving activity in adult-child dyads:* *A cross-cultural study.* Unpublished doctoral dissertation, Northwestern University, Evanston, IL, USA.

Ashton, P. (1996). The concept of activity. In L. Dixon-Krauss (Ed.), *Vygotsky in the classroom* (pp. 111-124). White Plains, N.Y: Longman Publisher.

Au, K. H. (1990). Changes in a teacher's view of interactive comprehesion instruction. In L. Moll (Ed.), *Vygotsky and education* (pp. 271-286). Cambridge: Cambridge University Press.

Au, K. H., & Kawakami, A. J. (1984). Vygotskian perspectives on discussion processes in small-group reading-lessons. In P. L. Peterson, L. C. Wilkinson & M. Hallinan (Eds.), *The social context of instruction: Group organization and group processes* (pp. 209-225). Academic Press.

Au, K. H., & Kawakami, A. J. (1986). Influence of the social organiza-tion on instruction on children text comprehension ability: A Vygotskian perspective. In T. E. Raphael (Ed.), *Contexts of school based literacy* (pp. 63-77). New York: Random House.

Ayman-Nolley, S. (1988). Piaget and Vygotsky on creativity. *Quarterly Newsletter of the Laboratory of Comparative Human Cognition, 10(*4), 107-111.

Ayman-Nolley, S. (1992). Vygotsky's perspective on the development of imagination and creativity. *Creativity Research Journal,* 5(1), 77-85.

Azmitia, M. (1988). Peer interaction and problem-solving: When are two heads better than one? *Child Development, 59,* 87-96.

Azmitia, M. (1989). Social influences on children's cognition: State of the art and future directions *Advances in Child Development and Behavior, 22,* 89-144.

Azmitia, M. (1992). Expertise, private speech, and the development of self-regulation. In R. M. Diaz & L. E. Berk (Eds.), *Private speech:* *From social interaction to self-regulation* (pp. 101-22). Lawrence Erlbaum Associates.

Bailes, K. (1986). Soviet science in the Stalin period: The case of V. I. Vernadskii. *Slavic Review, 45(*1), 20-37.

Bald, J. (1986, May 2). Mode making [case against the four modes theory of learning language]. *Times educational Supplement,* (3644) 55.

Baran, H. (Ed.). (1974). *Semiotics and structuralism: Readings from* *the Soviet Union.* White Plains, NY: International Arts and Science

Press.

Baron, R. M., & al. (1993). An integration of Gibsonian and Vygotskian perspectives on changing attitudes in group contexts. *British Journal of Social Psychology, 32*(1), 53-70.

Barritt, L., & Kroll, B. (1978). Some implications of cognitive developmental psychology for research in composing. In C. Cooper & L. Odell (Eds.), *Research on composing: Points of departure*. Urbana, IL: N.C.T.E.

Bartholomae, D., & Petrosky, A. (1986). *Facts, artifacts, and counterfacts*. Postsmouth, NH: Boynton/Cook.

Basch, M. F. (1981). Psychoanalytic interpretation and cognitive transformation. *International Journal of Psycho Analysis, 62*(2), 151-175.

Bator, P. G. (1980). *The impact of cognitive development upon audience awareness in the writing process*. Unpublished doctoral dissertation, University of Michigan, USA.

Bauer, R. A. (1952). *The new man in Soviet psychology*. Cambridge: Harvard University Press.

Bauer, R. A. (1955). *Nine Soviet portraits*. New York

Bauer, R. A. (Ed.). (1962). *Some views on Soviet psychology*. Washington: American Psychological Association.

Bazerman, C. (1988). Shaping written knowledge: The genre and activity of the experimental articlin science. Madison, WI: University of Wisconsin Press.

Beach, K. (1992). Scribner's uses of history: From field into the factory. *Quarterly Newsletter of the Laboratory of Comparative Human Cognition, 14*(4), 111-113.

Bearison, D. J. (1982). New directions in studies of social interaction and cognitive growth. In F. Serafica (Ed.), *Social cognitive development in context* (pp. 199-221). NY: Guilford Press.

Bearison, D. J. (1986). Transactional cognition in context: New models of social understanding. In D. J. Bearison & H. Zimiles (Eds.), *Thought and emotion: developmental perspectives* (pp. 129-146). Lawrence Erlbaum Associates. London.

Bearison, D. J. (1991). Interactional contexts of cognitive development: Piagetian approaches to sociogenesis. In L. Landsmann Tolchinsky (Ed.), *Culture, schooling and psychological development* (Vol. 4, pp. 56-70). Ablex Publishing Corp.

Bearison, D. J., & Weinstein, B. D. (1985). Social interaction, social observation and cognitive development in young children. *European Journal of Social Psychology, 15*, 333-343.

Bearison, D. J., Magzamen, S., & Filardo, E. K. (1986). Socio-cognitive conflict and cognitive growth in young children. *Merrill-*

Palmer Quarterly, 32(1), 51-72.

Beggs, W. D., & Howarth, P. N. (1985). Inner speech as a learned skill. *Journal of Experimental Child Psychology, 39,* 396-411.

Behrend, D., & al. (1992). The relation between private speech and parental interactive style. In R. M. Diaz & L. E. Berk (Eds.), *Private speech: From social interaction to self-regulation* (pp. 85-100). Lawrence Erlbaum Associates.

Bell, N., & Perret-Clermont , A. N. (1985). The social-psychological impact of school selection and failure. *International Review of Applied Psychology, 34,* 149-160.

Belmont, J. M. (1989). Cognitive strategies and strategic learning: The socio-instructional approach. *American Psychologist, 44,* 142-148.

Belmont, J. M. (1995). Discussion: A view from the empiricist's window. *Educational Psychologist, 30*(2), 99-102.

Belmont, J. M., Y Freeseman, L. J. (1988). *Journal references to Jean Piaget and Lev Vygotsky: Implications for the acculturation of American psychologists.* Unpublished manuscript, University of Kansas Medical Center, Kansas City.

Belmont, J. M., Mitchell, D. W. (1994, September). An empirical test of relations between psychometric intelligence and zone of proximal development. In J. Belmont & T. Akhutina (Cochairs), *The zone of proximal development in the diagnosis and training of mentally retarded children.* Symposium conducted at the International Conference: L. S. Vygotsky and the Contemporary Human Sciences, Golitsyno, Russia.

Benigni, L., & Valsiner, J. (1985). Developmental psychology without the study of developmental processes. *ISSBD Newsletter, 4.*

Bereiter, C., & Englemann, S. (1966). Teaching disadvantaged children in preschool. NJ: Englewood Cliffs, Prentice-Hall.

Berg, E. E. (1970). *L. S. Vygotsky's theory of the social and historical origins of consciousness.* PhD thesis. University of Wisconsin, USA.

Berk, L. E. (1985, July). Why children talk to themselves. *Young Children, 40*(5, 46-52.

Berk, L. E. (1986). Private speech: Learning out loud. *Psychology Today, 20*(5), 34-42.

Berk, L. E. (1986). Relationship of elementary school children's private speech to behavioral accompaniment to task, attention, and task performance. *Developmental Psychology, 22,* 671-680.

Berk, L. E. (1992). Chilren's private speech: An overview of theory and the status of research. In R. M. Diaz & L. E. Berk (Eds.), *Private speech: From social interaction to self-regulation* (pp. 17-53). Lawrence Erlbaum Associates.

Berk, L. E. (1993). *Infants, children and adolescents*. Boston: Allyn & Bacon.

Berk, L. E. (1994). Why children talk to themselves. *Scientific American, 271*(5), 78-83.

Berk, L. E. (1994). Vygotsky's theory: The importance of make-believe play. *Young Children, 50*(1), 30-39.

Berk, L. E., & Garvin, R. A. (1984). Development of private speech among low-income Appalachian children. *Developmental Psychology, 20*, 271-286.

Berk, L. E., & Potts, M. K. (1991). Development and functional significance of private speech among attention-deficit hyperactivity disordered and normal boys. *Journal of Abnormal Child Psychology, 19*(3), 357-377.

Berk, L. E., & Landau, S. (1991). Private speech of learning disabled and normally achieving children in classroom academic and laboratory contexts. *Child Development, 64*(2), 556-571.

Berk, L. E., & Winsler, A. (1995). *Scaffolding children's learning: Vygotsky and early childhood education.* NAEYC Research into Practice Series. Volume 7. Washington, D.C: National Association for the Education of Young Children.

Berlyne, D. E. (1970). Children's reasoning and thinking. In P. H. Mussen (Ed.), *Carmichael's manual of psychology.* (Vol. 1, pp. 939-981). New York: John Wiley & Sons.

Bernstein, L. E. (1981). Language as a product of dialogue. *Discourse Processes, 4*, 117-147.

Berthoff, A. E. (1978). Tolstoy, Vygotsky and the making of meaning. *College Composition & Communication, 29*, 249-255.

Best, L. (1993). *The interaction of cognition and context in the composing processes of first-year college writers.* Unpublished doctoral dissertation, University of Rochester, USA.

Bidell, T. (1988). Vygotsky, Piaget and the dialectic of development. *Human Development, 31*, 329-348.

Bidell, T. (1991). The constructive web: An alternative metaphor of development. *Genetic Epistemologist, 21*, 6-8.

Bidell, T. (1992). Beyond interactionism in contextualist models of development. *Human Development, 35*, 306-325.

Bidell, T., Fisher, K. W. (1992). Structure and variation in Piagetian theory and research: Beyond the stage debate. In R. J. Sternberg & C. A. Berg (Eds.), *Intellectual development.* New York: Cambridge University Press.

Bidell, T., Fisher, K. W. (in press). Developmental transitions in children's early on-line planning. In M. M. Haith, J. B. Benson, R. J. Roberts Jr., & B. F. Pennsington (Eds.), *Development of future-*

oriented processes. Chicago: Chicago University Press.

Biesta, G., & Miedema, S. (1989). Vygotskij in Harlem: De Barbara Taylor school. *Jeugd en Samenleving, 9,* 547-562.

Bivens, J. (1992). The representation of private speech in children's literature. In R. M. Diaz & L. E. Berk (Eds.), *Private speech: From social interaction to self-regulation* (pp. 159-77). Lawrence Erlbaum Associates.

Bivens, J. A. (1992). *International reciprocal teaching of math story problems: A qualitative analysis of the social origins of children's private speech.* Unpublished doctoral dissertation, Clark University, USA.

Bivens, J., & Berk, L. K. (1990). A longitudinal study of the development of elementary children's private speech. *Merrill-Palmer Quarterly, 36,* 443-463.

Bjornsen, C. A. (1992). *Friendship and social competence in preschool children.* Unpublished doctoral dissertation, Virginia Commonwealth University, USA.

Blackely, T. J. (1964). *Soviet theory of knowledge.* Dordrecht, Holland: Reidel.

Blackely, T. J. (Ed.). (1975). *Themes in Soviet Marxist philosophy.* Dordrecht, Holland: Reidel.

Blackely, T. J. (1976). The logic of Capital. *Studies in Soviet Thought, 16,* 281-288.

Bloch, M. (1983). *Marxism and anthropology.* Oxford: Oxford University Press.

Bloch, S., & Reddaway, P. (1984). *Soviet psychiatric abuse: The shadow over world psychiatry.* London: Victor Gollancz Ltd.

Bodrova, E., & Leong, D. (1994). *Vygoysky: An introduction (An overview of the work of the Soviet psychologist Lev Vygotsky, Vygotsky's developmental theory)* [Film]. Videorecording, Davis, CA: Davidson Film Inc, TRT: 27:35.

Bolotta, R. L. (1984). *Composing as becoming: From process to holomovement.* Unpublished doctoral dissertation, The Ohio State University, USA.

Bonkowski, N., Gavelek, J., & Akamatsu, T. (1991). Education and the social construction of mind: Vygotskian perspectives in the cognitive development of deaf children. In D. S. Martin (Ed.), *Cognition, education and deafness* (pp. 185-194). Washington DC: Gallaudet University Press.

Borden, R. C. (1987). *The magic and the politics of childhood: The childhood theme in the work of Iurii Olesha, Valentin Kataev and Vladimir Nabokov.* Unpublished doctoral dissertation, Columbia University, USA.

Bourassa, S. C. (1990). A paradigm for landscape aesthetics. *Conference of the Association of American Geographers* (1990, Toronto, Canada). *Environment and Behavior, 22*(6), 787-812.

Bradley, R. (1985). Social-cognitive development and toys. *Topics in Early Childhood Special Education, 5*(3), 11-29.

Brand, A. (1987). The why of cognition: Emotion and the writing process. *College Composition & Communication, 38*(4), 436-443

Branscombe, N. A. (1991). *Young children's use of social and narrative thought in the construction of literary awareness (social thought).* Unpublished doctoral dissertation, Auburn University, USA.

Brashear, N. L. (1993). *Sibling and parental behaviors in literacy development.* Unpublished doctoral dissertation, Claremont Graduate School, USA.

Braun, C., & Al. (1987). An examination of contexts for reading assessment. *Journal of Educational Research, 80*(5), 283-289.

Bretherton, I. (1991). What children know. *Science,* (254), 446.

Brinko, K. T. (1988). *Instructional consultation with feedback in higher education: A quantitative and qualitative analysis.* Unpublished doctoral dissertation, Northwestern University, USA.

Britain, L. P. (1992). *Having wonderful ideas together: Children's spontaneous collaboration in a self-directed play context (collaboration, play).* Unpublished doctoral dissertation, University of Oregon, USA.

Britton, J. (1970). *Language and learning.* Coral Gables, FL: University of Miami.

Britton, J. (1971). Introduction. In A. R. Luria & F. A. Yudovich, *Speech and development of the mental processes of the child.* Penguin.

Brondi, S. K. (1993). *An investigation of the application of Feuerstein's learning potential assessment device with school-identified adolescents with learning disabilities.* Unpublished doctoral dissertation, Philadelphia: Temple University, USA.

Bronfenbrenner, U. (1962). Soviet methods of character of education: Some implications for research. *American Psychologist, 17,* 550-565.

Bronfenbrenner, U. (1970). *Two worlds of childhood: USA and USSR.* New York: BAsic Books.

Bronfenbrenner, U. (1977). Towards an experimental ecology of human development. *American Psychologist, 32,* 513-531.

Bronfenbrenner, U. (1979). *The ecology of human development: Experiments by nature and design.* Cambridge: Harvard University Press.

Brooke, R. D. (1984). *Writing and commitment: Some psychosocial functions of college writing (deconstruction)*, Unpublished doctoral dissertation, University of Minnesota, USA.

Brooks, F. B., & Donato, R. (1992, August). *Vygotskian perspectives on understanding foreign language learner discourse during communicative tasks.* Paper presented at the Annual meeting of the American Association of Spanish and Portuguese, Cancun Mexico.

Brooks, F. B., & Donato, R. (1994). Vygotskian approaches to understanding foreign language earner discourse during communicative tasks. *Hispania, 77*, 262-274.

Brown, A. L. (1979). Vygotsky: A man of all seasons. *Contemporary Psychology, 24*(3), 161-163.

Brown, A. L., & French, L. A. (1979). The zone of potential development: Implications for intelligence testing in the year 2000. *Intelligence, 3 *, 255-273.

Brown, A. L., & Ferrara, R. A. (1985). Diagnozing zone of proximal development. In J. V. Wertsch (Ed.), *Culture, communication and cognition: Vygotskian perspectives* (pp. 273-305). New York: Cambridge University Press.

Brown, A. L. & Palinscar, A. S. (1989). Guided, cooperative learning and individual knowledge acquisition. In L. B. Resnick (Ed.), *Knowledge, learning and instruction: Essays in honor of Robert Glaser* (pp. 393-451). Hillsdale, New Jersey: Lawrence Erlbaum Associates.

Brown, A. L., Palinscar, A. S., & Armbruster, B. B. (1994). Instructing comprehension-fostering activities in interactive learning situations. In B. R. Ruddell, M. R. Ruddell & H. Singer (Eds.), *Theoretical models and processes of reading* (pp. 757-787). Newark, DE: International Reading Association.

Brown, A. L., Ash, D., Rutherford, M., Nakagawa, K., Gordon, A., & Compione, J. (1993). Distributed expertise in the classroom. In G. Salomon (Ed.), *Ditributed cognitions* (pp. 188-228). New York: Cambridge University Press.

Brown, P. G. (1980). *Kantian psycholinguistics: Wilfrid Sellars' philosophy of language as a theory of language development.* Unpublished doctoral dissertation, Emory University, USA.

Brown, J. S., Collins, A., & Duguid, P. (1989). Situated cognition and the culture of learning. *Educational Researcher, 18*(1), 32-42.

Brown, T. (1988). Why Vygotsky? The role of social interaction in constructing knowledge. *Quarterly Newsletter of the Laboratory of Comparative Human Cognition, 10*(4), 111-117.

Brownell, C. A., & Carriger, M. S. (1991). Collaborations amomg toddler peers: Individual contributions to social contexts. In L. Resnick, J. M. Leviner., & S. D. Teasley (Eds.), *Perspectives on socially shared cognition* (pp. 365-383). Washington DC: American Psychological Association.

Brownell, M. T. (1990). *Differences in transfer propensity and learning speed on balance-scale problems for students with learning disabilities and other low-achieving students.* Unpublished doctoral dissertation , University of Kansas, USA.

Brownell, M. T., Mellard, D. F., & Deshler, D. D. (1991, April). *Differences in transfer propensity and learning speed on balance-scale problems for students with learning disabilities and other low-achieving students.* Unpublished manuscript, University of Kansas: Institute for Research in Learning Disabilities, 40 pages.

Brozek, J. (1962). Current status of psychology in the USSR. *Annual Review of Psychology, 13,* 515-566.

Brozek, J. (1964). Recent developments in Soviet psychology. *Annual Review of Psychology, 15,* 493-594.

Brozek, J. (1966). Contemporary Soviet psychology. In N. O'Cnnor (Ed.), *Present-day Russian psychology* (pp. 178-198). Oxford: Pergamon Press.

Brozek, J. (1966). Soviet psychology in English: Translation of books. *Soviet psychology and Psychiatry(4),* 100-104.

Brozek, J. (1969). Soviet contributions to history. *Contemporary Psychology, 14,* 432-434.

Brozek, J. (1972). To test or not to test: Trends in Soviet views. *Journal of the History of the Behavioral Sciences, 8,* 243-248.

Brozek, J. (1972). Some significant historical events in the development of Soviet psychology. In J. Brozek & D. I. Slobin, Psychology in the USSR: A historical perspective (pp. 11-14). New York: White Pains: International arts & Sciences Press.

Brozek, J. (1979). Soviet psychology. I. In H. J. Eysenck, W. A. Würzburg, & R. M. Berne (Eds.), *Ecyclopedia of psychology* (pp. 1034-1037). The Seabury Press.

Brozek, J., Hoskovec, J., & Slobin, D. I. (1965/66). Reviews in English of recent Soviet psychology: A bibliography. *Soviet Psychology and Psychiatry (3-4),* 95-99.

Brozek, J., & Slobin, D. I. (1972). *Psychology in the USSR: A historical perspective.* New York: Wite Pains: International Arts & Sciences press.

Bruner, J. (1962). Preface. In L. S. Vygotsky, *Thought and language.* Cambridge, Mass: MIT. Presss.

Bruner, J. (1967). Preface to: Vygotsky memorial issue. *Soviet Psychology, 5(3),* 3-5.

Bruner, J. (1983). *Child's talk: Learning to use language.* New York: Norton.

Bruner, J. (1983). State of the child. *The New York Review of Books, Oct.27, 30*(16), 84-89.

Bruner, J. (1983). *Le développement de l'enfant: Savoir faire, savoire dire.* France, Paris: Presses Universitaires de France.

Bruner, J. (1983). La conscience, la parole et la "zone proximale": Refle-xions sur la théorie de Vygotsky. In J. Bruner, *Le développement de l'enfant: Savoir faire, savoire dire* (pp. 281-292). France, Paris: Presses Universitaires de France.

Bruner, J. (1984). Vygotsky's zone of proximal development: The hidden agenda. *New Directions for Child Development (*23), 93-97. (Translated into Arabic by Mohamed ELhammoumi)

Bruner, J. (1985). Vygotsky: A historical and a conceptual perspective. In J. V. Wertsch (Ed.), *Culture, communication and cognition: Vygotskian perspectives.* Cambridge University Press.

Bruner, J. (1986). Vygotskij: Una prospettiva storica e culturale. [Vygotsky: A historical and cultural perspective.]. *Studi di Psicologia dell'Educazione, 5*(3), 81-94.

Bruner, J. (1987, May). *Vygotsky revsited.* Paper presented at the Graduate School and University Center, City University of New York.

Bruner, J. (1987). Prologue to the english edition. In L. S. Vygotsky, *the collected works of L. S. Vygotsky: Problems of general psychology* (Vol. 1, pp.1-16). New York: Plenum Press.

Bruner, J. (1987). Foreword. In M. Hickmann (Ed.), *Social and functional approaches to language and thought* (pp. xi-xii). New York: Academic Press.

Bruner, J. (1990). *Acts of meaning. Cambridge.* MA: Harvard University Press.

Bruner, J. (1995). Reflecting on Russian consciousness. In L. Martin, K. Nelson & E. Tobach (Eds.), *Sociocultural psychology: Theory and practice of doing and knowning* (pp. 67-85). New York: Cambridge University Press.

Bruner, J., & Haste, H. (Eds.). (1987). *Making sense: The child's construction of the world.* London: Routledge.

Bullock, C. (1983). Using theory in the classroom: Vygotsky and the teaching of composition. *English Quarterly, 16*(2), 14-20.

Burkhalter, N. (1992). *Persuative writing: Analizing why and where students have problems.* Unpublished manuscript.

Burkhalter, N. (1992). *Applying Vygotsky: Teaching preformal-operational children a formal operational task.* Unpublished manuscript.

Burkhalter, N. (1995). A Vygotskian-based curriculum for teaching persuative writing in the elementary grades. *Language Arts, 72,* 192-

199.

Burnell, D. P. (1979). Egocentric speech: An adaptive function applied to developmental disabilities in occupational therapy. *American Journal of Occupational Therapy, 33(*3), 169-174

Buss, A. R. (1979). *A dialectical psychology.* New York: Irvington.

Buzzelli, C. A. (1993). Morality in context: A sociocultural approach to enhancing young children's moral development. *Child & Youth Care Forum, 22*(5), 375-386.

Cairns, R. B. (1992). The making of a developmental science: The contributions and intellectual heritage of James Baldwin. *Developmenal Psychology, 28(*1), 17-24.

Camperell, K. (1981). *Other to self-regulation, Vygotsky's theory cognitive development and its implications for improving comprehension instruction for unsuccessful students.* (ERIC Document Document Service No. ED 211 968)

Campione, J. C., Brown, A. L., Ferrera, R. A., & Bryant, N. R. (1984). The zone of proximal development: Implications for individual differences and learning. *New Directions for Child Development, (*23), 77-91.

Capps, D. (1991, October). *Revisioning Vygotsky.* Resources in Education, 44.

Carlin, M. E. (1994). The psychodynamic treatment of a disturbed adolescent: A Vygotskian perspective. *Bulletin of the Menninger Clinic, 58*(3), 355-374.

Cannella, G. S. (1993). Learning through social interaction: Shared cognitive experience, negotiation strategies, and joint concet construction for young children. *Early Childhood Research Quarterly, 8,* 427-444.

Carlson, J. (1994). Dynamic assessment of mental abilities. In R. J. Sternberg (Ed.), *Encyclopedia of human intelligence* (Vol. 1, pp. 368-372). New York: Macmillan Publishing Company.

Carver, T. (1980). Marx, Engels and dialectics. *Political Studies, 28(*3), 353-363.

Cassidy, D. J., & Myers, B. K. (1993). Mentoring in inservice training for child care workers. *Child & Youth Care Forum, 22*(5), 387-398.

Catàn, L. (1986). The dynamic display of process: Historical development and contemporary ises of the microgenetic method. *Human Development, 29,* 252-263.

Cazden, C. B. (1981). Performance before competence: Assistance to child discourese in the zone of proximal development. *Quarterly Newsletter of the Laboratory of Comparative Human Cognition, 3(*1), 5-8.

Cazden, C. B. (1980). Toward a social educational psychology -- with

Soviet help. *Contemporary Educational Psychology, 5,* 196-201.

Cazden, C. B. (1986). Classroom discourse. In M. C. Wittrock (Ed.), Hand*book of research teaching* (pp. 432-463). NY: Macmillan.

Cazden, C. B. (1988). *Classroom discourse.* Portsmouth, NH: Heinemann.

Cazden, C. B. (1992). Does practice with specific "Linguistic devices" matter? *Quarterly Newsletter of the Laboratory of Comparative Human Cognition, 14*(4), 113-114.

Cazden, C. B. (1993). Vygotsky, Hymes, and Bakhtin: from word to utterance and voice. In E. Forman, N. J. Minick, & C. A. Stone (Eds.), *Contexts for learning: Sociocultural dynamics in children's development* (pp. 197-212). New York: Oxford University Press.

Cazden, C. B. (1994). Vygotsky and literacy teaching. *TESOL, 28*(1), 172-172.

Cazden, C. B. (in press). Selective traditions: Readings on Vygotsky in writing pedagogy. In D. Hicks (Ed.), *Child discourse and social learning: An interdisciplinary perspective.* Cambridge: Cambridge University Press.

Chaplin, M. T. (1976). *Implications in the theories of Lev Vygotsky, Jean Piaget, George Kelly and Erik Erikson for the assessment of instruction in college reading.* Unpublished doctoral dissertation, New Brunswick: Rutgers University of State University of New Jersey, USA.

Chen, J. C. (1992). *One preschool teacher's approach to play intervention: An interpretive study based on Vygotsky's concept of activity.* Unpublished doctoral dissertation, University of Illinois at Urbana-Champaign, USA.

Chen, R. M. (1987). *The private speech of a chinese-english bilingual child: A naturalistic study.* Unpublished doctoral dissertation, University of Ilinois at Urbana-Champaign, USA.

Chiachiere, F. J. (1993). *The relationship of attitude to foreign language study, gender, grades and length of foreign language study to scores on the verbal scholastic aptitude test.* Unpublished doctoral dissertation. New York: New York University,USA.

Childe, V. G. (1979). Prehistory and marxism. *Antiquity, 53*(208), 93-95.

Chletsos, P. N. (1988). *An application of Vygotsky's theory to understanding formal operational strategies on Piaget's balance beam task.* Unpublished doctoral dissertation, New Brunswick: Rutgers University, The State University of New Jersey, USA.

Choi, S. (1992). *Mothers' and older siblings' scaffolding of preschool children's pretend play.* Unpublished doctoral dissertation, University of Wisconsin, USA.

Choi, S. Y. (1992). *Social origins of egocentric speech: An examination of language and cognition in bilingual Korean-American children (bilingual children)*. Unpublished doctoral dissertation, Columbia University, Teachers College, USA.

Chomsky, N. (1976). On the biological basis of language capacities. In R. W. Rieber (Ed.), *The neuropsychology of language: Essays in honor of Eric Lenneberg* (pp. 1-24). New York: Plenum Press. (A reply to Luria's critic)

Clark, K., & Holquist, M. (1984). *Mikhail Bakhtin*. Cambridge, MA: Harvard University Press.

Cobb, P., Wood, T., & Yackel, E. (1993). Discourse, mathematical thinking and classroom practice. In E. Forman, N. J. Minick, & C. A. Stone (Eds.), *Contexts for learning: Sociocultural dynamics in children's development* (pp. 91-119). NY: Oxford University Press.

Cohen, R. J. (1990). *The relationships between instruction and students' conceptions of mathematic*. Unpublished doctoral dissertation, University of California, Los Angeles, USA.

Cochran, S. M. (1988). Mediating: An important role for the reading teacher. In C. N. Hedley, & J. S. Hicks (Eds.), *Reading and the special learner* (pp. 109-139). Ablex Publishing Corp.

Cole, M. (1978). *Soviet developmental psychology*. White Plains, NY: Sharpe.

Cole, M. (Ed.). (1978). *The selected writings of A. R. Luria*. White Plains, NY: Sharpe.

Cole, M. (Ed.). (1979). Luria A. R. In D. L. Sills (Ed.), *International encyclopedia of the social sciences*, (Vol. 18, pp. 469-471). NY: Free Press.

Cole, M. (1980). The kharkov school of development psychology. *Soviet Psychology, 18*(2), 3-8.

Cole, M. (1985). The zone of proximal development: Where culture and cognition create each other. In J. V. Wertsch (Ed.), *Culture, communication and cognition: Vygotskian perspectives*. Cambridge University Press.

Cole, M. (1985). Mind as a cultural achievement: Implication for IQ testing. In E. Eisner (Ed.), *Learning and teaching the ways of knowning: Eighty-fourth yearbook of the National Society for the Study of Education*. Chicago: National Society for the Study of Education.

Cole, M. (1988). Cross-cultural research in the sociohistorical tradition. *Human Development, 31*, 137-152.

Cole, M. (1990). Alexandr Romanovich Luria: Cultural Psychologist. In E. Goldberg (Ed.), *Contemporary neuropsychology and the legacy of Luria. Institute for research in behavioral neuroscience* (pp. 11-28). Lawrence Erlbaum Associates.

Cole, M. (1990). *A cultural theory of development: What does it imply about the application of scientific research.* Paper presented at the Latin American Workshop on Applied Developmental Psychology, Recife, Brazil.

Cole, M. (1990). *Cultural psychology: Some general principles and concrete example.* Paper presented at the Second International Congress on Activity Theory, Lahti, Finland.

Cole, M. (1990). Cognitive development and formal schooling: The evidence from cross-cultural research. In L. Moll (Ed.),*Vygotsky and education.* Cambridge: Cambridge University Press.

Cole, M. (1991). On cultural psychology. *American Anthropologist, 93*(2), 435-439.

Cole, M. (1991). Conclusion. In L. Resnick, J. M. Leviner & S. D. Teasley (Eds.), *Perspectives on socially shared cognition* (pp. 398-417). Washington DC: American Psychological Association.

Cole, M. (1992). Sylvia Scribner at LCHC. *Quarterly Newsletter of the Laboratory of Comparative Human Cognition, 14*(4), 147-151.

Cole, M. (1993). Mind as a cultural achievement: Implications for IQ testing. *Journal of the Society of Accelerative Learning & Teaching, 18*(1-2).

Cole, M. (1994). Introduction. *Mind, Culture, and Activity: An International Journal, 1*(3), 133-134.

Cole, M. (1994). Introduction. *Journal of Russian & East European Psychology, 32*(4), 3-5.

Cole, M. (1994, June). *Cultural mechanisms of cultural development.* Peper presented at the meeting of the Jean Piaget Society, Chiacago, IL.

Cole, M. (1994). A conception of culture for a communication theory of mind. In D. R. Vocate (Ed.), *Intrapersonal communication: Different voices, different minds* (pp. 77-98). New Jersey: Lawrence Erlbaum Associates.

Cole, M. (1995). Socio-cultural-historical psychology: Some general remarks and a proposal for a new kind of cultural-genetic methodology. In J. Wertsch, P. del Rio & A. Alvarez (Eds.), *Sociocultural studies of mind* (pp. 187-214). New York: Cambridge University Press.

Cole, M. (1995). Cultural-historical psychology: A seso-genetic approach. In L. Martin, K. Nelson & E. Tobach (Eds.), *Sociocultural psychology: Theory and practice of doing and knowning* (pp. 168-204). New York: Cambridge University Press.

Cole, M. (1995). Culture and cognitive development: From cross-cultural research to creating systems of cultural mediation. *Culture*

& *Psychology.*

Cole, M. (1996). *Culture in mind.* Cambridge, MA: Harvard University Press.

Cole, M., Cole, S. (1977). *Soviet developmental psychology: An anthology.* White Plains, New York: E. M. Sharpe.

Cole, M., Cole, S. (1971). Three giants of Soviet psychology. *Psycho-logy Today, 4* (10), 43-50, 78-90, 94-98.

Cole, M., Gay, J., Glick, J., & Sharp, D. (Eds.). (1971). *The cultural context of learning and thinking.* New York: Basic Books.

Cole, M., & Maltzman, I. (Eds.). (1969). *Handbook of contemporary Soviet psychology.* New York: Basic Books.

Cole, M., & Scribner, S. (1974). *Culture and thought.* New York: Wiley.

Cole, M., & Scribner, S. (1978). Introduction. In L. S. Vygotsky, *Mind in society* (pp. 1-14). Cambridge, MA: Harvard University Press.

Cole, M., & Griffin, P. (1983). A socio-historical approach to re-mediation. *Quarterly Newsletter of the Laboratory of Comparative Human Cognition, 5(4),* 69-74.

Cole, M., & Engeström, Yrjö. (1993). A cultural-historical approach to distributed cognition. In G. Salomon (Ed.), *Distributed cognitions* (pp. 1-46). New York: Cambridge University Press.

Cole, M., & Engeström, Yrjö. (1994). Introduction. *Mind, Culture, and Activity: An International Journal, 1*(1&2), 3-7.

Cole, M., & Engeström, Yrjö. (1995). Commentary on Lucariello's article: Mind, culture, person: Elements in a cultural psychology. *Human Development, 38,* 19-24.

Collison, G. O. (1974). Concept formation in a second language: A study of Ghanian school children. *Harvard Educational Review, 44,* 441-457.

Combs, M. (1996). Emerging readers and writers.. In L. Dixon-Krauss (Ed.), *Vygotsky in the classroom* (pp. 25-41). White Plains, N.Y: Longman Publisher.

Comeaux, P. A. (1980). *Children performing poetry: A way of learning.* Unpublished doctoral dissertation, Southern Illinois University at Carbondale, USA.

Confrey, J. (1991). Steering a course between Vygotsky and Piaget. *Educational Researcher, 28*(8), 28-33.

Confrey, J. (1995). How compatible are radical constructivism, sociocultural approaches, and social constructivism. In L. P. Steffe & J. E. Gale (Eds.), *Constructivism in education* (pp. 185-225). Hillsdale, NJ: Lawrence Erlbaum Associates.

Conley, J. C. (1987). *The effects of aging, response delay, and stimulus word characteristics on word associations.* Unpublished doctoral dissertation, University of Southern Mississippi, USA.

Cornforth, M. (1967). *Marxism and the linguistic philosophy.* London: Routledge and Kegan Paul.

Conroy, M. S. (1985). Education of the blind, deaf, and mentally retarded in late tzarist Russia.
Slavic and East European Education review, (1-2), 29-49.

Cordeiro, P. (1994). Vygotsky in the classroom: An interactionist literacy framework in mathematics. In V. John-Steiner, C. P. Panofsky & L. W. Smith (Eds.), *Sociocultural approaches to language and literacy: An interactionist perspective* (pp. 265-297). NY: Cambridge University Press.

Corindia, N. S. (1982). *An investigation of the relatioship among students' questioning level, their cognitive level, and their teacher's questioning level.* Unpublished doctoral dissertation, Boston University School of Education USA.

Corsaro, W. A. (1985). Theoretical issues in research on peer culture. In CorsaroW. A., *Friendship and peer culture in the early years* (pp. 51-75). Norwood, NJ: Ablex

Corsaro, W. A. (1985). *Friendship and peer culture in the early years.* Norwood, NJ: Ablex

Corsaro, W. A., & Rizzo, T. A. (1988). Discussione and friendship: Socialization processes in the peer culture of Italian nursery schoolchildren. *American Sociological Review, 53*(6), 879-894.

Corsaro, W. A., & Edler, D. (1990). Children's peer cultures. *Annual Review of Sociology, 16,* 197-220.

Corson, S. A., & Corson, E. C. (Eds.). (1976). *Psychiatry and psychology in USSR.* New York: Plenum Press.
Costa, A. L. (1984, November). Mediating the metacognitive. *Educational Leadership,* 57-62.

Costa, A. L. (1991). *The school as a home for the mind.* Palatine. IL: IRI/Skylight Publishing, Inc.

Cox, M. L. (1987). *Two year-olds' symbol play as a function of maternal interaction.* Unpublished doctoral dissertation, City University of New York, USA.

Crain, I. J. (1995). Philosophy, politics, and psychoanalysis. *Nature, Society, & Thought, 8*(1), 79-99

Crane, L. L. (1987). *Evidence for parallel development of intuitive and procedural knowledge.* Unpublished doctoral dissertation, University of Maryland Baltimore County, USA.

Crook, C. (1991). Computers in the zone of proximal development: Implications for evaluation. *Computers & Education, 17,* 81-92.

Daiute, C., & Dalton, B. (in press). Collaborative between children learning to write: Can novices be masters? *Cognition & Instruction*

Dale, H. (1992). *Collaborative writing: A singular we.* Unpublished doctoral dissertation, University of Wisconsin-Madison USA.

Dale, H. (1994). Collaborative writing interactions in one nine-grade classroom. *Journal of Educational Research, 87*(6), 334-344.

Damon, W. (1984). Peer interaction: The untapped potential. *Journal of Applied Developmental Psychology, 5),* 331-343.

Damon, W. (1991). Problem of direction in socially shared cognition. In L. Resnick, J. M. Leviner., & S. D. Teasley (Eds.), *Perspectives on socially shared cognition* (pp. 384-397). Washington DC: Ameri-can Psychological Association.

Damon, W. (1994). Commentary on Verba's paper: The beginnings of collaboration in peer interaction. *Human Development, 37*), 140-142.

Damon, W., & Phelps, E. (1991). Peer collaboartion as a context of cognitive growth. In L. Landsmann, Tolchinsky (Ed.), *Culture, schooling and psychological development* (pp. 171-184). Human development. Vol.4. Ablex Publishing Corp.

Dance, F. E. (1964). Speech communication in the Soviet Union: The phylogenesis of speech according to Frederick Engels. *The Speech Teacher, Journal of Speech Association of America, 13*, 115-118.

Dance, F. E. (1994). Hearing voices. In D. R. Vocate (Ed.), *Intra-personal communication: Different voices, different minds* (pp. 195-212). New Jersey: Lawrence Erlbaum Associates.

Daniele, R. J. (1985). *A study of the development of the ability to produce deceptive strategies.* Unpublished doctoral dissertation, City University of New York, USA.

Danziger, K. (1990). *Constructing the subject: Historical origins of psychological research.* Cambridge: Cambridge University Press.

Daugherty, M. A. (1991). *Identifying creativity through young child-ren's private speech.* Unpublished doctoral dissertation, University of Georgia, USA.

Davidson, L., & Scripp, L. (1994). Conditions of giftedness: Musical development in the preschool and early elementary years. In R. F. Subotnik & K. D. Arnold (Eds.), *Beyond Terman: Contemporary longitudinal studies of giftedness and talent* (pp. 155-185).New Jerey: Ablex.

Davidson, P. M. (1992). The role of social interaction in cognitive development: A propaedeutic. In L. L. Winegar & J. Valsiner (Eds), *Children's development within social context: Methodology and Theory* (Vol. 1, pp. 19-35). Lawrence Erlbaum Asssociates.

Dazzi, N. (1986). The problem of concept formation in Vygotsky. *Revista de Historia de la Psicologia, 7*(1), 3-12.

Dean, A. L. (1994). Instinctal affective forces in the internalization process: Contributios of Hans Loewald. *Human Development. 37* (1), 42-57.

Deleclos, V., Vye, N., Burns, M., Bransford, J., & Hasselbring, T. (1992). Improving the quality of instruction: Roles for dynamic assessment. In. H. C. Haywood & D. Tzuriel (Eds.), *Interactive assessment* (pp. 317-331). New York: Springer-Verlag.

De Lisi, R. (1981). Landmarks in the literature: Children's thought and language. *New York University Education Quarterly, 13*(1), 29-32.

Derry, S., & Lajoie, S. (1993). A middle camp for (un) intelligent instructional computing: An introduction. In S. Derry & S. Lajoie (Eds.), *Computers as cognitive tools* (pp. 1-11). Hillsdale, NJ: Erlbaum.

Derry, S., & Hawkes, L. (1993). Local cognitive modeling of problem-solving behavior: An application of fuzzy theory. In S. Derry & S. Lajoie (Eds.), *Computers as cognitive tools* (pp. 107-140). Hillsdale, NJ: Erlbaum.

Deutsch, A. (1989). *An exploration of how children with attention-deficit hyperactivity disorders and their mothers use speech.* Unpubli-shed doctoral dissertation, The Brooklyn: Long Island City University, USA.

Diamant, R. J., & Bearison, D. J. (1991) Development of formal reasoning during successive peer interactions. *Developmental psychology, 27*(2), 277-284.

Diaz, R. M. (1985). The intellectual power of bilinguism. *Quarterly Newsletter of the Labora-tory of Comparative Human Cognition, 7*(1), 16-22.

Diaz, R. M. (1985). *The union of thought and language in children private speech: Recent empirical evidence for Vygotsky's theory.* Paper presented at the International Congress of Psychology, Mexico.

Diaz, R. M. (1986). The union of thought and language in children private speech. *Quarterly Newsletter of the Laboratory of Compara-tive Human Cognition, 8*(3), 90-97.

Diaz, R. M. (1992). Methodological concerns in the study of private speech. In R. M. Diaz & L. E. Berk (Eds.), *Private speech: From social interaction to self-regulation* (pp. 55-81). Lawrence Erlbaum Associates.

Diaz, R. M., & Klinger, C. (1991). Towards an explanatory model of the interaction between bilingualism and cognitive development. In E. Bialystok (Ed.), *Language processing in bilingual children* (pp. 167-192). Cambridge: Cambridge University Press

Diaz, R. M., & Padilla, K. A. (1985). Teoria e investigaciones empiricas sobre el lenguaje privado. [Theory and empirical investigations of private language]. Special Issue: About Vygotsky's thoughts. *Anuario de Psicologia, 33*(2), 43-58

Diaz, R., & al. (1990). The social origin of self-regulated. In L. Moll (Ed.), *Vygotsky and education.* Cambridge: Cambridge University Press.

Diaz, R. M., Moll. L., & Mehan. H. (1986). Sociocultural resources in instruction: A context-specific approach. In California State Depart-ment of Education (Ed.), *Beyond language: Social and cultural factors in schooling language minority children* (pp. 187-230). Los Angeles: California State University Evaluation, Dissemination and Assessment Center.

Diaz, R., Neal, C. J., & Vachio, A. (1991). Maternal teaching in the zone of proximal development: A comparison of law-and high-risk dyads. *Merrill-Palmer Quarterly, 37*(1), 83-108.

Diaz, R. M., & Berk, L. E. (1992). Introduction. In R. M. Diaz & L. E. Berk (Eds.), *Private speech: From social interaction to self-regulation.* (pp. 1-13). Lawrence Erlbaum Associates.

Diaz, R. M., & Berk, L. E. (Eds.). (1992). *Private speech: From social interaction to self-regulation.* Lawrence Erlbaum Associates.

Diaz, R. M., & al. (1995). A Vygotskian critique of self-instructional training. *Development & Psychopathology, 7*(2), 369.

Di Bello, L & Orlich, F. (1987). How Vygotsky's notion of "scientific concept" may inform contemporary studies of theory development. *Quarterly Newsletter of the Laboratory of Comparative Human Cognition, 9*(3), 96-99.

Di Bello, L. (1992). Looking for "what's leading": A legacy from Sylvia Scribner. *Quarterly Newsletter of the Laboratory of Compara-tive Human Cognition, 14*(4), 114-116.

Dinkler, P. D. (1991). *Recursive composing in freshmam composition: Case studies of four student writers in search of the self-made writer (writing instruction).* Unpublished doctoral dissertation, The ohio State University, USA.

Dixon [Krauss], L. A. (1985). *An investigation of the zone of proximal development for reading placement.* Unpublished doctoral disserta-tion, The University of Florida, USA.

Dixon-Krauss, L. (1994). *A mediation model for dynamic literacy instruction.* Paper presented at the International Conference on L. S. Vygotsky and the Contemporary Human Sciences, Moscow, Russia.

Dixon-Krauss, L. (1995). Partner reading and writing: Peer social dialogue and the zone of proximal development. *Journal of Reading Behavior, 27*(1), 45-64.

Dixon-Krauss, L. (1996). Vygotsky's sociohistorical perspective on leaning and its application to western literacy instruction. In L. Dixon-Krauss (Ed.), *Vygotsky in the classroom* (pp. 7-24). White Plains, N.Y: Longman Publisher.

Dixon-Krauss, L. (1996). Spontaneous and scientific concepts in content-erea instruction. In L. Dixon-Krauss (Ed.), *Vygotsky in the classroom* (pp. 43-58). White Plains, N.Y: Longman Publisher.

Dixon-Krauss, L. (Ed.). (1996). *Vygotsky in the classroom.* White Plains, N.Y: Longman Publisher.

Donaldson, M. (1978). *Children's minds.* London: Fontana / Collins.

Donato, R. (1988). *Beyond group: A psycholinguistic rationale for collective activity in second-language learning.* Unpublished doctoral dissertation, University of Delaware, USA.

Donato, R. (1994). Collective scaffolding in second language learning. In J. P. Lantolf & G. Appel (Eds.), *Vygotskian approaches to second language research* (pp. 33-56). New Jersey: Ablex.

Donato, R., & J. P. Lantolf. (1990). Dialogic origins of L2 monitoring. In L. F. Bouton & Y. Kachuri (Eds.), *Pragmatics and language learning* (Vol. 1, pp. 83-97). Urbana-Champaign, IL: Division of English as an International Language.

Donato, R., & McCormick, D. (1994). A sociocultural perspective on language learning strategies: The role of mediation. *Modern Language Journal, 78(4)*, 453-464.

Doolittle, P. E. (1995, June). *Understanding cooperative learning through Vygotsky's zone of proximal development.* Paper presented at the Lilly National Conference on Excellence in College Teaching, Columbia, SC.

Doughery, K. C. (1993). *Looking for a way out: Women on welfare and their educational advancement.* Unpublished doctoral dissertation, University of Colorado at Boulder, USA.

Drucker, L. (1982). *The effects of age, cognitive strategy, type of conrolling speech and reward preference on delay of gratification.* Unpublished doctoral dissertation, Hofstra University, USA.

Edwards, P. A., & Garcia, G. E. (1994). The implication of Vygotskian theory for the development of home-school programs: Afocus on storybook reading. In V. John-Steiner, C. P. Panofsky & L. W. Smith (Eds.), *Sociocultural approaches to language and literacy: An interactionist perspective* (pp. 243-264). NY: Cambridge University Press.

EL-Dinary, R. B. (1993). *Teachers learning, adapting and implementing strategies-based instruction in reading.* Unpublished doctoral dissertation, Baltimore: University of Maryland, USA.

EL-Dinary, R. B. (1994). Seven teachers' acceptance of transactional strategies instruction during their first year. *Elementary School*

Journal, 94(2), 207-219.

Ellis, S., & Gauvain, M. (1992). Social and cultural influences on children's collaborative interactions. In L. T. Winegar & J. Valsiner (Eds.), *Children's development within social context* (pp. 155-180). Hillsdale: Lawrence Erlbaum Associates.

Elsasser, N., & John-Steiner, V. (1983). An interactionist approach to advancing literacy. *Harvard Educational review, 44*, 355-369.

Emerson, C. (1983). The outer word and inner speech: Bakhtin, Vygotsky and the internalization of language. *Critical Inquiry, 10,* pp.245-264. Also in G. S. Morson (Ed.), *Bakhtin: Essays and dialogues on his work* (pp. 21-40). Chicago: Chicago University Press.

Emerson, C. (1983). Bakhtin and Vygotsky on internalization of language. *Quarterly Newsletter of the Laboratory of Comparative Human Cognition, 5*(1), 9-13.

Emery, A. (1935). Dialectics vs. mechanistics: A communist debate on scientific method. *Philosophy of Science, 2*, 9-38.

Emig, J. (1971). *The composing processes of twelfth graders.* Champaign IL: N.C.T.E.

Emig, J. (1971). Writing as a mode of learning. *College Composition & Communication, 28*(2), 122-128.

Emig, J. (1982). Nonmagical thinking: Presenting writing developmentally in the schools. In C. Frederiksen & J. Dominic (Eds.), *Writing: The nature, development, and teaching of written communication.* NJ: Erlbaum.

Englert, C. S. (1992). Writing instruction from a socioculural perspective: The holistic, dialogic, and social entreprise of writing. *Journal of Learning Disabilities, 25*(3), 153-172.

Englert, C. S., & Mariage, T. V. (1991). Shared understanding: Structuring the writing experience through dialogue. *Journal of Learning Disabilities, 6*(6), 330-342.

Englert, C., & Palincsar, A. S. (1991). Reconsidering instructional resarch in literacy from a sociocultural perspective. *Learning Disabilities Research & Practice, 24*, 225-229.

Englert, C. S., Rosendal, M. S., & Mariage, T. V. (1994). Fostering the search for understanding: A teacher's strategies for leading cognitive developmentin "zones of proximal development". *Learning Disability Quarterly, 17*, 187-204.

Englert, C. S., Raphael, T. E., & Anderson, L. M. (in press). Socially-mediated instruction: Students' knowledge and talk about writing. *Elementary School Journal.*

Epstein, H. T. (1980). Some biological bases of cognitive development. *Bulletin of the Orton Society, 30*, 46-62

Everson, B. J. (1991). Vygotsky and the teaching of writing. *Quarterly of the National Writing Project & the Center for the Study of Writing & Literacy, 13(3)*, 8-11.

Exner, C. (1990). The zone of proximal development in hand manipulation skills of nondysfunctional 3 and 4 year old children. *American Journal of Occupational Therapy, 44(10)*, 884-892.

Fairbanks, C. M. (1992). *Tyshun's great adventures in learning: Teachers and students as vicars of culture.* Unpublished doctoral dissertation, The University of Michigan, USA.

Faltis, C. (1990). Spanish for native speakers: Freirian and Vygotskian perspectives. *Foreign Language Annals, 23(2)*, 117-126.

Falmagne, R. F. (1995). The abstract and the concrete. In L. Martin, K. Nelson & E. Tobach (Eds.), *Sociocultural psychology: Theory and practice of doing and knowning* (pp. 205-228). New York: Cambridge University Press.

Farmer, F. (1991). *Dialogue imagination: Vygotsky, Bakhtin, and their internalization of voices (Vygotsky Lev, Bakhtin Mikhael, imitation).* Unpublished doctoral dissertation, University of Louisville, USA.

Farver, J. M. (1993). Cultural differences in scaffolding pretend play: A comparison of American and Mexican mother-child and sibling-child pairs. In K. MacDonald (Ed.), *Parent-child play* (pp. 349-366). Albany, NY: State University of New York Press.

Faulconer, J. E., & Williams, R. (Eds.). (1990). *Reconsidering psycho-logy.* PA: Duquesne University Press.

Faulkner, T. M. (1989). *Collaborative writing: Case studies of fourth and fifth-grade students at work.* Unpublished doctoral dissertation, The University of Iowa, USA.

Feierstein, R. E. (1991). *The use of guided imagery to increase attention and academic achievement in children with attention deficit hyperactivity disorder.* Unpublished doctoral dissertation, The Fielding Institute, USA.

Feigenbaum, P. (1989). *The development of the planning function and the discourse structure of "private" speech.* Unpublished doctoral dissertation, City University of New York, USA.

Feigenbaum, P. (1992). Development of the syntactic and discourse structures of private speech. In R. M. Diaz & L. E. Berk (Eds.), *Private speech: From social interaction to self-regulation* (pp. 181-98). Lawrence Erlbaum Associates.

Fein, G. G. (1979). Echoes from the nursery: Piaget, Vygotsky, and the relationship between language and play. *New Directions for Child Development, 6)*, 1-14.

Fein, G. (1984). New wine in old bottles. *New Directions for Child*

Development, (25), 71-84

Ferrara, R. A. (1987). *Learning mathematics in the zone of proximal development: The importance of flexible use of knowledge.* Unpublished doctoral dissertation, University of Illinois, Champagn, USA.

Ferrara, R. A., Brown, A. L., & Compione, J. C. (1986). Children's learning and transfer of inductive reasoning rules: Studies of proximal development. *Child Development, 57,* 1087-1099.

Fey, M. H. (1992). *Freeing voices: Literacy through computer conferencing and feminist collaboration.* Unpublished doctoral dissertation, The University of Rochester, USA.

File, N. (1993). The teacher as a guide of children's competence with peers. *Child & Youth Care Forum, 22*(5), 351-360.

Finkel, E. A., & Stewart, J. (1994). Strategies for model-revision in a high school genetics classroom. *Mind, Culture, and Activity: An International Journal, 1*(3), 168-195.

Fiore, K., & Elsasser, N. (1982). "Strangers no more": A liberatory literacy curriculum. *College English, 44*(2), 115-128.

Fitzpatrick, S. (Ed.). (1978). *The cultural revolution in Russia:1928-1932.* Blomington: Indiana University Press.

Fitzpatrick, S. (1990). Russians on the psyche. *Science,* (248), 881-883.

Flaherty, S. M. (1983). *Developing and interactive technical writing curriculum through action research.* Unpublished doctoral dissertation, The Ohio State University, USA.

Flavell, H. (1966). Le langage privé. *Bulletin de Psychologie, 19,* 698-701.

Fleer, M. (1992). Identifying teacher-child interaction with scaffolds scientific thinking in young children. *Science Education, 76*(4), 373-397.

Flower, L. (1979). Writer-based prose: A cognitive basis for problems in writing. *College English, 14*(1), 19-37.

Fodor, J. (1972). Some reflections on L. S. Vygotsky's thought and language. *Cognition, 1*(1), 83-95.

Foley, J. (1991). A psycholinguistic framework for task-based approaches to language teaching. *Applied Linguistics, 12*(1), 62-75.

Forman, E. A. (1987). Learning through peer instruction: A Vygotskian pertspective. *Genetic Epistemology, 15,* 6-15.

Forman, E. A. (1989). The role of peer interaction in the social construction of mathematical knowledge. *International Journal of Educational Research, 23*(3), 55-70.

Forman, E. A. (1992). Discourse, intersubjectivity and the development of peer collaboration: A Vygotskian approach. In L. Winegar & J.

Valsiner. (Eds), Children's development within social context: Methodology and Theory (Vol. 1, pp. 143-159). Lawrence Erlbaum Asssociates.

Forman, E. A., & Cazden, C. (1985). Exploring Vygotskian perspectives in education: The cognitive value of peer interaction. In J. V. Wertsch (Ed.), *Culture, communication and cognition: Vygotskian perspectives.* Cambridge University Press. Also, In B. R. Ruddell, M. R. Ruddell & H. Singer (Eds.), *Theoretical models and processes of reading* (pp. 155-178). Newark, DE: International Reading Association. 1994.

Forman, E. A., & Kraker, M. J. (1985). The social origin of logic: the constructions of Piaget and Vygotsky. Peer conflict and psychological growth). *New Directions for Child Development,* (29), 23-39.

Forman, E. A., & McPhail, J. (1989, March). *What we have learned about the cognitive benefits of peer interaction?: A Vygotskian critique.* Paper presented as a part of a symposium series."Extending Vygotskian theory III: Interpersonal relationships and the teaching-learning process" Annual meeting of the American Educational Research Association: San Francisco, California.

Forman, E. A., & McPhail, J. (1993). Vygotskian perspective on children's collaborative problem-solving acitivities. In E. Forman, N. J. Minick, & C. Stone (Eds.), *Contexts for learning: Sociocultural dynamics in children's development* (pp. 213-229). New York: Oxford University Press.

Forman, E. A., Minick, N., & Stone, C. A. (Eds.). (1993). *Contexts for learning: Sociocultural dynamics in children's development.* New York: Oxford University Press.

Fosberg, I. A. (1946). Multiple solutions to the Vigotsky test. *American Psychologist, 1*(7), 280.

Fosberg, I. A. (1948). A modification of the Vygotstky block test for the study of higher thought processes. *American Journal of Psychology, 61,* 558-561.

Fowler, L. S. (1992). *Computer-mediated communications in grades 3 through 12 education: Teacher reports of impact on social, cultural and writing development.* Unpublished doctoral dissertation, University of Cincinnati, USA.

Frauenglass, M., & Diaz, R. (1985). Self-regulatory functions of children's private speech: A critical analysis of recent challenges to Vygotsky's theory. *Developmental Psychology, 21*(2), 357-64.

Frawley, W., & Lantolf, J. (1985). L2 discourse: A Vygoskian perspec-tive. *Applied Linguistics, 6*(1), 19-44.

Frawley, W., & Lantolf, J. (1986). Private speech and Self-regulatory:

a commentary on Frauenglass and Diaz. *Developmental Psychology, 22*(5), 706-708.

Fredericks, S. C. (1974). Vygotsky on language skills. *The Classical World, 67,* 283-290.

Freedman, S. W. (1995). Rethinking the theories of Vygotsky and Bakhtin. *Written Communication, 12*(1), 74-92.

Freigenbaum, P. (1995). A Marx-Freud dialogue? *Nature, Society, & Thought, 8*(1), 101-109.

French, L. A. (1980). *Cognitive consequences of education: transfer of training in the elderly.* Unpublished doctoral dissertation, University of Illinois at Urbana-Champaign,USA.

Freund, L. S. (1988). *The child's transition from mother regulation to self-regulation during a problem-solving task.* Unpublished doctoral dissertation, University of Maryland Baltimore County, USA.

Fulani, L. B. (1984). *Children's understanding of number symbols in formal and informal contexts (Black, low income, mathematics).* Unpublished doctoral dissertation, City University of New York, USA.

Furrow, D. (1992). Developmental trends in the differentiation of social and private speech. In R. M. Diaz & L. E. Berk (Eds.), *Private speech: From social interaction to self-regulation* (pp. 143-158). Lawrence Erlbaum Associates.

Fuson, K. C. (1979). The development of self regulating aspects of speech: A review. In G. Zevin (Ed.), *The development of self-regulation through private speech* (pp. 135-217). New York: Wiley.

Galimore, R. (1990, September). *Mapping teachers' zones of proximal development: A Vygotskian perspective on teaching and teacher training.* Paper presented at th International Symposium on Research on Effective and Responsible Teaching. University of Fribourg, Fribourg, Switzerland.

Gallimore, R., Dalton, S., & Tharp, R. G. (1986). Self-regulation and interactive teaching: The effects of teaching conditions on teachers' cognitive activity. *Elementary School Journal, 86*(5), 612-631

Gallimore, R., Tharp, R. G., & Rueda, R. (1989). The social context of cognitive functioning in the lives of mildly handicapped persons. In D. Sugden (Ed.), *Cognitive approaches in special education* (pp. 51-81). Falmer Press.

Gallimore, R., & Tharp, R. (1990). Teaching mind in society: Teaching, schooling, and literate. In L. Moll (Ed.), *Vygotsky and education* (pp. 175-205). Cambridge: Cambridge University Press.

Gallimore, R., & Goldenberg, C. (1993). Activity settings of early literacy: Home and school factors in children's emergent literacy. In E. Forman, N. J. Minick, & C. A. Stone (Eds.), *Contexts for learning: Sociocultural dynamics in children's development* (pp. 315-335). New York: Oxford University Press.

Gannaway, G. J. (1988). *Toward a critical theory of teaching composition and cultural literacy (deconstructionism).* Unpublished doctoral dissertation, The University of Texas at Austin, USA.

Gaskill, M. (1985). *The effect of private speech on cognitive performance.* Unpublished Master's thesis, The University of New Mexico, USA.

Gaskill, M., & Diaz, R. M. (1991). The relation between private speech and cognitive performance. *Infancia y Aprendizaje, (*53), 45-58.

Gaskins, S. (1988). Children's play as representation and imagination: The case of Piaget and Vygotsky.
Quarterly Newsletter of the Laboratory of Comparative Human Cognition, 10(4), 104-107.

Gaskins, S. (1990). *Exploratory play and development in Maya infants.* Unpublished doctoral dissertation, University of Chicago, USA.

Gaskins, S., & Göncü, A. (1992). Cultural variation in play: A challenge to Piaget and Vygotsky. *Quarterly Newsletter of the Laboratory of Comparative Human Cognition, 14*(2), 31-35.

Gauvain, M. (1995). Thinking in niches: Sociocultural influences on cognitive development. *Human Development, 38,* 25-45.

Gelb, S. A. (1991). Street level and trickle-down psychology. *Quarterly Newsletter of the Laboratory of Comparative Human Cognition, 13*(1), 68-71.

Gellatly, A., Rogers, D., & Sloboda, J. A. (Eds.). (1989). *Cognition and social worlds.* Clarendon Press / Oxford University Press.

Gellner, E. (Ed.). (1980). *Soviet and Western anthropology.* London: Duckworth & Co. Ltd.

Gere, A. (1987). *Writing groups: History, theory, and implications.* Carbondale, IL: Southern Illinois U.P.

Gerineger, P. S. (1989). *Development of children's metacognition through parent involvement in higher level thinking activities.* Unpublished doctoral dissertation, Seattle University, USA.

Gibson, D. B. (1994). *A test of Vygotsky's higher and lower cognitive functions concept.* Unpublished doctoral dissertation, George Mason University, USA.

Gibson, J. T. (1980). Soviet pedagogical research: Classroom studies: I. Cognitive theories of development and instruction. *Contemporary Educational Psychology. 5,* 184-191.

Gibson, J. T. (1980). A comparison of Soviet and American approaches to special education. *Phi Delta Kappa, 62*(4), 264-267.

Gibson, S. S. (1988). *Classroom communities and global coherence: A sociocognitive model for composition theory, pedagogy, and research.* Unpublished doctoral dissertation, University of Louisville, USA.

Gillette, B. (1994). The role of learner goals in L2 success. In J. P. Lantolf & G. Appel (Eds.), *Vygotskian approaches to second language research* (pp. 195-213). New Jersey: Ablex.

Gindis, B. (1986). Special education in the Soviet Union: Problems and perspectives. *Journal of Special Education, 20*(3), 375-383.

Gindis, B. (1988). Children with mental retardation in the Soviet Union. *Mental Retardation, 26*(6), 381-384.

Gindis, B. (1991). Professional school psychology in the Soviet Union: Current status, problems, and perspectives. *School Psychology Quarterly, 6*(3), 186-199.

Gindis, B, (1992) Successful theories and practices from Russia: Can they be adopted in the United States? *AAMR News & Notes, 6*(6).

Gindis, B. (1995). A voice from the future. *School Psychology International, 16*(2), 99-103.

Gindis, B. (1995). Viewing the disabled child in the sociocultural milieu: Vygotsky's quest. *School Psychology International, 16*(2), 155-166.

Gindis, B. (1995). The social/cultural implication of disability: Vygots-ky's paradigm for special education. *Educational Psychologist, 30* (2), 77-81.

Glassman, M. (1990). The nature of Piaget and corss-cultural research. *Genetic Epistemologist, 18,* 25-32.

Glassman, M. (1990). Self, other and society: A Vygotskian view of creativity. *Quarterly Newsletter of the Laboratory of Comparative Human Cognition, 12*(4), 141-146.

Glassman, M. (1994). All things being equal: The two roads of Piaget and Vygotsky. *Developmental Review, 14*(2), 186-214.

Glassman, M. (1995). The difference between Piaget and Vygotsky: A response to Duncan. *Developmental Review, 15*(4), 473-482.

Glassman, M. (1996). The argument for constructivism. *American Psychologist, 51*(3), 264-265.

Glick, J. (1983). Piaget, Vygotsky, and Werner. In S. Wapner & B. Kaplan (Eds.), *Toward a holistic developmental psychology* (pp. 35-83). Lawrence Erlbaum Associates.

Glick, J. (1992). Steps in the long march: From principles to practices. *Quarterly Newsletter of the Laboratory of Comparative Human Cognition, 14*(4), 117-118.

Glick, J. (1995). Intellectual and manual labor: Implications for developmental theory. In L. Martin, K. Nelson & E. Tobach (Eds.), *Sociocultural psychology: Theory and practice of doing and knowning* (pp. 357-382). New York: Cambridge University Press.

Glock, H. J. (1986). Vygotsky and Mead on the self, meaning and internalisation. *Studies in Soviet Thought, 31*, 131-148.

Godfrey, T. E. (1980). *Literature in the elementary school: A developmental approach*. Unpublished doctoral dissertation, Univer-sity of Nebraska-Lincoln, USA.

Goldberg, L. H. (1980). *Self-verbalization and attentional behaviors of low socioeconomic urban four and five-year-old children during puzzle tasks*. Unpublished doctoral dissertation, Fordham University, USA.

Goldsmith, D. F., & Rogoff, B. (1995). Sensitivity and teaching by dysphoric and nondysphoric women in structured versus unstructured situations. *Developmental Psychology, 31*(3), 388-394.

Golstein, H. J. (Ed.). (1994). *Play, toys, and child development*. Cambridge University Press.

Goldstick, D. (1980). The Leninist theory of perception. *Dialogue, 19*(1), 1-19.

Göncü, A. (1987). The role of adults and peers in the socialization of play during preschool years. In G. Gasto, F. Ascione, & M. Salehi (Eds.), *Current perspectives in early childhood research* (pp. 33-41). Logan, UT: Early Intervention Research Institute Press.

Göncü, A. (1993). Development of intersubjectivity in the dyadic play of preschoolers. *Early Childhood Research Quarterly, 8*(1), 99-116.

Goodman, Y. M., & Goodman, K. S. (1990). Vygotsky in a whole-language perspective. In L. Moll (Ed.), *Vygotsky and education* (pp. 223-250). Cambridge: Cambridge University Press.

Gould, C. (1980). *Marx's social ontology: Individuality and community in Marx'z theory of social reality*. Cambridge, MA: MIT Press.

Gowen, J. W. (1983). *Creative symbolism of three-year-old high risk children playing alone and with a familiar playmate*. Unpublished doctoral dissertation, University of North Carolina at Chapel Hill, USA.

Gowen, J. W. (1995). The early development of symbolic play. *Young Children, 50*(3), 75-84.

Gowen, J. W., Goldman, B. D., Johnson-Martin, N., & Hussey, B. (1989). Object paly and exploration of handicapped and nonhandicapped infants. *Journal of Applied Developmental Psychology, 10*, 53-72.

Gowen, J. W., Goldman, B. D., Johnson-Martin, N., & Hussey, B. (1992). Object paly and exploration in children with and without handicaps. *American Journal of Mental Retardation, 97*(1), 21-28.

Graham, L. R. (1987). *Science, philosophy, and human behavior in the Soviet Union*. New York: Columbia University Press.

Graue, M. E., & Walsh, D. J. (1995). Children in context: Interpreting the here and now of children's lives. In J. A. Hatch (Ed.), *Qualitative research in early childhood settings* (pp. 135-154). Wesport & London: Praeger

Gray, J. (1966). Attention, consciousness, and voluntary control of behavior in Soviet psychology. In N. O'Connor (Ed.), *Present-day Russian psychology* (pp. 1-38). Oxford: Pergamon Press.

Greenfield, P. (1992). On the cognitive consequences of literacy by Sylvia Scribner. *Quarterly Newsletter of the Laboratory of Compara-tive Human Cognition, 14*(4), 118-120.

Greeno, J. (1988, November). The situated activities of learning and knowing mathematics. In M. J. Behr, C. B. Lacampagne, & M. M. Wheeler (Eds.), *North American chapter of the International Group for the Psychology of Mathematics Education, 10th Annual Meeting* (pp. 481-521). Dekalb, IL.

Griffin, P., & Cole, M. (1984). Current activity for the future : The Zo-ped. *New Directions for Child Development,* (23), 45-64.

Griffin, P., King, C., Diaz, E., & Cole, M. (1989). A socio-historical approach to learning and instruction (in Russian). Moscow: Pedago-gika.

Griffin, P., Belyaeva, A., Soldatova, G. (1992). Socio-historical concepts applied to observations of computer use. *European Journal of Educational Psychology, 7*(4), 269-286.

Griffin, P., Belyaeva, A., Soldatova, G., & the Velikhov-Hamburg Collective. (1993). Creating and reconstituting contexts for educational interactions, including a computer program. In E. Forman, N. J. Minick, & C. A. Stone (Eds.), *Contexts for learning: Sociocultural dynamics in children's development* (pp. 120-152). New York: Oxford University Press.

Groff, K. (1985). *Perception and context: Language acquisition grounded on activity theories of Lev Vygotsky.* Unpublished doctoral dissertation, The Ohio State University, USA.

Grubb, M. H. (1983). *The writing proficiency of selected ESL and monolingual english writers at three grade levels.* Unpublished doctoral dissertation, University of California, Los Angeles, USA.

Gruikshank, W. M., & Hallihan, D. P. (Eds.). (1975). *Research and theory in minimal cerebral dysfunction and learning disability.* NY: Syracuse University Press.

Gunnels, J. A. (1992). *"Man, you know you be reading good. You know all dem words." Young children's literacy acquisition during a small group intervention program (remediation, social interaction).* Unpublished doctoral dissertation, Auburn University, USA.

Hagstrom, F. (1992). Creativity as interaction. *Proceedings of the*

Conference on New Directions in Child and Family Research: Shaping Head Start for the Nineties (pp.396-398). Washington, DC: Administration on Children, Youth and Families.

Hall, E. A. (1992, February). An examination of the process of teaching reading to learning disabled children: Vygotskian perspectives. *Resources in Education,* 65

Hall, L. K., & Day, J. D. (1982). *A comparison of the zone of proximal development in learning disabled, mentally retarded, and normal children.* Paper presented at the meeting of the American Educational Research Association, New York.

Hanfmann, E. (1941). A study of personal patterns in an intellectual performance. *Character & Personality, 9,* 315-325.

Hanfmann, E., & Kasanin, J. (1937). A method for the study of concept formation. *Journal of Psychology,* 251-240.

Hanfmann, E., & Kasanin, J. (1942). Conceptual thinking in schizophrenia. *Nervous and Mental Disorders, Monograph ,* (67).

Harding, C. G., & Safer, L. A. (1990). Constructing the thinker: The integration of developmental research with educational practice. *Journal of Human Behavior and Learning, 7(2),* 35-39.

Harmston, R. K. (1987). *A writing-based, phenomenological approach to english teacher preparation.* Unpublished doctoral dissertation, The University of Michigan, USA.

Harris, A. (1979). Hstorical development of the Soviet theory of self regulation. In G. Zevin (Ed.), *The development of self-regulation through private speech.* New York: Wiley.

Harrs-Schmidt, G., & McNamee, G. D. (1986). Children as authors and actors: Literacy development through basic activities. *Child Learning, Teaching and Therapy, 2(1),* 63-73.

Hart, D., Kohlberg, L., & Wertsch, J. (1987). The development of social-self theories of James Mark Baldwin, George Herbert Mead, and Lev Semenovich Vygotsky. In L. Kohlberg, R. Devries, G. Fein, D. Hart, R. Mayer, G. Noam, J. Snarcy, & J. Wertsch (Eds.), *Child psychology & childhood education: A cognitive-developmental view* (pp. 223-258). New York: Longman.

Harvey, F. A. (1980). *The interaction of television viewing and experience with manipulable materials in children's science concept development.* Unpublished doctoral dissertation, Harvard University, USA.

Haste, H. (1987). Growing into rules. In J. Bruner & H. Haste (Eds.), *Making sense: The child's construction of the world.* London: Routledge.

Hatch, T., & Gardner, H. (1993). Finding cognition in the classroom: An expanded view of human intelligence. In G. Salomon (Ed.),

Ditributed cognitions (pp. 164-187). New York: Cambridge University Press.

Hatfield, F. M. (1981). Analysis and remediation of aphasia in the USSR: The contribution of A. R. Luria. *Journal of Speech and Hearing Disorders, 46*(4), 338-347.

Heath, S. B. (1983). *Ways with words: Language, life, and work in communities and classrooms.* Cambridge: Cambridge University Press.

Heath, S. B. (1986). Sociocultural contexts of language development. In California State Department of Education (Ed.), *Beyond language: Social and cultural factors in schooling language minority children* (pp. 143-186). Los Angeles: California State University Evaluation, Dissemination and Assessment Center.

Henderson, B. B. (1984). Social support and exploration. *Child Development, 55*(4), 1246-1251

Henderson, B. B. (1984). Parents and exploration: The effect of context onindividual differences in exploratory behavior. *Child Development, 55*(4), 1237-1245.

Henderson, R.W. (1993). The interactive videodisc system in the zone of proximal development: Academic motivationand learning outcomes in precalculus. *Journal of Educational Computing Research, 9*(1), 29-44.

Hewes, D. E., & Evans, D. (1978). Three theories of egocentric speech: A contrastive analysis. *Communication Monographs, 45*(1), 18-32

Hirst, W. (1992). From tools to practice. *Quarterly Newsletter of the Laboratory of Comparative Human Cognition, 14*(4), 124-126.

Hirst, W., & Manier, D. (1995). Opening vistas for cognitive psychology. In L. Martin, K. Nelson & E. Tobach (Eds.), *Sociocultural psychology: Theory and practice of doing and knowning* (pp. 89-124). New York: Cambridge University Press.

Hodapp, R., & Goldfield, E. (1985). Self-and other regulation during the infancy period. *Developmental Review, 5*(3), 274-288.

Hodnett, E. D. (1986). *Aspekte der sprachgestaltung bei Paul Celan (German text, semantics, linguistics).* Unpublished doctoral dissertation, University of California San Diego, USA.

Hoffman, J. (1977). The dialectic of nature: The natural-historical foundation of our outlook. *Marxism Today, 21*(1), 11-18.

Holaday, B., laMontagne, L., & Marciel, J. (1994). Vygotsky's zone of proximal development: Implications for nurse assistance of children's learning. *Issues in Comprehensive Pediatric Nursing, 17*(1), 15-28.

Holland, D., & Valsiner, J. (1988). Cognition, symbols and Vygotsky's developmental psychology. *Ethos, 16,* 247-272.

Holland, D., & Reeves, J. R. (1994). Activitiy theory and view from somewhere: Team perspectives on the intellectual work of programming. *Mind, Culture, and Activity: An International Journal, 1*(1&2), 8-24.

Holland, D., & Cole, M. (1995). Between discourse and schema: Reformulating a cultural-historical approach to culture and mind. *Anthropology & Education Quarterly, 26*(4), 475-490.

Holowinsky, I. Z. (1988). Vygotsky and the history of pedology. *School Psychology International, 9*(3), 123-128

Holzman, L. (1985). Pragmatism and dialectical materialism in language development. In K. E. Nelson (Ed.), *Children's language* (Vol. 5, pp.345-367). Lawrence Erlbaum Associates.

Holzman, L. (1989). Vygotsky in Harlem, somerset and on capitol hill. *Newsletter of the Association of Progressive Helping Professionals, 1,* 1-3.

Holzman, L. (1990). Lev and let Lev: A dialogue on the life and work of renowed psychologist / methodologist Lev Vygotsky. *Practice: the magazine of psychology and political economy, 7,* 11-23.

Holzman, L. (1992). When learning leads development: Building a humane learning environment. *Community Psychologist, 25*(3), 9-11.

Holzman, L. (1992). Stop working and get to play. *Lib Ed,* (11), 8-12.

Holzman, L. (1995). Creating developmental learning environments. *School Psychology International, 16*(2), 199-212.

Holzman, L. (1995). Creating the zone: Reflections on the International Conference on L. S. Vygotsky an contemporary human sciences. *School Psychology International, 16*(2), 213-216.

Holzman, L. (in press). Newman's practice of method completes Vygotsky. In I. Parker & R. Spears (Eds.), *Psychology and Marxism: Coexistence and contradiction.* London: Pluto Press.

Holzman, P. (1976). Theoretical models and the treatment of schizophrenia. In P. Holzman, & M. Gill (Eds.), *Psychology versus metapsychology.* NY: International University Press.

Hood, L., Fiess, K., & Aron, J. (1982). Growing up explained: Vygotskian look at the language of causality. In C. J. Brained & M. Pressley (Eds.), *Verbal processes in children. Progress in cognitive developmental research* (pp. 265-285). New York: Springer.

Houchins, S. C. (1991). *Parental scaffolding of early adolescents' interpersonal negotiation skills (social skills).* Unpublished doctoral dissertation, The University of Texas at Austin, USA.

Howe, A. C. (1996). Development of science concepts within a vygotskian framework. *Science Education, 80,* 35-51.

Howie, D., & Peters, M. (1996). Positioning theory: Vygotsky,

Socio-historicocultural Psychology

Wittgenstein and social constructionist psychology. *Journal of the Theory of Social Behaviour, 26*(1), 51-64.

Hoy, E. A. (1975). Measurement of egocentrism in children's communication. *Developmental Psychology, 11*(3), 392.

Hsu, T. L. (1993). *Young children's concepts of visual forms and reality and fantasy in illustrations (children's literature).* Unpublished doctoral dissertation. Texas, Austin: The University of Texas at Austin, USA.

Hull, G., Rose, M., Fraser, L. R., & Caslellana, M. (1991). Remediation as social construct: Perspective from an analysis of classroom discourse. *College Composition & Communication , 42*(3, 299-329.

Hull, G., & Rose, M. (1989). Rethinking remediation: Toward a social cognitive understanding of problematic reading and writing. *Written Communication, 8,* 139-154.

Hutchins, E. (1989). Mediation and automatization. *Quarterly Newsletter of the Laboratory of Comparative Human Cognition, 8,* 47-57.

Hutchins, E. (1991). The social organization of distributed cognition. In L. Resnick, J. Leviner., & S. D. Teasley (Eds.), *Perspectives on socially shared cognition* (pp. 283-307). Washington DC: American Psychological Association.

Hutchins, E. (in press). Distributed cognition. Cambridge, MA: MIT Press.

Hvitfeldt, C. (1986). Traditional culture, perceptual style, and learning: The classroom behavior of Hmong adults. *Adult Education Quarterly, 36*(2), 65-77.

Innis, R. (1982). *Karl Bühler: Semantic foundations of language theory.* New York: Plenum.

Innis, R. E. (1994). *Consciousness and the play of signs.* Blomington: Indiana University Press.

Isaacson, S. L. (1985). *Assessing the potential syntax development of third and fourth grade writers (learning disability, Vygotsky, sentence combining).* Unpublished doctoral dissertation, Arizona State University, USA.

Isenberg, J., & Jacob, E. (1983). Literacy and symbolic play: A review of the literature. *Childhood Education, 59*(4), 272-276

Jacob, S. (1990). Scaffolding children's conscious-ness as thinkers. *Quarterly Newsletter of the Laboratory of Comparative Human Cognition, 12*(2), 70-75.

Janc, H. (1992). *Metaphoric comprehension: A higher psychological process mediated by signs.* Unpublished doctoral dissertation, The Brooklin: Long Island University, USA.

Jennings C. M., & Xu Di. (1996). Collaborative learning and thinking: The Vygotskian approach. In L. Dixon-Krauss (Ed.), *Vygotsky in the classroom* (pp. 77-91). White Plains, N.Y: Longman Publisher.

John-Steiner, V. (1985). *Notebooks of the mind: Explorations of thinking*. New York: Harper & Row.

John-Steiner, V. (1990). A Vygotskian perspective on verbal thinking and writing. In C. Hedley, J. Houtz & A. Baratta (Eds.), *Cognition, curriculum and literacy* (pp. 35-45). Ablex Press.

John-Steiner, V. (1992). Private speech among adults. In R. M. Diaz & L. E Berk (Eds.), *Private speech: From social interaction to self-regulation* (pp. 285-296). Lawrence Erlbaum Associates.

John-Steiner, V. (1992). Creative lives, creative tensions. *Creativity Research Journal, 5*(1), 99-108.

John-Steiner, V. (1992). Scribner: Rigor and creativity. *Quarterly Newsletter of the Laboratory of Comparative Human Cognition, 14*(4), 126-127.

John-Steiner, V. (1993). Afterword: Vygotskian approaches to mathematical education. *Focus on Learning Problems in Mathematics, 15*(2-3), 108-112.

John-Steiner, V., & Tatter, P. (1983). An interactional model of language development. In B. Bain (Ed.), *The sociogenesis of language and human conduct* (pp. 79-97. New York: Plenum Press.

John-Steiner, V., & Panofsky, C. P. (1985). Processus sociogénétiques de la communication verbale. In B. Schneuwly & J. P. Bronckart (Eds.),*Vygotski aujourd'hui* (pp. 203-219). Neuchâtel-Paris: Delachaux & Niestlé (Collection Textes de Base en Psychologie).

John-Steiner, V., Panofsky, C. P., & Smith, L. W. (Eds.). (1994). *Sociocultural approaches to language and literacy: An interactionist perspective*. NY: Cambridge University Press.

John-Steiner, V., Panofsky, C. P., & Smith, L. W. (Eds.). (1994). Introduction. In V. John-Steiner, C. P. Panofsky & L. W. Smith (Eds.), *Sociocultural approaches to language and literacy: An interactionist perspective*. New York: Cambridge University Press.

John-Steiner, V., & Souberman, E. (1978). Afterword. In L. S. Vygotsky, *Mind in society* (pp.121-133). Cambridge, MA: Harvard University Press.

Johnson, J. R. (1981, November). *Spoken language and Vygotsky and Sokolov's concept of inner speech.* Paper presented at the meeting of the Ntaional Speech Communication Associatio, Anaheim, CA.

Johnson, J. R. (1984). The role of inner speech in human communi cation. *Communication Education 33,* 211-222.

Johnson, J. R. (1994). Intrapersonal spoken language: A n attribute of extarpersonal competency. In D. R. Vocate (Ed.), *Intrapersonal communication: Different voices, different minds* (pp. 169-192). New Jersey: Lawrence Erlbaum Associates.

Johnson, M. H. (1988). *Dialogue and dialectic: Developing visual art concepts through classroom art criticism.* Unpublished doctoral dissertation, The Florida Sate University, USA.

Johnston, P. (1985). Investigating reading failure as an integrated human activity: A Vygotskian approach to reading disabilities research. *Research Communications in Psychology, Psychiatry & Behavior, 10*(1&2), 99-127.

Johnston, P. (1986). A Vygotskian perspective on assessment in reading. *Reading-Canada-Lecture,* (4), 82-92.

Johnston, P. (1990). A Vygotskian perspective on assessment in reading. In S. B. Sigmon (Ed.), *Critical voices on special education: Problems and progress concerning the mildly handicapped* (pp. 103-119). State University of New York Press.

Jones, D. M. (1991). Alexithymia: Inner speech and linkage impairment. *Clinical social Work Journal, 19*(3, 237-249.

Jones, G. A., & Thornton, C. A. (1993). Vygotsky revisited: Nurturing young children's understanding of number. *Focus on Learning Problems in Mathematics, 15*(2-3), 18-28.

Jones, M. A. (1990). *Art/writing connection: An ethnographic study of the relationship between art and writing for special education high school students'.* Unpublished doctoral dissertation, University of Louisville, USA.

Joravsky, D. (1962). *Soviet marxism and natural science:1917-1932.* NY: Columbia University Press.

Joravsky, D. (1966). Soviet ideology. *Soviet Studies, 18*(1), 2-19.

Joravsky, D. (1974, May 16). The great Soviet psychologist. *New York Review of Books.*

Joravsky, D. (1983). The Stalinist mentality and the higher learning. *Slavic Review, 42*(4), 575-600.

Joravsky, D. (1987). L. S. Vygotsky: The muffled deity of Soviet psychology. In M. G. Ash & W. R. Woodward (Eds.), *Psychology in twentieth century, thought and society* (pp. 189-211). Cambridge: Cambridge University Press.

Joravsky, D. (1989). The Stalinist mentality and the treatment of schizophrenia. In M. O. McCagg, & L. Siegelbaum (Eds.), *The disabled in the Soviet Union: Past and present, theory and practice* (pp. 119-149). University of Pittsburg Press.

Joravsky, D. (1989). *Russian psychology: A critical history.* Oxford: Basil Blackwell.

Kabasakalian, R. D. (1988). *Conversations in mathematics: Fractions and nonfractions: Rule shifts across teachers and topics.* Unpublished doctoral dissertation, Columbia University Teachers College, USA.

Kanner, B., & Wertsch, J. (1991). Beyond a transmission model of communication. *Educational Psychology Review, 3*(2), 103-109.

Karoly, P. (1993). Mechanisms of self-regulation: A systems view. *Annual Reiew of Psychology, 44*, 23-52.

Kasanin, J., & Hanfmann, E. (1938). An experimental study of concept formation in schizophrenia. *American Journal of Psychiatry, 95*, 35-52.

Katz. S., & Lesgold, A. (1993). The role of the tutor in computer-based collaborative learning situations. In S. Derry & S. Lajoie (Eds.), *Computers as cognitive tools* (pp. 289-317). NJ: Erlbaum.

Kazemek, F. E. (1983). *Toward a theoretical framework of adult literacy.* Unpublished doctoral dissertation, Southern Illinois University at Carbondale, USA.

Keating, D. (1994). Contextualist theories of intelligence. In R. J. Sternberg (Ed.), *Encyclopedia of human intelligence* (Vol. 1, pp. 293-298). New York: Macmillan Publishing Company.

Kelly, A. (1981). Empiriocriticism: A Bolshevik philosophy? *Cahiers du Monde Russe et Soviétique, 22*), 89-118.

Kendler, T. S. (1972). An ontogeny of mediational deficiency. *Child Development(43)*, 1-17.

Kennell, R. P. (1989). *Three cheacher scaffolding strategies in college instrumental applied music instruction.* Unpublished doctoral dissertation, The University of Wisconson-Madison, USA.

Kessen, W. (1979). The American child and other cultural inventions. *American Psychologist, 34*, 815-820.

Kimball, J. (1990). *Implications of theory for collaborative invention in college composition.* Unpublished doctoral dissertation, Harvard University, USA.

Kindermann, T. A., & Valsiner, J. (Eds.). (1995). *Development of person-context relations.* Hillsdale, NJ: Erlbaum.

Klingler, C. (1985). *The self-regulatory speech of children in an additive bilingual situation (Mexico).* Unpublished doctoral dissertation, University of New Mexico, USA.

Knox, J. E. (1989). The changing face of Soviet defectology: A study in rehabilitating the handicappped. *Studies in Soviet Thought, 37*, 217-236.

Knox, J. E. (1993). Translator's introduction. In L. S. Vygotsky & A. R. Luria, *Studies on the history of behavior: Ape, premitive   and child* (pp. 1-35). New Jersey: Lawrence Erlbaum Associates

Knox, J. E., & Kozulin, A. (1989). Vygotskian tradition in Soviet psychological study of deaf children. In W. O. Mc Caggy & L. Siegelbaum (Eds.), *The disabled in the Soviet Union: Past and present, theory and practice.* (pp. 63-84). University of Pittsburg Press.

Knox, J. E., & Stevens, C. B. (1993). Vygotsky and soviet russian defectology: An introduction. In L. S. Vygotsky, *The collected works of L. S. Vygotsky. The fundamentals of defectology: Abnormal psychology and learning disabilities* (Vol. 2, pp. 1-25). New York: Plenum Press.

Kohlberg, L., Yaeger, J., & Hjertholm, E. (1968). Private speech: Four studies and a review of theories. *Child Development, 39*), 691-736.

Kohlberg, L., & Fein, G. G. (1987). Play and constructive work as contributors to development. In L. Kohlberg, R. Devries, G. Fein, D. Hart, R. Mayer, G. Noam, J. Snarcy, & J. Wertsch (Eds.), *Child psychology & childhood education: A cognitive-developmental view* (pp. 392-440). New York: Longman.

Kohlberg, L., & Wertsch, J. (1987). Language and the development of thought. In L. Kohlberg, R. Devries, G. Fein, D. Hart, R. Mayer, G. Noam, J. Snarcy, & J. Wertsch (Eds.), *Child psychology & childhood education: A cognitive-developmental view* (pp. 179-221). New York: Longman.

Konold, C. (1995). Social and cultural dimensions of knowledge and classroom teaching. In L. P. Steffe & J. E. Gale (Eds.), *Constructivism in education* (pp.1 75-183). NJ: Lawrence Erlbaum Associates.

Kontos, S. (1983). Adult-child interaction and the origins of metacognition. *Journal of Educational Research, 77*(1), 43-54.

Kozulin, A. (1982). Pavel Blonsky and Russia progressivism: The early years. *Studies in Soviet Thought, 24*, 11-21.

Kozulin, A. (1983). Review of Historical meaning of the crisis in psychology by Lev Vygotsky. *Studies in Soviet Thought, 26*), 249-256.

Kozulin, A. (1984). Lev Vygotsky: The continuing dialogue. In *Psychology in utopia: Toward a social history of Soviet psychology* (pp. 102-120). Cambridge, Mass.: The MIT Press.

Kozulin, A. (1984). Pavel Blonsky and the failure of progressive education. In *Psychology in utopia: Toward a social history of Soviet psychology* (pp. 121-136). Cambridge, Mass.: The MIT Press.

Kozulin, A. (1984). *Psychology in utopia: Toward a social history of Soviet psychology.* Cambridge, Mass.: The MIT Press.

Kozulin, A. (1985). Chelpanov and the establishment of Moscow Institute of Psychology. *Journal of the History of the Behavioral Sciences, 21*, 23-32.

Kozulin, A. (1986). The concept of activity in Soviet psychology:

Vygotsky, his disciples and critics. *American Psychologist, 41*, 246-274.

Kozulin, A. (1986). Vygotsky in context. In L. Vygotsky,In L. S. Vygotsky, *Thought and language*. Cambridge, Mass.: MIT Presss.

Kozulin, A. (1987). A study of the ethos of the 1920s as reflected in architectural projects. *Studies in Soviet Thought, 34)*, 111-116.

Kozulin, A. (1987). Social contexts misconstructed: The case of Soviet development psychology. *Human Development, 30*, 336-340.

Kozulin, A. (1988). Reality monitoring, psychological tools, and cognitive flexibility in bilinguals: Theoretical synthesis and pilot experimental investigation. *International Journal of Psychology, 23*(1), 79-92

Kozulin, A. (1989). The changing face of Soviet psychology. *Studies in Soviet Thought, 37*(3), 185-189.

Kozulin, A. (1989). Soviet studies in the psychodynamics of the unconscious. *Studies in Soviet Thought, 37*(3), 237-245.

Kozulin, A. (1990). The concept of regression and Vygotskian developmental theory. *Developmental Review, 10*, 218-238. (Translated into Arabic by Mohamed ELhammoumi)

Kozulin, A. (1990). Mediation: psychological activity and psychological tools. *International Journal of Cognitive Education & Medicated Learning, 1*(2), 151-159.

Kozulin, A. (1990). *Vygotsky's psychology: A biography of ideas*. Harvester.

Kozulin, A. (1991). Introduction: Lev Vygotsky and the contemporary social thought. *Studies in Soviet Thought, 42*(2), 71-72.

Kozulin, A. (1991). Life as authoring: The humanistic tradition in Russian psychology. *New Ideas in Psychology, 9*(3), 335-351.

Kozulin, A. (1993). Apes, primitives and children and ... Translators. A review of Studies on the history of behavior: Ape, primitive and child by Vygotsky, L. S., & Luria, A. R. (1993), (Translated and edited by V. Golod & J. Knox) New Jersey: Lawrence Erlbaum Associates; and Ape, primitive man and child: Essays in the history of behavior by Luria, A. R., & Vygotsky, L. S. (1992), (Translated by E. Rossiter). Brighton, England: Harvester Wheatsheaf. *Human Development, 36)*, 368-372.

Kozulin, A. (1993). 'Literature as a psychological tool'. *Educational Psychologist, 28*, 253-264.

Kozulin, A. (1995). The learning process: Vygotsky's theory in the mirror of its interpretations.
School Psychology International, 16(2), 117-129.

Kozulin, A., & al. (1995). Mediated learning experience and psychological tool: Vygotsky's and Feuernstein's perspectives in a study of student learning. *Educational Psychologist, 30*(2), 67-76.

Kragler, S. (1986). *Dynamic versus static testing: Impact of reading placement of reading underachievers.* Unpublished doctoral dissertation, The University of Florida, USA.

Kragler, S. (1996). Vygotsky and at-risk readers: Assessment and instructioal implications. In L. Dixon-Krauss (Ed.), *Vygotsky in the classroom* (pp. 149-160). White Plains, N.Y: Longman Publisher.

Kraker, M. J. (1987). *Use of writing as a notation system by normally achieving and learning-disabled first grade children.* Unpublished doctoral dissertation, Northwestern University, USA.

Krancberg, S. (1981). The 'science of logic' in Soviet philosophy and reading in Hegelian dialectics. *Studies in Soviet Thought, 22*, 83-109.

Krepner, K., Valsiner, J., & Van Der Veer, R. (Forthcoming). Too close for comfort: Some puzzling similarities between William Stern and Lev Vygotsky.

Kroll, D. L. (1988). *Cooperative mathematical problem solving and metacognition: A case study of three pairs of women.* Unpublished doctoral dissertation, Indiana University, USA.

Kuslansky, L. R. (1992). *Component skills in the development of referential commuincation skill.* Unpulished doctoral dissertation. New York: Columbia University, USA.

Kussmann, T. (1976). The Soviet concept of development and the problem of activity. In K. F. Riegel & J. A. Meacham (Eds.), *The developing individual in a changing world: Historical and cultural issues* (Vol. 1), 122-130). Chicago: Aldine.

Kutzik, D. M. (1990). *Hereditarian IQ versus human intelligence.* Unpublished doctoral dissertation, Temple University, USA.

Kvale, S. (1975). Memory and dialectics: Some reflections on Ebbinghaus and Mao Tse-Tung. *Human Development, 18*, 205-222.

Labarca, A. (1985). La estructura de la competencia oral en una segunda lengua: Un analisis Vigotskiano. [The structure of oral competence in a second language: A Vygotskyan analysis]. Special Issue: About Vygotsky's thought. *Anuario de Psicologia, 33*(2), 91-105.

Laboratory of Comparative Human Cognition. (1976). Memory span for nouns, verbs and function words in low SES children: A replication and critique of Schuts and Keislar. *Journal of Verbal Learning & Verbal Behavior, 15*, 431-435.

Laboratory of Comparative Human Cognition. (1978). Cogniton as a residual category in anthropology. *Annual Review of Anthropology, 7*, 51-69.

Laboratory of Comparative Human Cognition. (1979). What's cultural about cross-cultural cognitive psychology? *Annual Review of Psychology, 30,* 145-172.

Laboratory of Comparative Human Cognition. (1982). Culture and intelligence. In R. Sterneberg (Ed.), *Handbook of human intelligence* (pp. 642-719). Cambridge: Cambridge University Press.

Laboratory of Comparative Human Cognition. (1982). A model system for the remediation of learning disabilities. *Quarterly Newsletter of the Laboratory of Comparative Human Cognition, 4*(3), 39-66.

Laboratory of Comparative Human Cognition. (1983). Culture and cognitive development. In P. H. Mussen & W. Kessen (Eds.), *Handbook of child psychology* (Vol. 1, pp. 295-356). New York: Wiley & Sons, Inc.

Laboratory of Comparative Human Cognition (The Quarterly Newsletter of the). (1987). *Special issue on Vygotsky, 9*(3.

Laboratory of Comparative Human Cognition (The Quarterly Newsletter of the). (1988). *Special issue on Vygotsky. 10*(4).

Lachicotte. W. S. (1992). *On the borderline: Profession, imagination and authority in the practice of mental health care.* Unpublished doctoral dissertation. Chapel Hill, NC: University of North Carolina at Chapel Hill, USA.

Lalinscar, A. M., David, Y. M., Winn, J. A., & Stevens, D. D. (1991). Examining the context of strategy instruction. *Remedial and Special Education, 12*(3), 43-53.

Lambdin, D. (1993). Monitoring moves and roles in cooperative mathematical problem solving.
Focus on Learning Problems in Mathematics, 15(2-3), 48-64.

Lamport-Hughes, N. (1991). *An empirical investigation of learning potential and other predictors of cognitive rehabilitation (brain injury, rehabilitation, neurotraining).* Unpublished doctoral dissertation, Saybrook Institute, USA.

Landa-Neimark, M. (1980). Soviet pedagogical research: Classroom studies: II. Critical analysis of Davydov's approach to cognitive theories of development and instruction. *Contemporary Educational Psychology, 5,* 192-195.

Langer, J. (1988). A note on the comparative psychology of mental development. In S. Strauss (Ed.), *Ontogeny, phylogeny, and historical development. Human development* (Vol. 2, pp. 68-85). Ablex Publishing Corp.

Lantolf, J. P. (1993, February). *Sociocultural theory and second langauge classroom: The lesson of strategic interaction.* Paper, Georgetown University Roundtable. Washington, DC.

Lantolf, J. P. (1994). Sociocultural theory and second langauge learning. *Modern Language Journal, 78*(4), 418-420.

Lantolf, J. P., & Frawley, W. (1984). Second language performance and Vygotskian psycholinguistics: Implications for L2 instruction. In A. Maning, P. Marin and K. McCalla (Eds.), *The tenth LACUS forum, 1983* (pp. 425-440). Columbia, SC: Hornbeam Press.

Lantolf, J. P., & Frawley, W. (1985). On communicative strategies: A functional perspective. *Issues in Applied Psycholinguitics, 17*(2-3), 143-157.

Lantolf, J. P., Labarca, A., & den Tuinder, J. (1985). Strategies for accessing bilingual dictionaries: A question of regulation. *Hispania, 68*(4), 858-864.

Lantolf, J. P., & Ahmed, M. (1989). Psycholinguistic perspectives on interlanguage variation: A Vygotskian analysis. In S. Gass, C. Madden, D. Preston & L. Selinker (Eds.), *Variation in second language acquisition: Psycholinguistic issues* (pp. 93-108). Clevedon: multilingual Matters

Lantolf, J. P., & Appel, G. (Eds.). (1994). *Vygotskian approaches to second language research.* New Jersey: Ablex.

Lantolf, J. P., & Appel, G. (1994). Theoretical framework: An introduction to Vygotskian perspectives on second language research. In J. P. Lantolf & G. Appel (Eds.), *Vygotskian approaches to second language research* (pp. 1-32). New Jersey: Ablex.

Lantolf, J. P., & Appel, G. (1994). Speaking as mediation: A study of L1 and L2 text recall tasks. *Modern Language Journal, 78*(4), 437-452.

Lantolf, J. P., & Aljaafreh, A. A. (1994). Negative feedback as regulation and second langauge learning in the zone of proximal development. *Modern Language Journal, 78*(4), 465-483.

Larramendy, J. L. (1990, July). Parier sur le français fonctionnel (Betting on functional french). *Français dans le Monde (le), (234)*, 66-70.

Lave, J. (1988). *Cognition in practice: mind, mathematics and culture in every life.* Cambridge University Press.

Lave, J. (1992). Comments on Sylvia Scribner's "The cognitive consequences of literacy" and "Mind in action: A functional approach to thinking". *Quarterly Newsletter of the Laboratory of Comparative Human Cognition, 14*(4), 127-128.

Lave, J., & Wenger, E. (1991). Situated learning: Legitimate peripheral participation. Cambridge University Press.

Laszlo, E. (Ed.). (1967). *Philosophy in the Soviet Union.* Dortrecht: D. Reidel.

Lawler, J. (1975). Dialectic philosophy and developmental psychology: Hegel and Piaget on contradiction. *Human Development, 18*, 1-17.

Lee, B. (1985). Intellectual origins of Vygotsky's semiotic analysis. In

J. V. Wertsch (Ed.), *Culture, communication and cognition: Vygotskian perspectives.* Cambridge University Press.

Lee, B., & Hickmann, M. (1983). Language, thought, and self in Vygotsky's developmental theory. In B. Lee & G. G. Noam (Eds.), *Developmental approches to the self* (pp. 343-378). New York: Plenum Press.

Lee, W. S. (1989). *Intercultural communication: A testbench of the theory of activity.* Unpublished doctoral dissertation, University of Southern California, USA.

Leeds, J. I. (1989). *Repetition, science and psychoanalysis: Theoretical considerations and an empirical study.* Unpublished doctoral dissertation, The Institute of Advanced Psychological Studies, Adelphi University, USA.

Lefevre, K. (1987). *Invention as a social act.* Carbondale, IL: Southern Illinois U. P.

Lemons, M. P. (1990). *Evaluation of a jointly created educational computer game.* Presented to the Psychology Department, University of California at San Diego.

Leong, D., & Bodrova, E. (1996). *Tools of the mind: The Vygotskian approaches to early childhood education.* Englewood Cliffs, NY: Merrill.

Lethbridge, D. (1986). A Marxist theory of self-actualization. *Journal of Humanistic Psychology, 26*(2), 84-103.

Lethbridge, D. (1987). Fromm and Marx: On human nature. *Journal of Humanistic Psychology, 27*(1), 93-108.

Lethbridge, D. (1992). *Mind in the world: The Marxist psychology of self-actualization.* (Studies in Marxism, Vol. 26). Minneapolis: MEP Publications.

Lethbridge, D. (1992). The social ontology of the individual. In D. Lethbridge, *Mind in the world: The Marxist psychology of self-actualization* (pp. 57-66). (Studies in Marxism, Vol. 26). Minneapolis: MEP Publications.

Lethbridge, D. (1992). The internalization of social speech. In D. Lethbridge, *Mind in the world: The Marxist psychology of self-actualization* (pp. 69-83). (Studies in Marxism, Vol. 26). Minneapolis: MEP Publications.

Lethbridge, D. (1992). The internalization of the world. In D. Lethbridge, *Mind in the world: The Marxist psychology of self-actualization* (pp. 85-93). (Studies in Marxism, Vol.26). Minneapolis: MEP Publications.

Lethbridge, D. (1992). The ontegenesis of the self. In D. Lethbridge, *Mind in the world: The Marxist psychology of self-actualization* (pp. 95-120). (Studies in Marxism, Vol. 26). Minneapolis: MEP

Publications.

Lethbridge, D. (1992). Epilogue: Marxist psychology as a humanistic psychology. In D. Lethbridge, *Mind in the world: The Marxist psychology of self-actualization* (pp. 147-155). (Studies in Marxism, Vol.26). Minneapolis: MEP Publications.

Letto, M., & al. (1994). Application of Vygotskian developmental theory to language acquisition in a young child with cerebral palsy. *Augmentative & Alternative Communication, 10*(3), 151-160

Levine, J. M., & Resnick, L. B. (1993). Social foundations of cognition. *Annual Reiew of Psychology, 44,* 585-612.

Levine, L. R. (1988). *'Everyone else ... including me': Learning to value diversity in school.* Unpublished doctoral dissertation, University of Pennsylvania, USA.

Levy, E. (1987). A Vygotskian perspective on discourse: from complex to concept. *Quarterly Newsletter of the Laboratory of Comparative Human Cognition, 9*(3), 100-105.

Lewis, R. (1986). Science, non science, and cultural revolution. *Slavic Review, 45*(2), 286-292.

Lidz, T. (1990). The origin and treatment of schizophrenic disorders. Madison, CT: International Universities Press, Inc.

Lidz, C.S. (1995). Dynamic assessment and the legacy of L. S. Vygotsky. *School Psychology International, 16*(2), 143-153.

Lightfoot, C. G. (1990). *Adolescent adventures and peer group culture (risk-taking).* Unpublished doctoral dissertation, University of North Carolina at Chapel Hill, USA.

Lima, M. G. (1995). From aesthetics to psychology: Notes on Vygotsky's psychology of art. *Anthropology & Education Quarterly, 26*(4), 410-424.

Lindesmith, A. R., Srauss, A. L., & Denzin, N. K. (1978). *Social psychology.* Holt, Rinehart & Winston. (Discussion of the divergence of Piaget's and Vygotsky's egocentric speech: pp.352-356)

Lipman, M. (1991). Squaring soviet theory with american practice. *Educational Leadership, 48*(8), 72-76.

Lipman, M. (1996). Natasha: Vygotskian dialogue. New York: Teaches College Press.

Litowitz, B. E. (1988). Early writing as transitional phenomena. In P. C. Horton, H. Gewirtz, & K. J. Kreutter (Eds.), *The solace paradigm: An eclectic search for psychological immunity* (pp. 321-338). New York: I.U. P.

Litowitz, B. E. (1989). Patterns of internalization. In K. Field, B. Cohler, & G. Wool (Eds.), *Learning and education: Psychoanalytic perspectives* (pp. 305-328). New York: I.U.P.

Litowitz, B. E. (1990). Just say no: Responsibility and resistance. *Quarterly Newsletter of the Laboratory of Comparative Human Cognition, 12*(4), 135-141.

Litowitz, B. E. (1993). Deconstruction in the zone of proximal development. In E. Forman, N. J. Minick, & C. A. Stone (Eds.), *Contexts for learning: Sociocultural dynamics in children's development* (pp. 184-196). New York: Oxford University Press.

Lodhi, S. S. (1988). *An analysis of automatic verbal behavior of young children.* Unpublished doctoral dissertation, Columbia University Teachers College, USA.

London. I. D. (1949). A historical survey of psychology in the Soviet Union. *Psychological Bulletin, 46*(3), 241-277.

London. I. D. (1950). A reply to Razran's note. *Psychological Bulletin, 47*, 150-151.

London. I. D. (1951). Psychology in the USSR.
American Journal of Psychology, 64, 422-428.

London. I. D. (1951). Contemporary psychology in the Soviet Union. *Science,* (114), 227-233.

London. I. D. (1960). Reflections of a Soviet psychologist. *Contemporary psychology*(3), 98-99.

Lonning, R. A. (1991). *The effect of cooperative learning strategies on student verbal interactions and achievement during conceptual change instruction.* Unpublished doctoral dissertation, University of Minnesota, USA.

Losey, K. M. (1995). Mexican american students and classroom interaction: An overview and critique.
Review of Educational Research, 65(3), 283-318.

Lucariello, J. (1995). Mind, culture, person: Elements in a cultural psychology. *Human Development, 38,* 2-18.

Lucid, D. (Ed.). (1977). *Soviet semiotics: An anthology.* MD: Johns Hopkins University Press

Lucy, J. (1988). The role of language in the development of representation: A comparison of views of Piaget and Vygotsky.*Quarterly Newsletter of the Laboratory of Comparative Human Cognition, 10*(4), 99-103.

Lucy, J. (in press). *Reflexive language: Reported speech and metapragmatics.* New York: Cambridge University Press.

Lucy, J., & Wertsch, J. V. (1987). Vygotsky and Whorf: A comparative analysis. In M. Hickmann (Ed.), *Social and functional approaches to language and thought* (pp. 67-86). New York: Academic Press.

Lunsford, A. (1979). Cognitive development and the basic writer. *College English, 41*(1), 38-47.

Lunsford, A. (1980). The content of basic writers' essays. *College Composition & Communication, 31*(3), 278-290.

Lunsford, A. (1985). Cognitive studies and teaching writing. In B. McCeland & T. Donovan (Eds.), *Perspectives on research and scholarship in composition.* NY: M.L.A.

Lyles, A. E. (1989). *Social competence of three-and four-year-olds and parental involvement in prekindergarten programs in New York.* Unpublished doctoral dissertation, Fordham University, USA.

Lyons. B. G. (1983). *Defining the zone of proximal development for four-year-olds simulating the use of absent objects: A methodology for observing cognitive capacities.* Unpublished doctoral dissertation, Northwesten University, USA.

Lyons, B. G. (1984). Defining a child's zone of proximal development: Evaluating process for treatment planning. *American Journal of Occupational Therapy, 38*(7), 446-451.

Mack, N. (1986). *False consciousness and the composing process.* Unpublished doctoral dissertation, The Ohio State University, USA.

Maguire, R. A. (1968). *Red virgin soil: Soviet literature in the 1920's.* Princeton.

Maher, E. D. (1986). *Speech produced during problem-solving: A comparative study of language disordered and normally achieving child dyads (Vygotsky).* Unpublished doctoral dissertation, Northwestern University, USA.

Maldonado, N. S. (1991). *A short term developmental study of bilingual social and self directed speech (self directed, social interaction).* Unpublished doctoral dissertation, Columbia University Teachers College, USA.

Manning, B., & Payne, B. (1993). A Vygotskian-based theory of teacher cognition: Toward the acquisition of mental reflection and self-regulation. *Teaching & Teacher Education, 9*(4), 361-371.

Marsh, D. (1993). Freire, Vygotsky, special education and me. *Journal of Special Education, 17*(2), 119-134.

Marshall, M. J. (1991). *Progress, culture and democracy: Public discourse and rhetoric of education (Adaams Jane, Rice Joseph Mayer, Arnold Matthew, Du Bois W. E. B.).* Unpublished doctoral dissertation, University of Michigan, USA.

Martin, D. S. (Ed.). (1991). *Cognition, education and deafness.* Washington, DC: Gallaudet University Press.

Martin, L. (1983). *Children's problem-solving as inter-individual outcome.* Unpublished doctoral dissertation, University of California, San Diego, USA.

Martin, L. (1985). The role of social interaction in children's problem solving. *Quarterly Newsletter of the Laboratory of Comparative*

Human Cognition, 7(2), 40-46.

Martin, L. (1990). Detecting and defining science problems: A study of video-mediated lessons. In L. Moll (Ed.), *Vygotsky and education* (pp. 372-402). Cambridge: Cambridge University Press.

Martin, L. (1992). Sylvia, the technical, and the symbolic. *Quarterly Newsletter of the Laboratory of Comparative Human Cognition, 14*(4), 128-129.

Martin, L. (1995). Linking thought and setting in the study of workplace learning. In L. Martin, K. Nelson & E. Tobach (Eds.), *Sociocultural psychology: Theory and practice of doing and knowning* (pp. 150-167). New York: Cambridge University Press.

Martin, L., & Scribner, S. (1991). Laboratory for cognitive studies of works: A case study of the intellectual implications of a new techno-logy. *Teachers College Record, 92*(4), 582-602.

Martin, L., Nelson, K., & Tobach, E. (Eds.). (1995). *Sociocultural psychology: Theory and practice of doing and knowning.* New York: Cambridge University Press.

Matthews, M. (1996). Vygotsky and writing: Children using langauge to learn and learnign from the child's language what to teach. In L. Dixon-Krauss (Ed.), *Vygotsky in the classroom* (pp. 93-110). White Plains, N.Y: Longman Publisher.

McCafferty, S. G. (1992). The use of private speech by adult second language learners: A cross-cultural study. *Modern Language Journal, 76*), 177-189.

McCafferty, S. G. (1994). Adult second language learners' use of private speech: A review of studies. *Modern Language Journal, 78*(4), 421-436.

McCafferty, S. G. (1994). The use of private speech by adult ESL learners at different levels of proficiency. In J. P. Lantolf & G. Appel (Eds.), *Vygotskian approaches to second language research* (pp. 117-134). New Jersey: Ablex.

McCagg, M. O. (1989). The origins of defectology. In M. O. McCagg, & L. Siegelbaum (Eds.), *The disabled in the Soviet Union: Past and present, theory and practice* (pp. 39-61). Pittsburg: University of Pittsburg Press.

McCagg, M. O., & Siegelbaum, L. (Eds.). (1989). *The disabled in the Soviet Union: Past and present, theory and practice.* Pittsburg: University of Pittsburg Press.

McCaslin, M. M. (1989). Whole language: Theory, instruction, and future implementation. *Elementary School Journal, 90*(2), 223-229

McCaslin, M. M. (1990). Motivated literacy. Annual Meeting of the National Reading Conference (1989, Austin, Texas). *National Reading Conference Yearbook, 39,* 35-50.

McCreary, D. R. (1984). *Communicative strategies in Japanese-American negotiations (Vygotsky, sociolinguistics, psycholinguisti-cs).* Unpublished doctoral dissertation, University of Delaware, USA.

McCreary, D. (1985). A Vygotskian psycholinguistic persepective on the acquisition and loss of Japanese. *Rassegna Italiana di Linguistica Applicata, 17(*2-3), 159-171.

McCreary, D. R. (1985). La teoria psicolinguistica de Vigotski aplicada al desarrollo temprano bilingue Japonesn-Ingles. [Vygotsky's psycholinguistic theory applied to the early development of Japanese-English bilingualism]. Special Issue: About Vygotsky's thought. *Anuario de Psicologia, 33(*2), 107-115.

McCutchen, L. B. (1990). *The social language of dialectics and irony: Freud, Lacan and clinical practice.* Unpublished doctoral dissertation, Berkeley: California School of Professional Psychology, USA.

McDermott, R. (1992). From mental capacities to activities in context: The evolution of Sylvia Scribner's cultural psychology. *Quarterly Newsletter of the Laboratory of Comparative Human Cognition, 14(*4), 129-131.

McFarland, K. P. (1992). *The use of the dialogue journal in multicultural education.* Unpublished doctoral dissertation, Texas A&M University, USA.

McLane, J. B. (1981). *Dyadic problem-solving: A comparison of child-child and mother-child interaction.* Unpublished doctoral dissertation, Northwestern University, Evanston, IL, USA.

McLane, J. B. (1987). Recontextualizing Vygotsky. In M. Hickmann (Ed.), *Social and functional approaches to language and thought* (pp. 87-104). New York: Academic Press.

McLane, J. B. (1987). Interaction, context and the zone of proximal development. In M. Hickmann (Ed.), *Social and functional approaches to language and thought* (pp. 267-285). New York: Academic Press.

McLane, J. B. (1990). Writing as a social process. In L. Moll (Ed.), *Vygotsky and education* (pp. 304-318). Cambridge: Cambridge University Press.

McLane, J. B., & Wertsch, J. V. (1986). Child-child and Adult-child interaction: A Vygotskian study of dyadic problem systems. *Quarterly Newsletter of the Laboratory of Comparative Human Cognition, 8(*3), 98-105.

McMahon, S. I. (1996). Book club: The influence of a Vygotskian perspective on a literature-based reading program. In L. Dixon-Krauss (Ed.), *Vygotsky in the classroom* (pp. 59-76). White Plains,

N.Y: Longman Publisher.

McNamee, G. D. (1979). The social interaction origin of narrative skills.
Quarterly Newsletter of the Laboratory of Comparative Human Cognition, 1(4), 63-68.

McNamee, G. D. (1980). *The social origin of narrative skills.* Unpublished doctoral dissertation, North-western University, Evanston, IL, USA.

McNamee, G. D. (1987). The social origin of narrative skills. In M. Hickmann (Ed.), *Social and functional approaches to language and thought* (pp. 287-304). New York: Academic Press.

McNamee, G. D. (1995). A Vygotskian perspective on literacy development.
School Psychology International, 16(2), 185-198.

McNamee, G. D. (1990). Learning to read and write in an inner-city setting: A longitudinal study of community change. In L. Moll (Ed.), *Vygotsky and education* (pp. 287-303). Cambridge: Cambridge University Press.

McNamee, G. D., & Harris-Schmidt, G. (1985). Narration and dramatization with learning disabled children. *Quarterly Newsletter of the Laboratory of Comparative Human Cognition, 7*(1), 6-15.

McNamee, G. D., McLane, J. B., Cooper, P., & Kerwin, S. M. (1985). Cognition and affect in early literacy development.
Early Childhood Development and Care, 20, 229-244.

McNamee, G. D., & McLane, J. B. (1990). Early literacy. Cambridge, MA: Cambridge University Press.

McNeill, D. (1981). Action, thought and language. *Cognition, 10* (1-3), 201-208

Meacham, J. A. (1979). The role of verbal activity in remembering the goals of actions. In G. Zevin (Ed.), *The development of self-regulation through private speech.* New York: Wiley.

Meece, R. S., & Rosenblum, S. (1965). Conceptual thinking of sixth-grade children as measured by the Vygotsky block test. *Pyschological Reports, 17,* 195-202.

Melby, J. R. (1988). *Maternal behavior and child competence.* Unpublished doctoral dissertation, Iowa State University, USA.

Mertz, E., & Parmentier, R. J. (Eds.) (1985). *Semiotic mediation: Sociocultural and Psychological perspectives.* New York: Academic Press.

Millard, M. K. (1992). *The dialectic transformation: Process and product.* Unpublished doctoral dissertation, New Brunswick: Rutgers University the State University of New Jersey, USA.

Miller, A. O. (1965). New use for the Vygotsky blocks. *Journal of*

Clinical Psychology, 11, 87-89.

Miller, G. M. (1978). Comment. In L. S. Vygotsky. Mind in society. Cambridge, MA: Harvard University Press.

Miller, G. M. (1983). *Factors related to book-sharing behaviors of parents and young children.* Unpublished doctoral dissertation, University of Georgia, USA.

Miller, J. (1972). *Word, self, reality: The rhetoric of imagination.* NY: Dodd, Mead.

Miller, J. K. (1991). *Fantasy and symbols in the play of young children: An investigation into the influence of emotional development.* Unpublished doctoral dissertation, Boston University, USA.

Miller, M. A. (1984). The theory and practice in Soviet psychiatry. *Psychiatry, (1)*, 13-24.

Miller, M. A. (1985). Freudian theory under Bolshevik rule: The theoretical controversy during the1920s. *Slavic Review, 44*(4), 625-646.

Miller, M. A. (1986). The origins and development of Russian psychoanalysis 1890-1930. *Journal of the American Academy of Psychoanalysis, 14*(1), 125-135.

Miller, M. A. (1986). The reception of psychoanalysis and the problem of the unconscious in Russia. *Social Research, 57*, 875-888.

Minick, N. (1985). *L. S. Vygotsky and soviet activity theory: New perspectives on the relation between mind and society.* Unpublished doctoral dissertation. Northwestern University, USA.

Minick, N. (1986). The early history of the Vygotskian school: the relationship between mind and activity.
Quarterly Newsletter of the Laboratory of Comparative Human Cognition, 8(4), 119-125.

Minick, N. (1987). Implications of Vygotsky's theories for dynamic assessment. In C. S. Lidz (Ed.), *Dynamic assessment: An interactional approach to evaluating learning potential* (pp. 116-140). N.Y: Guilford Press.

Minick, N. (1987). The development of Vygotsky's thought: an introduction. In L. S. Vygotskt, *The collected works of L. S. Vygotsky: Problems of general psychology* (Vol. 1, pp. 17-36). New York: Plenum Press.

Minick, N. (1989). Vygotsky and Soviet activity theory: New perspectives on the relationship between mind and society. Literacies Institute, Special Monograph Series No.1. Newton, Massachussetts: Educational Development Center, Inc.

Minick, N. (1989). Mind and activity in Vygotsk's work: an expanded frame of reference. *Cultural Dynamics, 2*(2), 162-187.

Minick, N., Stone, C. A., & Forman, E. (1993). Introduction: Integration of individual, social, and institutional processes in accounts of children's learning and development. In E. Forman, N. J. Minick, & C. A. Stone (Eds.), *Contexts for learning: Sociocultural dynamics in children's development* (pp. 3-16). New York: Oxford University Press.

Mintz, A. (1958). Recent developments in psychology in the USSR. *Annual Review of Psychology, 9*, 453-5o4.

Mintz, A. (1959). Further developments in psychology in the USSR. *Annual Review of Psychology, 10*, 455-487.

Mirskin, J. (1992). *Writing as a process of valuing (writing process, social value).* Unpublished doctoral dissertation, University of Wisconsin-Madison, USA.

Moffett, J. (1982). Writing, inner speech, and mediation. *College English, Vol44*(3), 231-246.

Moll, L. (1989). Teaching second language students: A Vygotskian perspective. In D. M. Johnson & D. H. Roen (Eds.), *Richness in writing: Empowering ESL students* (pp. 55-69). New York: Longman

Moll, L. (1990). Intrduction. In L. Moll (Ed.), *Vygotsky and education.* Cambridge: Cambridge University Press.

Moll, L. (Ed.). (1990). *Vygotsky and education: Instructional implications and applications of sociohistorical psychology.* Cambridge: Cambridge University Press.

Moll, L. (1992). Bilingual classroom studies and comminuty analysis: Some recent trends. *Educational Researcher, 21*(3), 20-24.

Moll, L. (1992). Biliteracy and thinking. *Quarterly Newsletter of the Laboratory of Comparative Human Cognition, 14*(4), 132-134.

Moll, C. (1994). Literacy research in community and classrooms: A sociocultural approach. In B. R. Ruddell, M. R. Ruddell & H. Singer (Eds.), *Theoretical models and processes of reading* (pp. 179-207). Newark, DE: International Reading Association.

Moll, L., & Diaz, S. (1987). Change as the goal of educational research. *Anthropology & Education Quarterly, 18*(4), 300-311.

Moll, L., & Greenberg, J. (1990). Creating zones of possibilities: Combining social contexts for instruction. In L. Moll (Ed.), *Vygotsky and education* (pp. 319-348). Cambridge: Cambridge University Press.

Moll, L., Tapia, J., & Whitmore, K. (1993). Living knowledge: The social distribution of cultural resources for thinking. In G. Salomon (Ed.), *Ditributed cognitions* (pp. 139-163). New York: Cambridge University Press.

Moll, L., & Whitmore, K. (1993). Vygotsky in classroom practice:

Moving from individual transmission to social interaction. In E.
Forman, N. Minick, & C. A. Stone (Ed.), *Contexts for learning:
Sociocultural dynamics in children's development* (pp. 19-42). New
York: Oxford University Press.

Mortenson, R. (1972). Review: The psychology of arts. *College
Composition & Communication, 23*(1), 93-94.

Mosenthal, P. (1975). Language and thought. *Theory into Practice,
14*(5), 306-311.

Moskovitz, S. (1975, Jan.). Research in early childhood: Do
preschoolers learning to sort prefer to help of Vygotsky or Piaget?
Report. *Science & Children, 12,* 30.

Moss, E. (1990). Social interaction and metacognitive development in
gifted preschoolers. *Gifted Child Quarterly, 34*(1), 16-20.

Mukhopadhyay, S. (1989). *Spatial skills amomg three different occupational groups in India.* Unpublished doctoral dissertation, Syracuse
University, USA.

Murfin, B. (1994). Constructing a MEZOPD (Multiple Electronic
Zone of Proximal Development). *Journal of Computers in
Mathematics & Science Teaching, 13*(4), 405-414.

Nelson, D. S. (1993). *An evaluation study of the implemention of the
"cognitive curriculum for young children" in a rural special
educational preschool classroom.* Unpublished doctoral dissertation,
State University of New York at Buffalo, USA.

Nelson, K. (1992). Sylvia Scribner's "The cognitive consequences of
literacy". *Quarterly Newsletter of the Laboratory of Comparative
Human Cognition, 14*(4), 135-136.

Nelson, K. (1995). From spontaneous to scientific concepts:
Continuities and discontinuities from childhood to adulthood. In L.
Martin, K. Nelson & E. Tobach (Eds.), *Sociocultural psychology:
Theory and practice of doing and knowning* (pp. 229-249). New
York: Cambridge University Press.

Newman, D., Griffin, P., & Cole, M. (1989). *The construction zone:
Working for cognitive change in school.* Cambridge: Cambridge
University Press.

Newman, F. (1991). *The myth of psychology.* New York: Castillo
International.

Newman, F. (1992). Surely Castillo is left-but is it wright or wrong?
The Drama Review, 36, 24-27.

Newman, F., & Holzman, L. (1993). *Lev Vygotsky: Revolutionary
scientist.* New York: Routledge.

Nickerson, R. (1993). On the distribution of cognition: Some
reflections. In G. Salomon (Ed.), *Ditributed cognitions* (pp. 229-
261). New York: Cambridge University Press.

Nicolopoulou, A. (1991). Play and the social context of development in early care and education. In B. Scales, M. Almy, A. Nicolopoulou, S. E. Tripp (Eds.), *Early childhood education* (pp. 129-142). NY: Teachers College Press.

Nicolopoulou, A. (1993). Play, cognitive development, and the social world: Piaget, Vygotsky, and beyond. *Human Development, 36,* 1-23.

Nicolopoulou, A., & Cole, M. (1993). Generalization and transmission of shared knowledge in the culture of collaborative learning: The fifth dimension, its play-world, and its institutional contexts. In E. Forman, N. J. Minick, & C. A. Stone (Eds.), *Contexts for learning: Sociocultural dynamics in children's development* (pp. 283-314). New York: Oxford University Press.

Nobre, M. J. (1986). *Inner speech as the basis for artistic conceptualization: Soviet psycholinguistics and semiotics of art.* Unpublished doctoral dissertation, The Ohio State University, USA.

Nord, W. (1977). A Marxist critique of humanistic psychology. *Journal of Humanistic Psychology, 17*(1), 75-83.

Norman, R. D., Baker, C. A., & Doehring, D. G. (1950). The Hanfmann-Kasanin concept formation test as a measure of rigidity in relation to college aptitude and achievement. *Journal of Clinical Psychology, 6,* 365-369.

Norvell, C. M. (1990). *The functional aspects of private speech of children at age five.* Unpublished doctoral dissertation, The Brooklyn Center: Long Island University, USA.

Nunes, T. (1992). Sylvia Scribner: A mind in action. *Quarterly Newsletter of the Laboratory of Comparative Human Cognition, 14*(4), 136-138.

Nunn, G. G. (1984). *Peer interaction during collabo-rative writing at the 4th/5th grade level.* Unpub-lished doctoral dissertation, The Ohio State University, USA.

Nwachukwu, D. N. (1993). *A comparative investigation of the received of influence of significant others on the academic achievement of children.* Unpublished doctoral dissertation, Loyola University of Chicago, USA.

O'Connor, M. (Ed.). (1991). *Educational psychology.* Orlando, FL: Paul M. Deutsch Press (Classics in Soviet Psychology Series).

Ogbu, J. U. (1981). Origins of human competence: A cultural ecological approach. *Child Development, 52*), 413-429.

Ogbu, J. U. (1988). Culture, development and education. In A. D. Pelligrini (Ed.), *Psychological bases for early education* (pp. 245-273). New York: John Wiley.

Olson, L. H. (1988). *Infant object exploration in the social context.*

Unpublished doctoral dissertation, Tulane University, USA.

Ost, L. J. (1991). *Study of socio-cognitive conflict in cognitive development*. Unpublished doctoral dissertation, Auburn University, USA.

Pacifici, C. (1989). *The regulation of task activities in natural and idealized dyadic interactions with adults and preschool children: A Vygotskian approach*. Unpublished doctoral dissertation, City University of New York, USA.

Pacifici, C., & Bearison, D. J. (1987). The regulation of activity in the zone of proximal development: A microgenetic approach. Unpublished manuscript. The Graduate School and University of the City University of New York.

Pacifici, C., & Bearison, D. J. (1991). Development of children's self-regulations in idealized and mother-child interactions. *Cognitive Development, 6*, 261-277.

Packer, M. J. (1993). Commentary: Away from internalization. In E. Forman, N. J. Minick, & C. A. Stone (Eds.), *Contexts for learning: Sociocultural dynamics in children's development* (pp. 254-265). New York: Oxford University Press.

Palincsar, A. S. (1986). The role of dialogue in providing scaffolding instruction. *Educational Psychologist, 21*, 73-98.

Palincsar, A. S. (1991). Scaffolded instruction of listening comprehension with first graders at risk for academic difficulty. In A. Mc Keough and J. L. Lupart (Eds.), *Toward the practice of theory-based instruction* (pp. 50-65). Lawrence Erlbaum Associates.

Palincsar, A. S., & Brown, A. L. (1984). Reciprocal teaching of comprehension-fostoring and comprehension-monitoring activities. *Cognition and Instruction, 1*(2), 117-175.

Palincsar, A. S., & Brown, A. L. (1988). Teaching and practicing thinking skills to promote comprehension context of group problem solving. RASD: *Remedial and Special Education, 9*(1), 53-59.

Palincsar, A. S., & Brown, A. L. (1989). Classroom dialogues to promote self-regulated comprehension. In J. Brophy (Ed.), *Advances in research on teaching* (Vol. 1, pp. 35-72). Greenwich, CT: JAI Press.

Palincsar, A. S., Brown, A. L., Campione J. C. (1993). First-grade dialogues for knowledge acquisition and use. In E. Forman, N. J. Minick, & C. A. Stone (Eds.), *Contexts for learning: Sociocultural dynamics in children's development* (pp. 43-57). New York: Oxford University Press.

Panofsky, C. P., John-Steiner, V., & Blackwell, P. J. (1985). El desarrollo de los conceptos cientificos: una incursion en la teoria de

Vigotski. [The development of scientific concepts: An exploration of Vygotsky's theory]. Special Issue: About Vygotsky's thought. *Anuario de Psicologia, 33*(2), 81-90.

Panofsky, C. P., John-Steiner, V., & Blackwell, P. J. (1990). The development of scientific concepts and discourse. In L. L. Moll (Ed.), *Vygotsky and education* (pp. 251-267). Cambridge University Press.

Pappadis, T. J. (1984). *Evolving dialogues in the analytic situation.* Chicago Psychoanalytic Society and the Chicago Institute for Psychoanalysis Conference: Psychoanalysis: The vital issues (1981, Chicago, Illinois). *Emotions and Behavior Monographs, Mono. (*3), 97-122

Paris, S. G., & Cross, D. R. (1988). The zone of proximal development: virtues and pitfalls of a metaphorical representation of children's learning. *Genetic Epistemologist, 16* (1), 27-37.

Paris, S. G., & Winograd, P. (1990). How metacognition can promote academic learning and instruction. In B. F. Jones (Ed.), *Dimensions of thinking and cognitive instruction* (pp. 15-51). Lawrence Erlbaum Associates.

Park, C. (1992). *Young children's representation of replay: Developmental stages and effects of mediated computer environments (representational competence).* Unpublished doctoral dissertation, State University of New York at Buffalo, USA.

Parke, R. D., Ornstein, P. A., Rieser, J. J., & Zahn-Waxler, C. (Eds.). (1994). *A century of developmental psychology 1884-1994.* Washington DC: American Psychological Association.

Parmentier, R. J. (1994). *Signs in society: Studies in semiotic anthropology.* Bloomington: Indiana University Press.

Pasamanick, J. R. (1982). *The proverb moves the mind: Abstraction and metaphor in children six-nine.* Unpublished doctoral dissertation, Yeshiva University, USA.

Pasamanick, J. R. (1983). Talk does cook rice: Proverb abstraction through social interaction. *International Journal of the Sociology of Language, 44*, 5-25.

Payne, C. B. (1982). *A comparison study of high school teachers' attitudes toward error in written composition compared with key principles of Mina Shaughessy's theory of composing.* Unpublished doctoral dissertation, The Ohio State University, USA.

Pea, R. D. (1993). Practices of distributed intelligence and designs for education. In G. Salomon (Ed.), *Ditributed cognitions* (pp. 47-87). New York: Cambridge University Press.

Pellegrini, A. D. (1981). The development of preschoolers' private speech. *Journal of Pragmatics, 5*, 278-292.

Pellegrini, A. D. (1982). Learning through verbal interaction. *Journal of Applied Developmental Psychology, 1*, 39-46.

Pellegrini, A. D. (1982). Applying a self-regulating private speech model to classroom settings. *Language, Speech and Hearing Services in Schools, 13*(2), 129-133

Pellegrini, A. D. (1984). The development of the functions of private speech: A review of the Piaget-Vygotsky debate. In A. D. Pellegrini & T. D. Waykey (Eds.), *The development of oral and written language in social contexts* (pp. 57-69). New Jersey: Ablex.

Pellegrini, A. D. (1987). Learning and cognition. In A. D. Pellegrini, *Applied child study* (pp. 108-139). Lawrence Erlbaum Associates.

Pellegrini, A. D., Brody, G. H., & Sigel, I. E. (1985). Parents' book reading habits with their children. *Journal of Educational Psychology, 77*(3), 332-340.

Pellegrini, A. D. (1992). Rough-and-tumble play and social problem solving flexibility. *Creativity Research Journal, 5*(1), 13-26.

Penuel, W. R., & Wertsch, J. (1995). Vygotsky and identity formation: A sociocultural approach. *Educational Psychologist, 30*(2), 83-92.

Perez, M. (1990). *Vocabulary learning through educational preschool television program viewing.* Unpublished doctoral dissertation, Columbia University Teachers College, USA.

Perkins, D. N. (1993). Person-plus: A distributed view of thinking and learning. In G. Salomon (Ed.), *Distributed cognitions* (pp. 88-110). New York: Cambridge University Press.

Peters, J. M. (1996). Vygotsky in the future: Technology as a mediation tool and assessment. In L. Dixon-Krauss (Ed.), *Vygotsky in the classroom* (pp. 175-189). White Plains, N.Y: Longman Publisher.

Phelps, L. (1988). Compostion as a human science. NY: Oxford.

Pick, H. (1980). Perceptual and cognitive development of pre-schoolers in Soviet psychology. *Contemporary Educational Psychology, 5*(2), 140-149.

Pick, H., & Gippenreiter, J. (1994). Vygotskian theories of intelligence. In R. J. Sternberg (Ed.), *Encyclopedia of human intelligence* (Vol. 2, pp. 1122-1126). New York: Macmillan.

Pick, H., & Gippenreiter, J. (1994). Lev Vygotsky (1896-1934). In R. J. Sternberg (Ed.), Encyclopedia of human intelligence (Vol. 2, pp. 1126-1129). New York: Macmillan Publishing Company.

Pikas, A. (1966). Abstraction and concept formation. Cambridge: Harvard University Press.

Pittman, J. P. (1995). Comments on the papers on Marx-Freud. *Nature, Society, & Thought, 8*(1), 110-115.

Platt, E., & Brooks, F. B. (1994). The "Acquisition-rich environment" revisited. *Modern Language Journal, 78*(4), 497-511.

Play, Vygotsky, and imagination. Special Issue. (1992). *Creativity Research Journal, 5*(1.

Plumert, J. M., & Nicholas-Whitehead, P. (1996). Parental scaffolding of young children's spatial communication. *Developmental Psychology, 32*(3), 523-532.

Ponafsky, C. P. (1987). *The interactionsit roots of literacy: Parent-child bookreading and the processes of cognitive socialization.* Unpublished doctoral dissertation, The University of New Mexico, Albuquerque, NM, USA.

Portes, P. R. (1985). The role of language in the development of intelligence: Vygotsky revised. *Journal of research & development in education, 18*(4), 1-10.

Portes, P. R. (1991). Assessing children's cognitive environment through parent-child interactions. *Journal of Research & Development in Education, 24*(3), 30-37.

Portes, P. R. (Ed.). (1993). A cultural-historical approach to learning and teaching: New perspectives on advancing development. *Journal of the Society for Accelerative Learning and Teaching, 18*(1-2).

Posner, M. V. (1992). *International moments of discovery: An analysis of student-teacher language, interactions, and meaning-making during "insight" events in classes and student-teacher conferences in secondary english.* Unpublished doctoral dissertation, New York University, USA.

Presseisen, B. Z. (1992). *Mediating learning: The contributions of Vygotsky and Feuerstein in theory and practice.* Paper presented at the Annual Meeting of the American Educational Research Association, San Francisco, CA.

Prior, P. A. (1992). *Contextualizing writing and response in graduate seminars: A sociohistoric perspective on academic literacies* (2 volumes). Unpublished doctoral dissertation, University of Minneso-ta, USA.

Proffer, C. R., Proffer. E., Meyer, R., & Szpprlul, M. A. (1987). Russian literature of the 1920s. Ann Arbor, MI: Ardis.

Prucha, J. (Ed.). (1972). *Soviet psycholinguistics.* The Hague: Mouton.

Prucha, J. (Ed.). (1976). *Soviet studies in language and language behavior.* NY: North-Hlland.

Pudis, B. M. (1981). *The effects of three instructional activities on children's concept of word: A study of metaliguistic awareness.* Unpublished doctoral dissertation, Northwestern University, USA.

Pyman, A. (1994). A history of Russian symbolism. New Yrok:

Cambridge University Press.

Ratner, C. (1989). A social constructionist critique of naturalist theory of emotion. *Journal of Mind & Behavior, 10*, 211-230.

Ratner, C. (1989). A sociohistorical critique of naturalist theories of color perception. *Journal of Mind & Behavior. 10*, 361-377.

Ratner, C. (1991). Cultural variation in cognitive processes from a sociohistorical psychological perspective. *Journal of Mind & Behavior, 12*(3), 281-296.

Ratner, C. (1991). Vygotsky's sociohistorical psychology and its contemporary applications. New York: Plenum Press.

Ratner, C. (1993). A sociohistorical psychological approach to contextualism. In C. Steven, L. J. Hayes, H. W. Reese & T. R. Sarbin (Eds.), *Varieties of scientific contextualism* (pp. 169-186). Reno, NV: Context Press.

Ratner, C. (1993). Reconstructing the unconscious: A sociohistorical account. In T. R. Sarbin & J. Kitsuse (Eds.), *Constructing the social*. Newbury Park. CA: Sage.

Ratner, C. (1993). Review of: Understanding Vygotsky: A quest for synthesis by Van Der Veer, R., & Valsiner, J. Oxford: Basil Blackwell. 1991. *Journal of the History of Behavioral Sciences, 29*, 274-276.

Ratner, H., & al. (1991). Thinking and feeling: Putting Humpty Dumpty together again. *Merrill-Palmer Quarterly, 37*(1), 1-29.

Razran, G. (1935). Psychology in the USSR. *Journal of Philosophy, 32*, 19-24.

Razran, G. (1939). A quantitative study of meaning by conditioned salivary technique (semantic conditioning). *Science, 90*, 89-91.

Razran, G. (1942). Current psychological theory in the USSR. *Psychological Bulletin, 39*), 445-446.

Razran, G. (1950). A note on London's historical survey of psychology in the Soviet Union. *Psychological Bulletin, 47*, 146-149.

Razran, G. (1957). Soviet psychology since 1950. *Science, 125*, 1106-1113.

Razran, G. (1957). Recent Russian psychology: 1950-1956. *Contemporary Psychology, (2)*, 93-100.

Razran, G. (1958). Soviet psychology and physiology. *Science, 128*, 1187-1196.

Razran, G. (1961). The observable unconscious and he inferable conscious in current Soviet psychophysiology. *Psychological Review, 68*, 81-147.

Razran, G. (1978). Systematic psychology and dialectical materialism: A Soviet story with non-Soviet imports. *Behaviorism, 6*(1), 81-126.

Reder, S. (1992). No nestling in small niches: Seeing ideas in little places. *Quarterly Newsletter of the Laboratory of Comparative Human Cognition, 14*(4), 139-140.

Reese, H. W. (1992). Contextualism and dialectical materialism. In C. Steven, L. J. Hayes, H. W. Reese & T. R. Sarbin (Eds.), *Varieties of scientific contextualism* (pp. 71-105). Reno, NV: Context Press.

Reese, H. W. (1994). The data/theory dialectic: The nature of scientific progress. In S. T. Cohen & H. W. Reese (Eds.), *Life-span developmental psychology: Methodological contributions* (pp. 1-27). New Jersey: Lawrence Erlbaum Associates.

Reid, D. K., & Stone, C. A. (1991). Why is cognitive instruction effective? Underlying learning mechanisms. Special Issue: Cognitive instruction and problem learners. *RASE: Remedial and Special Education, 12*(3), 8-19

Resnick, L. (1991). Shared cognition: Thinking as social practice. In L. Resnick, J. M. Leviner., & S. D. Teasley (Eds.), *Perspectives on socially shared cognition* (pp. 1-20). Washington DC: American Psychological Association.

Resnick, L., Leviner, J. M., & Teasley, S. D. (Eds.). (1991). *Perspectiveson socially shared cognition.* Washington DC: American Psychological Association.

Resnick, L., Salmon, M., Zeitz, C., Wathen, H., & Holowchak. (1993). Reasoning in conversation. *Cognition & Instruction, 11*(3-4), 347-364.

Resnick, L. B., Pontecorvo, C., & Saljo, R. (Eds.). (in press). *Discourse, tools, and reasoning: Situated cognition and technologically supported environments.* Heidelberg, Germany: Springer-Verlag.

Riccillo, S. C. (1994). Phylogenesis: Understanding the biological origins of intrapersonal communication. In D. R. Vocate (Ed.), *Intrapersonal communication: Different voices, different minds* (pp. 33-56). New Jersey: Lawrence Erlbaum Associates.

Richardson, K., & Sheldon, S. (Eds.). (1988). *Cognitive development to adolescence: A reader.* NJ: Lawrence Erlbaum Associates.

Rieff, M. L. (1984). *First steps toward interpsychological communication: How mothers and eighteen-month-olds manage social interaction (prematures, Vygotsky, Soviet psychology).* Unpublished doctoral dissertation, Northwestern University, USA.

Riegel. K. F. (1972). Influence of economic and political ideologies on the development of developmental psychology. *Psychological Bulletin, 78*, 129-141.

Riegel. K. F. (1975). Toward a dialectical theory of development. *Human Development, 18*, 50-64.

Riegel. K. F. (1975). Subject-object alienation in psychological experiments and testing. *Human Development, 18,* 181-193.

Riegel. K. F. (1975). Structure and transformation in modern intellectual history. In K. F. Riegel& G. C. Rosenwald (Eds.), *Structure and transformation: Developmental and historical aspects* (pp. 3-45). New York: John Wiley & Sons.

Riegel. K. F. (1976). The dialectics of human development. *American Psychologist, 31(*10), 689-700.

Riegel. K. F. (1976). A manifesto for dialectical psychology. *American Psychologist, 31*(10), 696-697.

Riegel. K. F. (1979). *Foundations of dialectical psychology.* New York: Academic Press.

Riegel. K. F., & Rosenwald, G. C. (Eds.). (1975). *Structure and transformation: Developmental and historical aspects.* New York: John Wiley & Sons.

Rivers, W. J. (1987). *Problems in composition: A Vygotskian perspec-tive.* Unpublished doctoral dissertation, University of Delaware, USA.

Rivers, W. J. (1987). Story writing: A comparison of native and L2 discourse. In J. P. Lantolf & A Labarca (Eds.), *Research in second language learning: Focus on the classroom.* Delaware Symposium 6 (pp. 195-211). New Jersey: Ablex.

Rizzo, T. A. (1989). *Friendship development among children in school.* Norwood, NJ: Ablex

Rizzo, T. A., & Corsaro, W. A. (1988). Toward a better understanding of Vygotsky's process of internalization: Its role in the development of the concept of friendship. *Developmental Review, 8,* 219-137.

Roberts, R. N. (1979). Private speech in academic problem-solving: A naturalistic perspective. In G. Zevin (Ed.), *The development of self-regulation through private speech* (pp. 295-323). New York: Wiley.

Rody, J. (1989). *A polyphony of voices: The dialectics of social interaction and ESL literacy practices.* Unpublished doctoral dissertation, University of Southern California, USA.

Roe, A. (1963). Psychological definitions of man. In S. L. Washburn (Ed.), *Classification and human evolutions* (pp. 320-331). Chicago: Chicago University Press.

Roegholt, S. (1993). Towards a concept of multiperspective education. *Journal of Curriculum Studies, 25(*2), 153-167.

Rogoff, B. (1990). Apprenticeship in thinking: cognitive development in the social context. Oxford University Press.

Rogoff, B. (1991). Social interaction as apprenticeship in thinking: Guidance and participation in spatial planning. In L. Resnick, J. M. Leviner., & S. D. Teasley (Eds.), *Perspectives on socially shared cognition* (pp. 349-364). Washington DC: American Psychological Association.

Rogoff, B. (1992). Three ways to relate person and culture: Thoughts sparked by Valsiner's review of apprenticeship in thinking: Cognitive development in social context by B. Rogoff. *Human Development, 35,* 316-320.

Rogoff, B. (1993). Commentary on Nicolopoulou's article, Play, cognitive development, and the social world: Piaget, Vygotsky, and beyond. *Human Development, 36,* 24-26.

Rogoff, B. (1993). Children's guided participation and participatory appropriation in sociocultural activity. In R. Wozniak & K. Fisher (Eds.), *Development in context: Acting and thinking in specific environments* (pp. 121-153). Hillsdale, NJ: Erlbaum

Rogoff, B. (1995). Observing sociocultural activity on three planes: Participatory appropriation, guided participation, and apprenticeship. In J. Wertsch, P. del Rio & A. Alvarez (Eds.), *Sociocultural studies of mind* (pp. 139-164). New York: Cambridge University Press.

Rogoff, B. (in press). Development transitions in children's participation in sociocultural activities. In A. Sameroff & M. Haith (Eds.), *Reason and responsability: The passage through childhood.* Chicago: University of Chicago Press.

Rogoff, B., Malkin, C., & Gilbride, K. (1984). Interaction with babies as guidance in development. *New Directions for Child Development,* (23), 31-44.

Rogoff, B., & Wertsch, J. V. (1984). Editors' notes. *New Directions for Child Development,* (23), 1-6

Rogoff, B., & Wertsch, J. V. (Eds.). (1984). Children's learning in the "zone of proximal development". *New Directions for Child Development*(23

Rogoff, B., & Morelli, G. (1989). Perspectives on children's development from cultural psychology. *American Psychologist, 44*(2), 343-348.

Rogoff, B., Gauvin, M., & Ellis, S. (1991). Development viewed in its cultural context. In P. Light, S., Sheldon & M. Woodhead (Eds.), *Learning to think.* London: Routledge.

Rogoff, B., Mistry, Y, C., Göncü, A., & Mosier. (1993). Guided participation in cultural activity by toddlers and caregivers. *Monographs of the Society for Research in Child Development, 58* (7, Serial No. 236).

Rogoff, B., Mosier, C., Mistry, Y., & Göncü, A. (1993). Toddlers's guided participation with their caregivers in cultural activity. In E. Forman, N. J. Minick, & C. A. Stone (Eds.), *Contexts for learning: Sociocultural dynamics in children's development* (pp.

230-253). New York: Oxford University Press.

Rogoff, B., & Moreli, G. A. (1994). Cross-cultural perspectives on children's development. In P. K. Bock (Ed.), *Psychological anthropology* (pp. 231-242). Westport, CT: Praeger Publishers.

Rogoff, B., Baker-Sennett, J., Lacasa, P., & Goldsmith, D. (1995). Development through participation in socioculural activity. In J. Goodnow, P. Miller & F. Kessel (Eds.), *Cultural practices as contexts for development* (pp. 45-65). San Francisco: Jossey-Bass.

Rogoff, B., & Chavajas, P. (1995). What's become of research on the cultural basis of cognitive development?*American Psychologist, 50*(10), 859-877.

Rogoff, B., Radziszewski, B., & Masiello, T. (1995). The analysis of developmental processes in sociocultural activity. in L. Martin, K. Nelson & E. Tobach (Eds.), *Sociocultural psychology: Theory and practice of doing and knowning* (pp. 125-149. NY: Cambridge University Press.

Rohrkemper, M. (1989). Self-regulated learning and academic achievement: A Vygotskian view. In B. J. Zimmerman & D. H. Schunk (Ed.), *Self-regulated learning and academic achievement: Theory, Research and practice* (pp. 143-167). New York: Springer.

Rommetveit, R. (1985). Language acquisition as increasing linguistic structuring of experience and symbolic behavior control. In J. V. Wertsch (Ed.), *Culture, communication and cognition: Vygotskian perspectives.* Cambridge University Press.

Roschelle, J., & Behrend, S. D. (in press). The construction of shared knowledge in collaborative problem solving. In C. O'Malley (Ed.), *Computer supported collaborative learning.*

Rose, M. (1988). Narrowing the mind and page: Remedial writers and cognitive reductionism. *College Composition & Communi-cation, 39*), 267-302.

Rosen, H. (1994). Commentary on Dean's article: Instinctal affective forces in the internalization process: Contributions of Hans Loewald. *Human Development. 37*(1), 58-60.

Rosenshine, B., & Meister, C. (1992). The use of scaffolds for teaching higher-level cognitive strategies. *Educational Leadership,* 26-33.

Rossi. R. (1994, May). Following Vygotsky's quest for social justice. *Communique, 22*(7.

Roter, A. (1987). The concept of consciousness: Vygotsky's contribution. *Quarterly Newsletter of the Laboratory of Comparative Human Cognition, 9*(3), 105-111.

Roth, A. J. (1986). Monitoring in a coordination-mediation framework: A case study of situational constraint in early childhood (speech socialization, Yugoslavia). Unpublished Diss., The University of

Texas at Austin.

Roy, A. (1989). Developing second literacy: A Vygotskian perspective. *Journal of Teaching Writing, 8*(1), 91-98.

Rueda, R. (1990). Assisted performance in writing instruction with learning-disabled students. In L. Moll (Ed.), *Vygotsky and education* (pp. 403-426). Cambridge: Cambridge University Press.

Rueda, R. (1993). Book review of Tharp and Gallimore's "Rousing minds to life: Teaching, learning and schooling in social context". *Journal of the Society of Accelerative Learning & Teaching, 18*(1-2)

Russell, D. (1993). Vygotsky, Dewey, and externalism: Beyond the student/discipline dichotomy. *Journal of Advanced Composition, 13*(1), 173-198.

Ruvolo, T. (1986). *The effet of self-instructional training component of a cognitive-behavioral intervention for impulsive, educationally handicapped children (private speech).* Unpublished doctoral dissertation, Fordham University, USA.

Rychlak, J. F. (Ed.). (1976). *Dialectic: Humanistic rationale for behavior and development.* Basel: Karger.

Rychlak, J. F. (1976). The multiple meanings of 'dialectic'. In J. F. Rychlak (Ed.), *Dialectic: Humanistic rationale for behavior and development.* Basel: Karger.

Rychlak, J. F. (1976). Psychological science as humanist view it. *Nebraska Symposium on Motivtion, 34.*

Sacks, O. W. (1995). An anthropologist on Mars. New York: Alfred A. Knopf

Salomon, G. (1990). Cognitive effects with and of computer technology. Special Issue: Children in a changing media environment. *Communication Research, 17*(1), 26-44

Salomon, G. (1993). On the nature of pedagogic computer tools: The case of the writing partner. In S. Derry & S. Lajoie (Eds.), *Computers as cognitive tools* (pp. 179-196). Hillsdale, NJ: Erlbaum.

Salomon, G. (1993). No distribution without individuals' cognition: A dynamic interactional view. In G. Salomon (Ed.), *Ditributed cognitions* (pp. 111-138). New York: Cambridge University Press.

Salomon, G. (Ed.). (1993). *Distributed cognitions.* New York: Cambridge University Press.

Salomon, G., Globerson, T., & Guterman, E. (1989). The computer as a zone of proximal development: Internalizing reading-related metacognitions from a reading partner. *Journal of Educational Psychology, 81*(4), 620-227.

Sammarco, J. G. (1984). *Joint problem-solving activity in mother-child dyads: A comparative study of normally achieving amd l anguage disordered preschoolers.* Unpublished doctoral dissertation, Northwestern University, Evanston IL, USA.

Sapir, S. G. (1984). *The psychological foundation of a developing methodology: The clinical teaching model.* Unpublished doctoral dissertation, Columbia University Teachers College, USA.

Saracho, O. N. (1992). Preschool children's cognitive style and play and implications for creativity. *Creativity Research Journal, 5*(1), 35-47.

Savage, L. B. (1995). Testing the limits: Tool for assessing metacogni-tive skills and the zone of proximal development. *Resources in Education, 30*(2), 162 (ED 375 168)

Sawyers, J. K., Moran, J. D., Fu, V. R., Horm-Wingerd, D. M. (1992). Correlates of metaphoric comprehension in young children. *Creativity Research Journal, 5*(1), 27-33.

Saxe, G. B. (1992). Studying children's learning in context: Problems & prospects. *Journal of the Learning sciences, 2*(2), 215-234.

Saxe, G. B. (1994). Studying cognitive development in sociocultural context: The development of a practice-based approach. *Mind, Culture, and Activity: An International Journal, 1*(3), 135-157.

Saxe, G. B., Gearhart, M., & Guberman, S. R. (1984). The social organization of early number development. *New Directions for Child Development,* (23), 19-30.

Saxe, G. B., Gearhart, M., Note, M., & Paduano, P. (1993). Peer interaction and the development of mathematical understandings: A new framework for research and educational practice. In H. Daniels (Ed.), *Charting the agenda: Educational activity after Vygotsky* (pp. 107-144). London: Routledge.

Schaff, A. (1973). *Language and cognition.* NY: McGraw Hill.

Schaff, A. (1978). *Structuralism and Marxism.* NY: Pergamon Press.

Schetz, K. F. (1994). Teacher-assisted computer implementation: A Vygotskian perspective. *Early Education & Development, 5*(1), 18-26.

Schinke-Llano. L. (1986). Foreigner talk in joint cognitive activities. In R. Day (Ed.), *Talking to learn: Conversation in second language acquisition* (pp. 99-117). Rowley, Massachusetts: Newbury House.

Schinke-Llano. L. (1993). On the value of a Vygotskian framework for SLA theory and research. *Language Learning, 43*(1), 121-129.

Schinke-Llano. L. (1994). Linguistic accommodation with LED and LD children. In J. P. Lantolf & G. Appel (Eds.), *Vygotskian approaches to second language research* (pp. 57-68). New Jersey: Ablex.

Schmittau, J. (1991). A theoreticla conceptual analysis of US and Soviet students understanding of multiplication. In R. G. Underhill (Ed.), *Proceedings of the 13th Annual Meeting of North American*

Chapter of the International Group for the Psychology of Mathematics Education (pp. 153-159). Blacksburg, VA: Virginia Technological Institute.

Schmittau, J. (1993). Connecting mathematical knowledge: A dialectical perspective. *Journal of Mathematical Behavior, 12*(2), 179-201.

Schmittau, J. (1993). Vygotskian psychology and dialectical logic: A psychological-epistemological foundation for contemporary psychology. *Review of Education, 16*(1), 13-20.

Schmittau, J. (1993). Vygotskian scientific concepts: Implications for mathematics education. *Focus on Learning Problems in Mathematics, 15*(2-3), 29-39.

Schneider, P., Hyland, J., & Gallimore, R. (1985). The zone of proximal development in eighth grade social studies. *Quarterly Newsletter of the Laboratory of Comparative Human Cognition, 7*(4), 113-119.

Schneider, P., & Gearhart, M. (1988). The ecocultural niche of families with mentally retarded children: Evidence from mother-child interaction studies. *Journal of Applied Developmental Psychology, 9*(1), 85-106

Schoenberg, E. (1991). Individual and society in cognitive development. *Contemporary Psychoanalysis, 27*(1), 179-186.

Schreiber, L. L. (1987). Vygotsky and Montessori: The process of learning in the preschooler. *American Montessori Society,* 5-11.

Scribner, S. (1985). Vygotsky's use history. In J. V. Wertsch (Ed.), *Culture, communication and cognition: Vygotskian perspectives.* Cambridge University Press.

Scribner, S. (1986). Thinking in action: Some characteristics of practical thought. In R. Stenberg, & R. Wagner (Eds.), *Practical intelligence: Nature and origins of competencies in the everyday world* (pp. 13-30). Cambridge, UK: Cambridge University Press.

Scribner, S. (1987). On reading Vygotsky. *Quarterly Newsletter of the Laboratory of Comparative Human Cognition, 9*(3), 94-96.

Scribner, S. (1990). A socio-cultural approach to the study of mind. In G. Greenberg, & E. Tobach (Eds.), *Theories of the evolution of knowing* (pp. 107-120). Hillsdale, NJ: Lawrence Erlbaum.

Scribner, S. (1990). Reflections on a model. *Quarterly Newsletter of the Laboratory of Comparative Human Cognition, 12*(2), 90-95.

Scribner, S. (1992). The cognitive consequences of literacy. *Quarterly Newsletter of the Laboratory of Comparative Human Cognition, 14*(4), 84-102.

Scribner, S. (1992). Mind in action: A functional approach to thinking. *Quarterly Newsletter of the Laboratory of Comparative Human*

Cognition, 14(4), 103-110.

Scribner, S., & Cole, M. (1981). The psychology of literacy. Cambridge: Harvard University Press.

Scribner, S., & Beach, K. (1993). An activity theory approach to memory. *Applied Cognitive Psychology, 7*), 185-190.

Scwartz, S. S. (1991). *Facilitating the acquisition of executive control processes in young children: A study of teachers' instructional discourse in a problem-solving task.* Unpublished doctoral dissertation, University of Maryland, USA.

Searle, D. (1984). Scaffolding: Who's building whose building. *Language Arts, 61*(5), 480-483.

Searson, M. P. (1989). *Thinking goes to the ballpark: Baseball cognition and its development.* Unpublished doctoral dissertation, Rutgers University, The State University of New Jersey, USA.

Serpell, R. (1993). Commentary: Interface between sociocultural and psychologiacl aspects of cognition. In E. Forman, N. J. Minick, & C. Stone (Eds.), *Contexts for learning: Sociocultural dynamics in children's development* (pp. 357-368). New York: Oxford University Press.

Serpell, R. (1993). *The significance of schooling: life-journeys in an African society.* Cambridge: Cambridge University Press.

Serpell, R. (1994). Negociating a fusion of horizons: A process view of cultural validation in developmental psychology. *Mind, Culture, and Activity: An International Journal, 1*(1&2), 43-68.

Shaughnessy, M. (1976). Basic writing. In G. Tate (Ed.), *Teaching composition: Ten bibliographic essays.* Fort Worth, TX: T.C.U.

Shaughnessy, M. (1977). *Errors and expectations.* NY: Oxford.

Shaukman, A. (1977). Literature and semiotics: A study of the writing of Yuri M. Lotman. NY: North-Holland.

Shepel, E. N. L. (1995). Teacher self-identification in culture from Vygotsky's developmental perspective. *Anthropology & Education Quarterly, 26*(4), 425-442.

Shin, E. J. (1989). *Young children's use of decontextualized language as a function of parents' mediation of storybook reading.* Unpublished doctoral dissertation, The University of Michigan, USA.

Shipman, S. R. (1992). *A theoretical paradigm for a developmentally based kindergarten through twelfth-grade writing program.* Unpublished doctoral dissertation, Middle Tennessee Sate University, USA.

Shotter, J. (1986). Realism and relativism, rules and intentionality, theories and accounts: A response to Morss. *New Ideas in Psychology, 4*(1), 71-84

Shotter, J. (1987). Remembering and forgetting as social institutions. *Quarterly Newsletter of the Laboratory of Comparative Human Cognition, 9*(1), 11-19.

Shotter, J. (1989). Vygotsky's psychology: Joint activity in a developmental zone. *New Ideas in Psychology, 7*(2), 185-204.

Shotter, J. (1990). Knowing of the third kind: Essays on rhetoric, psychology and the culture of everyday social life. Utrecht: ISOR.

Shotter, J. (1992). Social constructionism: Relativism, moral sources, and judgments of adequacy. In D. N. Robinson (Ed.), *Social discourse and moral judgment* (pp. 181-205). Academic Press.

Shotter, J. (1993). Vygotsky: The social negotiation of semiotic mediation. *New Ideas in Psychology, 11*(1), 61-76.

Shotter, J. (1993). Bakhtin and Vygotsky: Internalization as a boundary phenomenon. *New Ideas in Psychology, 11*(3), 379-390.

Shotter, J. (1993). Harre, Vygotsky, Bakhtin, Vico, Wittgenstein: Academic discourses and conventional realities. *Journal for The Theory of Social Behavior, 23*(4), 459.

Shotter, J. (1994). The sociogenesis of processes of sociogenesis, and the sociogensis of their study. In W. de Graaf & R. Maier (Eds.), *Sociogenesis reexamined* (pp. 73-91). New York: Springer-Verlag.

Shotter, J. (1995). Talk of saying, showing, gesturing, and feeling in Wittgenstein and Vygotsky. E-mail Message, XLCHC, Vygotsky Project Page, Nevember 8.

Shreve, R. O. (1993). *Friends in the process of meaning-making: A of Vygotsky's concept of internalization.* Unpublished doctoral dissertation, The University of North Dakota, USA.

Siegel, A. W., & Cohen, R. (1991). Why a house is not a home: Constructing contexts for development. In R. Cohen, & A. W. Siegel (Eds.), *Context and development* (pp. 305-316). Lawrence Erlbaum Associates.

Silgailis, M. D. (1990). *Scientific and everyday concepts of pregnancy and childbirth.* Unpublished doctoral dissertation, City University of New York, USA.

Silvertein, M. (1985). The functional stratification of language and ontogenesis. In J. V. Wertsch (Ed.), *Culture, communication and cognition: Vygotskian perspectives.* Cambridge University Press.

Simon , B., & J. (Eds.). (1963). *Educational psychology in the USSR.* London: Routlege & Kegan Paul.

Simon , B. (Ed.). (1957). *Psychology in the Soviet Union.* Stanford: Stanford University Prsess.

Simon, J. L. (1986). *Early language skills and symbolic play development (mother influence, two-year olds, american).* Unpublished doctoral dissertation, Sate University of New York at Albany,

USA.

Sincoff, J. B., & Sternberg, R. J. (1989). The development of cognitive skills: An examination of recent theories. In A. M. Colley, & J. R. Beech (Eds.), *Acquisition and performance of cognitive skills. Wiley series in human performance and cognition* (pp. 19-60). John Wiley & Sons.

Skotko, D. (1992). Structural properties of verbal commands and their effects on the regulation of motor behavior. In R. M. Diaz & L. E. Berk (Eds.), *Private speech: From social interaction to self-regulation.* (pp. 225-242). Lawrence Erlbaum Associates.

Slobin, D. I. (1966). Noted figures in the history of Soviet psychology: Pictures and brief biographies. *Soviet Psychology & Psychiatry, 15*(2-3), 105-112.

Smagorinsky, P. (1995). The social construction of data: Methodological problems of investigating learning in the zone of proximal development. *Review of Educational Research, 65*(3), 191-212.

Smagorinsky, P., & Fly. P. K. (1993). The social environment of the classroom: A Vygotskian perspective on small group process. *Communication Education, 42*(2), 159-171.

Smith, A. B. (1993). Early childhood educare: Seeking a theoretical framework in Vygotsky's work. *International Journal of Early Years Education, 1*(1), 47-61.

Smith, S. R. (1981). *Written composition as symbolic transformation of thought: A theory derived from Langer and Vygotsky.* Unpublished doctoral dissertation, Auburn University, USA.

Smolucha, F. (1992). Social origins of private speech in pretend play. In R. M. Diaz & L. E. Berk (Eds.), *Private speech: From social interaction to self-regulation* (pp. 123-141). Lawrence Erlbaum

Smolucha, F. (1992). A reconstruction of Vygotsky's theory of creativity. *Creativity Research Journal, 5*(1), 49-67.

Smolucha, F. (1992). The revelance of Vygotsky's theory of creative imagination for contemporary research on play. *Creativity Research Journal, 5*(1), 69-76.

Smolucha, L. W., & Smolucha, F. (1986). L. S. Vygotsky's theory of creative imagination. *Siegener Periodicum Internationalen Empirishcen Literaturwissenschaft, 5,* 299-308.

Smolucha, L. W., & Smolucha, F. (1992). Vygotskian theory: An emerging paradigm with implication for a synergistic psychology. *Creativity Research Journal, 5*(1), 87-97.

Solso, R. L. (1985). The citation of Soviet scholars by Western psychologists. *American Psychologist, 40,* 1264-1265.

Solso, R. L. (1991). The institute of psychology, USSR: A 20-year retrospective. *Psychological Science, 2(*5), 312-320.

Solso, R. L., Lomov, B. F. (1985). An interview with Boris Lomov. *Soviet Psychology, 23,* 3-23.

Solso, R. L., & Hoffman, C. A. (1991). Influence of Soviet scholars. *American Psychologist, 46*(3), 251-253.

Somerville, J. (1938, April). Ontological problems of contemporary dialectical materialism. *Journal of Philosophy.*

Somerville, J. (1945). Soviet science and dialectical materialism. *Philosophy of Science, (*12), 23-29.

Somerville, J. (1946). The human mind: The dialectical method of thinking. In Soviet philosophy: A study of theory and practice (pp.178-212). New York: Philosophical Library.

Somerville, J. (1946). Our universe: General theory of dialectical materialism. In Soviet philosophy: A study of theory and practice (pp.149-177). New York: Philosophical Library.

Somerville, J. (1946). Soviet philosophy: A study of theory and practice. New York: Philosophical Library.

Spargo, P. K. (1990). *Vygotsky revisited: The effect of familiarity and level of object representation on the expression of assumptions about others in language.* Unpublished doctoral dissertation, New York: New School for Social Research, USA.

Spuhler, J. N. (Ed.). (1959). The evolution of man's capacity for culture. *Human Biology, 31(*1.

Stanback, A. M. (1992). *The testing of a new integrative model of cognition within the context of a continually existing educational problem.* Unpublished doctoral dissertation, California: School of Intercultural Studies, Biola University, USA.

Stanley, N. V. (1986). *A conccurent validity study of the emergent reading level (diagnosis, tests, placement, measurement).* Unpublished doctoral dissertation, The University of Florida, USA.

Stanley, N. V. (1996). Vygotsky and multicultural assessment and instruction. In L. Dixon-Krauss (Ed.), *Vygotsky in the classroom* (pp. 133-48). White Plains, N.Y: Longman Publisher.

Stawarski, C. A. (1986). *The zone of proximal development in the family learning system.* Unpublished doctoral dissertation, University of Georgia, USA.

Steffey, M. S. (1992). *Evidence of sociodramatic play during kindergarten housekeeping playtime (play activities).* Unpublished doctoral dissertation, University of San Francisco, USA.

Stein, N., & Yussen, S. (1985). Review of Werysch's analysis. In S.

R. Yussen (Ed.), *The growth of reflection in children* (pp. 69-101). New York: Academic Press.

Sternberg, R. J. (1990). The sociological metaphor: Lev Vygotsky and the theory of internalization. In R. J. *Sternberg. Metaphors of mind: Conceptions of the nature of intelligence* (pp.242-246). New York: Cambridge University Press.

Sternberg, R. J., & Wagner, R. K. (1994). *Mind in context: Interactionist perspectives on human intelligence.* NY: Cambridge University Press.

Stevens, J. A. (1982). Children of the revolution: Soviet Russia's homeless children (Besprizorniki) in the 1920's. *Russian History/ Histoire Russe, 9,* pts.2-3), 242-264.

Stewart, E. P. (1995). *Beginning writers in the zone of proximal development.* New Jersey: Lawrence Erlbaum Associates.

Still, A., & Costall, A. (1989). Mutual elimination of dualism in Vygotsky and Gibson. *Quarterly Newsletter of the Laboratory of Comparative Human Cognition, 11*(4), 131-136.

Still, A., & Costall, A. (1991). The mutual elimination of dualism in Vygotsky and Gibson. In A. Still & A. Costall (Eds.), *Against cognitivism: An alternative foundations for cognitive psychology* (pp. 225-236). London: Harvester Wheatsheaf.

Stone, C. A. (1985). Vygotsky's developmental model and the concept of proleptic instruction:some implication for theory and research in the field of learning disabilities. *Research Communications in Psychology, Psychiatry & Behavior. 10*(1&2), 129-152.

Stone, C. A. (1993). What is missing in the metaphor of scaffolding?. In E. Forman, N. J. Minick, & C. A. Stone (Eds.), *Contexts for learning: Sociocultural dynamics in children's development* (pp. 169-183). New York: Oxford University Press.

Stone, C. A., & Day, M. C. (1980). Competence and performance models and the characterization of formal operational skills. *Human Development, 23*(5), 323-353.

Stone, T. J. (1993). Whole-language reading processes from a Vygotskian perspective. *Child & Youth Care Forum, 22*(5), 361-373.

Stott, F. M. (1989). Making meaning together: Motivation for learning to write. In K. Field, B. J. Cohler, & G. Wool (Eds.), Learning and education: Psychoanalytic perspectives. Emotions and behavior monographs (Vol. 6. pp.329-353). International Universities Press.

Stremmel, A. J., Fu, V. R., Stone, T. J. (1992). The role of intersubjectivity in teaching culturally diverse children. *Proceedings of the Conference on New Directions in Child and Family Research: Shaping Head Start for the Nineties* (pp. 57-59). Washington, DC: Administration on Children, Youth and Families.

Stremmel, A. J., & Fu, V. R. (1993). Teaching in the zone of proximal development: Implications for responsive teaching practice. *Child & Youth Care Forum, 22*(5), 337-350.

Stremmel, A. J. (Ed.). (1993). A new perspective for child and youth care practice: Vygotsky's theory in action. *Child & Youth Care Forum, 22*(5), 333-398.

Strickland, G., & Holzman, L. (1988). Developing poor and minority children as learners with the Barbara Taylor School Educational Model. *Journal of Negro Education, 58(3),* 383-398.

Sufritz, E. R. (1992). *Early socialization as a foundation for bilingual literacy development.* Unpublished doctoral dissertation, Loyola University of Chicago, USA.

Sullum, D. M. (1991). *Individual differences in knowledge of delay strategies and verbally-regulated motor control and their relationship to delay of gratification in kindergartners.* Unpublished doctoral dissertation, State University of New York at Albany, USA.

Supancheck, P. M. (1989). *Effects of a dynamic assessment approach with developmentally delayed children.* Unpublished doctoral dissertation, University of California, Los Angeles, USA.

Sutton-Smith, B. (1992). The role of toys in the instigation of playful creativity. *Creativity Research Journal, 5*(1), 3-11.

Szekely, B. (1976). *The establishment of the academy of pedagogical sciences of the USSR.* Unpublished doctoral dissertation, Columbia University, Canada.

Tami-LeMonda, C. S., & Bornstein, M. H. (1993). Play and its relations to other mental functions in the child. *New Directions for Child Development, 59,* 17-27.

Tami-LeMonda, C. S., & Bornstein, M. H. (1994). Specificity in mother-toddler language-play relations across the second year. *Developmental Psychology, 30*(2), 283-292.

Tappan, M. B. (1992). Texts and contexts: Language, culture, and the development of moral functioning. In T. L. Winegar and J. Valsiner (Eds.), *Children's development within social context,* (Vol. 1, pp. 93-117). NJ, Hillsdale: Lawrence Erlbaum Associates.

Tappan, M. B. (1994). The Kohlberg-Vygotsky connection: Exploring the road not taken in studying moral development. In Tappan. M (Chair), *Biographical explorations: The life and the work of Lawrence Kohlberg.* Symposium conducted at the Associatopn of

Moral Education 20th Annual Conference. Banff, Alberta

Taylor, L. (1992). Mathematical attitude development from a Vygoskian perspective. *Mathematics Education Research Journal, 4*(3), 8-23.

Taylor, L. (1993). Vygotskian influences in mathematics education, with particular reference to attitude development. *Focus on Learning Problems in Mathematics, 15*(2-3), 3-17.

Teasley, S. D. (1992). *Communication and collaboration: The role of talk in children's peer collaborations.* Unpublished doctoral dissertation, University of Pittsburgh, Pittsburg, Pennsylvania, USA

Teasley, S. D. (1995). The role of talk in children's peer collaborations. *Developmental Psychology, 31*(2), 207-220.

Teasley, S. D. (in press). Talking about reasoning: How important is the peer collaborations?. In L. B. Resnick, C. Pontecorvo & R. Saljo (Eds.), *Discourse, tools, and reasoning: Situated cognition and technologically supported environments.* Heidelberg, Germany: Springer-Verlag.

Teasley, S. D., Rochelle, J. (1993). Constructing a joint problem space: The computer as a tool for sharing knowledge. In S. Lajoie & S. Derry (Eds.), *Computers as cognitive tools* (pp. 229-258). Hillsdale, NJ: Erlbaum.

Tent, J. F. (1988). *The Free University of Berlin: A political history.* Bloomington, IN: Indiana University Press.

Tenzer, A. (1990). Vygotsky and Piaget. *Contemporary Psychoanalysis, 26*(1), 46-52.

Tharp, R. C. (1989). Psychocultural variables and constants: Effects on teaching and learning in schools. *American Psychologist, 44*(2), 349-359.

Tharp, R. C. (1993). Institutional and social context of educational practice and reform. In E. Forman, N. J. Minick, & C. A. Stone (Eds.), *Contexts for learning: Sociocultural dynamics in children's development* (pp. 269-282). New York: Oxford University Press.

Tharp, R. C., & Gallimore, R. (1988). *Rousing minds to life: Teaching, learning and schooling in social context.* Cambridge: Cambridge University Press.

Thomas, R. M. (1979). Vygotsky's theory of thought and language. In R. M. Thomas, *Comparing theories of child development* (pp. 331-346). Wadsworth Publishing Co.

Thomas, R. M. (1992). *Comparing theories of child development.* Wadsworth Publishing Co.

Tobach, E. (1994). ... Personal is political is personal is political ... *Journal of Social Issues, 50*(1), 221-244.

Tobach, E. (1995). The uniqueness of human labor. In L. Martin, K. Nelson, & E. Tobach (Eds.), *Sociocultural psychology: Theory and practice of doing and knowning* (pp. 43-66). New York: Cambridge University Press.

Tobach, E., Flamagne, R. J., Parlee, M., Martin, L., & Kapelman, A. S. (Eds.). (in press). *Mind and social practice: Selected papers of Sylvia Scribner*. New York: Cambridge University Press.

Tomasello, M. (1995). Commentary on Gauvain's article: Thinking in niches: Sociocultural influences on cognitive development. *Human Development, 38*, 46-52.

Tomic, W. (1992). The action-theoretical approach in educational psychology. *Journal of Instructional Psychology, 19*(4), 302-311.

Toulmin, S. (1969). Ludwig Wittgenstein. *Encounter, 32)*, 58-71.

Toulmin, S. (1978, September 28). The Mozart of psychology. *The New York Review of Books, 25*(14), 51-57.

Toulmin, S. (1979). The Inwardness of mental life. *Critical Inquiry, 6*(1), 1-16

Toulmin, S. (1985). The inner life: the outer mind, 15 (1984 Heinz Werner Lecture Series). Worcester, MA: Clark University Press.

Troxel, R. D. (1983). *Models of cognition in the mathematical preparation of special educators*. Unpublished doctoral dissertation, Columbia University Teachers College, USA.

Trueba, H. T. (1991). Linkages of macro-micro analytical levels. *Journal of Psychohistory, 18*(4), 457-468.

Tudge, J. (1983). Moral development in the Soviet Union: A conceptual framework. *Soviet Psychology, 22*(1), 3-12.

Tudge, J. (1985). The effect of social interaction on cognitive development : How creative is conflict? *Quarterly Newsletter of the Laboratory of Comparative Human Cognition, 7*(2), 33-40.

Tudge, J. (1989). When collaboration leads to regression: Some negative consequences of socio-cognitive conflict. *European Journal of Social Psychology, 19*, 123-138.

Tudge, J. (1990). Vygotsky, the zone of proximal develpoment, and peer collaboration: implications for classroom practice. In L. Moll (Ed.), *Vygotsky and education*. Cambridge University Press.

Tudge, J. (1992). Processes and consequences of peer collaboration : A Vygotskian analysis. *Child Development. 63*, 1364-1379.

Tudge, J., & Rogoff, B. (1989). Peer influences on cognitive development: Piagetian and Vygotskian perspectives.In M. Bornstein, & J. Bruner (Eds.), *Interaction in human development*. Hillsdale, NJ: Erlbaum.

Tudge, J., & Winterhoff, P. (1993). Vygotsky, Piaget and Bandura: Perspectives on the relations between the social world and cognitive development. *Human Development, 36*, 61-81.

Tudge, J., Putnam, S., & Valsiner, J. (1992, April). *Reading in contextualist perspective: A Vygotskian apporach*. Paper presented at Conference on Human Development, Atlanta, GA.

Tudge, J., Putnam, S., & Sidden, J. (1993). Preschoolers activities in socio-cultural contexts. *Quarterly Newsletter of the Laboratory of Comparative Human Cognition, 15*(2), 71-84.

Tudge, J., Putnam, S., & Sidden, J. (1994). Everyday activities of American preschoolers: Lessons and work in two socio-cultural contexts. In A. Alvarez & P. del Rio (Eds.), *Perspectives in socio-cultural research: Education as cultural construction* (Vol. 4), 110-121). Madrid: Fundacion Infancia y Aprendizaje

Tudge, J., Putnam, S., & Valsiner, J. (1994). A socio-cultural approach to reading: A context-sensitive methodology. In C. Coll & N. Mercer (Eds.), *Perspectives in socio-cultural research, Vol.3: Interaction* (pp. 73-81). Madrid: Fundacion Infancia y Aprendizaje

Turkheimer, M. E. (1987). *Development of skills with objects: Infant play at 12, 15, and 18 months of age with mothers, peers, and alone*. Unpublished doctoral dissertation, Georgia State University, USA.

Turkle, S. (1994). Constructions and reconstructions of self in virtual reality: Playing in the MUDs. *Mind, Culture, and Activity: An International Journal, 1*(3), 157-167.

Turner, Ann. M. A. (1990). Lev Vygotsky and higher mental functions. *Contemporary Psychoanalysis, 26*(1), 41-45.

Utley, C., Haywood, H., & Masters, J. (1992). Policy implications of psychological assessment of minority children. In. H. C. Haywood & D. Tzuriel (Eds.), *Interactive assessment* (pp. 445-469). New York: Springer-Verlag.

Valsiner, J. (1984). Two alternative epistemological frameworks in psychology: The typological and variational modes of thinking. *Journal of Mind & Behavior, 5*(4), 449-470.

Valsiner, J. (1984). Conceptualizing intelligence: From an internal static attribution to the study of the process structure of organism-environment relationship. *International Journal of Psychology, 19*, 363-389.

Valsiner, J. (1984). Construction of the zone of proximal development in adult-child joint action: The socialization of meals. *New*

Directions for Child Development, (23), 65-76.

Valsiner, J. (1985). Parental organization of children's cognitive development within home environment. *Psychologia: An International
Journal of Psychology in the Orient, 28*(3), 131-143.

Valsiner, J. (1985). Common sense and psychological theories: The
historical nature of logical necessity. *Scandinavian Journal of
Psychology, 26,* 97-109.

Valsiner, J. (1986). The individual subject and scientific psychology.
NY: Plenum Press.

Valsiner, J. (1987). Culture and the development of children's actions.
Chichester, U. K: Wiley.

Valsiner, J. (1988). Developmental psychology. Brighton, UK: Harvester Press.

Valsiner, J. (1988). Children's social development within culturally
structured environments. In J. Valsiner (Ed.), *Child development
within culturally structured environments* (Vol. 1, pp. vii-xi). Norwood, N.J: Ablex.

Valsiner, J. (Ed.). (1988). *Child development within culturally structured environments* (Vol. 1). Norwood, N.J: Ablex.

Valsiner, J. (Ed.). (1988). *Child development within culturally structured environments Social co-construction and environmental guidance
of development* (Vol. 2). Norwood, N.J: Ablex.

Valsiner, J. (1988). Ontogeny of co-construction of culture within
socially organizad environmental settings. In J. Valsiner (Ed.),
*Child development within culturally structured environments: Social
co-construction and environmental guidance of development* (Vol. 2,
pp. 283-297). Norwood, N.J: Ablex.

Valsiner, J. (1989). *Human development and culture: The social nature
of personality and its study.* Lexington MA: Lexington Books.

Valsiner, J. (1989). From group comparisons to knowledge: A lesson
from cross-cultural psychology. In J. P. Forgas & J. M. Innes
(Eds.), *Recent advances in social psychology: An international
perspective* (pp. 501-510). North Holland: Elsevier Publishers.

Valsiner, J. (1989). Preserving habits: On the limits of usefulness of
statistics in psychologists' reasoning. In J. A. Keats, R. Taft, R. A.
Heath & S. H. Lovibond (Eds.), *Mathematical and theoretical
systems* (pp. 59-67). North Holland: Elsevier Publishers.

Valsiner, J. (Ed.). (1989). *Child development in a cultural context.*
Gottingen: Hogrefe.

Valsiner, J. (1989). How can psychology become "culture inclusive".
In J. Valsiner (Ed.), *Child development in a cultural context.*

Gottingen: Hogrefe.

Valsiner, J. (1991). Construction of teh mental: From the 'cognitive revolution' to the study of development. *Theory & Psychology, 1*(2), 477-494.

Valsiner, J. (1991). Building theoretical bridges over a lagoon of everyday events. A review of apprenticeship in thinking: Cognitive development in social context by B. Rogoff. *Human Development, 34,* 307-315.

Valsiner, J. (1991). Theories and methods in the service of data construction in developmental psychology. In P. Van Geert & L. P. Mos (Eds.), *Annals of theoretical psychology: Developmental psychology* (Vol. 7). New York: Plenum Press.

Valsiner, J. (1993). Comparative-cultural research in Soviet psychology. *Journal of Russian & East European Psychology, 31*(1), 5-10.

Valsiner, J. (1994). Irreversibility of time and the construction of historical developmental psychology. *Mind, Culture, and Activity: An International Journal, 1*(1&2), 25-42.

Valsiner, J. (1994). Replicability in context: The problem of generalization. In R. Van Der Veer., M. H. Van Ijzendoorn., & J. Valsiner (Eds.), *Reconstructing the mind: Replicability in research on human development* (pp. 173-181). New Jersey: Ablex Publishing Company.

Valsiner, J. (1994). Narratives in the making of history of psychology. In R. A. Rosa & J. Valsiner (Eds.), *Historical and theoretical discourse in socio-cultural studies.* Madrid: Fundacion Infancia y Aprendizaje.

Valsiner, J. (1994). Commentary on Van Geert's article: Vygotskian dynamics of development. *Human Development, 37*(6), 366-369.

Valsiner, J. (1994). Bi-directional cultural transmission and constructive sociogenesis. In W. de Graaf & R. Maier (Eds.), *Sociogenesis reexamined* (pp. 47-70. New York: Springer.

Valsiner, J. (1994). What is "natural" about "natural contexts"? Cultural construction of human development. *Infancia y Aprendizaje,* (66), 11-19.

Valsiner, J. (1994). Interactionist views of intelligence. In R. J. Sternberg (Ed.), *Encyclopedia of human intelligence* (Vol. 1, pp. 592-596). New York: Macmillan Publishing Company.

Valsiner, J. (Ed.). (1995). *Child development within culturally structured environments: Comparative-cultural and constructivist perspectives* (Vol. 3). Norwood, N.J: Ablex.

Valsiner, J. (1996). Sociogenetic perspectives on personality. In J. Valsiner (Ed.), *Personality: A sociogenetic approach*. Cambridge, MA: Harvard University Press.

Valsiner, J. (Ed.). (1996). *Personality: A sociogenetic approach*. Cambridge, MA: Harvard University Press.

Valsiner, J., & Benigni, L. (1986). Naturalistic research and ecological thinking in the study of child development. *Developmental Review, 6*, 208-233.

Valsiner, J., & Van Der Veer, R. (1988). On the social nature of human cognition: An analysis of the shared intellectual roots   of Herbert Mead and Lev Vygotsky. *Journal for the Theory of the Behavioral Sciences, 18*, 117-136.

Valsiner, J., & Oppenheimer, L. (1991). *The origins of action: Interdisciplinary and international perspectives*. Berlin: Springer-Verlag.

Valsiner, J., & Van Der Veer, R. (1992). The encoding of distance: the concept of the "zone of proximal development" and its interpretations. In R. R. Cocking & K. A. Renninger (Eds.), *The development and meaning of psychological distance*. Hillsdale, N.J: Lawrence Erlbaum Associates.

Valsiner, J., & Lawrence, J. A. (1993). Conceptual roots of internalization: From transmission to transformation. *Human Development, 36*, 150-167.

Valsiner, J., & Winegar, L. T. (1992). A cultural-historical context for social 'context'. In L. T. Winegar & J. Valsiner (Eds.), *Children's development within social context: Metatheory and theory* (Vol. 1, pp. 1-17). Hillsdale: Lawrence Erlbaum Associates.

Valsiner, J., & Maier, R. (1996). Presuppositions in tutoring: Rhetorics in the concepts. *Archives de Psychologie, 64*, 27-39.

Valverde, J. A. (1991). *An exploratory study of the use of "inner spoken language" for performance regulation by highly ranked tennis players (behavior regulation)*. Unpublished   doctoral dissertation, University of Kansas, USA.

Vandenberg, B. (1981). Play: Dormant issues and new perspectives. *Human Development, 24)*, 357-365.

Vare, J. F. W. (1992). *Learning to teach: Apprenticeship in a micro-teaching laboratory (teaching skill development, co-constructioon, rites of passage)*. Unpublished doctoral dissertation, University of North Carolina at Chapel Hill, USA.

Varelas, M. (1992). *Inducting students into science: A conceptual framework and a study of its classroom application (Science induction).* Unpublished doctoral dissertation, University of Illinois at Chicago, USA.

Vocate, D. R. (1980). *Higher mental processes and spoken language: implications of the work of A. R. Luria.* Unpublished doctoral dissertation, University of Denver, USA.

Vocate, D. R. (1987, December). *Inner speech and the domain of human communication.* Paper presented at the Annual Convention of the Soeech Communication Association, Boston, MA.

Vocate, D. R. (1987). *The theory of A. R. Luria.* Hillsdale: Lawrence Erlbaum.

Vocate, D. R. (1990). Luria on language and mind. *Language Communication, 10*(4), 267-284.

Vocate, D. R. (Ed.). (1994). *Intrapersonal communication: Different voices, different minds.* New Jersey: Lawrence Erlbuam Associates.

Vocate, D. R. (1994). self-talk in inner speech: Understanding the uniqueky human aspects of intrapersonal communication. In D. R. Vocate (Ed.), *Intrapersonal communication: Different voices, different minds* (pp.3-31). New Jersey: Lawrence Erlbaum Associates.

Vygotsky and the bad speller's * nightmare. (1991). *English Journal, 80*(8), 65-70.

Vygotsky's theory in action: A new perspective for child care and youth care practice. Special issue. *Child & Youth Care Forum, 22*(5.

Wagner, L. R., & Brock, D. (1996). Using portfolios to mediate literacy instruction and assessment. In L. Dixon-Krauss (Ed.), *Vygotsky in the classroom* (pp. 161-174). White Plains, N.Y: Longman Publisher.

Waldo, M. L. (1982). *The rhetoric of Wordsworth and Coleridge: Its place in current compostion theory.* Unpublished doctoral dissertation, Michigan Sate University, USA.

Wang, P. L. (1987). Concept formation and frontal lobe function: The search for a clinical frontal lobe test. In E. Perecman (Ed.), *The frontal lobes revisited* (pp. 189-205). NY: The IRBN Press.

Warnock, J. (1976). New rhetoric and grammar of pedagogy. *Freshman English News, 5*(2), 1-22.

Warren, A. R., & Tate, C. S. (1992). Egocentrism in children's telephone conversations. In R. M. Diaz & L. E. Berk (Eds.), *Private speech: From social interaction to self-regulation* (pp. 245-264). Hillsdale, NJ: Lawrence Erlbaum Associates.

Wartofsky, M. W. (1981). "The unhappy consciousness": Review of L. Kolakowski's, Main currents of marxism. *Praxis International, 1*(3), 288-306.

Wartofsky, M. W. (1982). Piaget's genetic epistemology and the marxist theory of knowledge. *Revue Internationale de Philosophie,* (142-143), 470-507.

Wartofsky, M. W. (1983). From genetic epistemology to historical epistemology: Kant, Marx, and Piaget. In L. Liben (Ed.), *Piaget and the foundations of knowledge* (pp. 1-17). Hillsdale, NJ: Lawrence Erlbaum Associates.

Washburn, G. (1990). Using Vygotskian theory to study fossilization in SLA. Paper Presented at the Second Language Acquisition-Foreign Language Learning II Conference, April. Urbana Illinois.

Washburn, G. (1994). Working in the ZPD: Fossilized and nonfossilized normative speakers. In J. P. Lantolf & G. Appel (Eds.), *Vygotskian approaches to second language research* (pp. 69-81). New Jersey: Ablex.

Washburn, S. L. (Ed.). (1963). *The classification and human evolution.* Chicago: Chicago University Press.

Washburn, S. L., & Moore, R. (1974). *Ape into man.* Boston: Little, Brown.

Watson, E. (1992). *Meaning, metaphysics and society: A critic of covariantional and conceptual role semantics and a proposal for a social theory of meaning.* Unpublished doctoral dissertation, University of California, San Diego, USA.

Weaver, C. (1988). *Reading process and practice: From socio-psycholinguistics to whole language.* Portsmouth, NH: Heinemann.

Weinstein, E. A. (1990). Vygotsky revisited. *Contemporary Psychoanalysis. 26*(1), 1-15.

Weis, L. (1990). Working class without work. New York: Routledge.

Wells, S. (1985). *Vygotsky reads 'Capital'.* Correspondences: Two.

Wertsch, J. (1977, March). *Inner speech revisisted.* Paper presented to Society for Research in Child Development, New Orleans, LA.

Wertsch, J. (1978). *Recent trends in Soviet psycholinguistics.* White Plains, New York: Sharpe.

Wertsch, J. (1978). Adult-child interaction and the roots of metacognition. *Quarterly Newsletter of the Institute for Comparative Human Development, 2*(1), 15-18.

Wertsch, J. (1979). *A state of the art review of Soviet research in cognitive psychology.* Department of Linguistics Northwestern University Evanstons, Illinois. Also in (ERIC ED 186-293), 43-47.

Wertsch, J. (1979). The regualtion of human action and the given-new organization of orivate speech. In G. Zivin (Ed.), *The development of self-regulation through private speech* (pp. 79-98). NY: Wiley.

Wertsch, J. (1979). From social interaction to higher psychological processes: a clarification and application of Vygotsky's theory. *Human Development, 22),* 1-22.

Wertsch, J. (1980). *Semiotic mechanisms in cognitive activity.* Paper presented at the Joint US-USSR Conference on the Theory of Activity, Institute of Psychology, USSR, Academy of Sciences, Moscow.

Wertsch, J. (1980). The significance of dialogue in Vygotsky's account of social egocentric and inner speech". *Contemporary Educational Psychology, 5,* 150-162.

Wertsch, J. (1981). Trends in Soviet cognitive psychology. *Storia e Critica della Psicologia, 2(2),* 219-295.

Wertsch, J. (Ed.). (1981). The concept of activity in Soviet psychology: An introduction. In J. V. Wertsch (Ed.), *The concept of activity in Soviet psychology.* Armonk, N.Y: M. E Sharpe.

Wertsch, J. (Ed.). (1981). *The concept of activity in Soviet psychology.* Armonk, N.Y: M. E Sharpe.

Wertsch, J. (1983). The role of semiosis in L. S. Vygotsky's theory of human cognition. In B. Bain (Ed.), *The sociogenesis of language and human conduct* (pp. 17-33). New York: Plenum Press.

Wertsch, J. (1984). Comment. In G. Blanck (Ed.), *Vigotski: Memoria y vigencia* [Vygotsky: Memory and actuality] (pp. 205-206). Buenos Aires: Cultura y Cognicion.

Wertsch, J. (1984). The zone of proximal development: some conceptual issues. *New Directions for Child Development, (23),* 7-18.

Wertsch, J. (1985). Adult-child interaction as a source of self-regulation in children. In S. R. Yussen (Ed.), *The growth of reflection in children* (pp. 69-97). New York: Academic Press.

Wertsch, J. (Ed.). (1985). *Culture, communication and cognition: Vygotskian perspectives.* Cambridge: Cambridge University Press.

Wertsch, J. (1985). The semiotic mediation of mental life: L. S. Vygotsky et M. M. Bakhtin. In E. Mertz & R. J. Parmentier (Eds.), *Semiotic mediation: Sociocultural and Psychological perspectives.* New York: Academic Press. Translated in French as: La médiation sémiotique de la vie mentale: L. S. Vygotsky et M. M. Bakhtine. In B. Schneuwly & J. P. Bronckart (Eds.), *Vygotski aujourd'hui* (pp. 139-168). Neuchâtel-Paris: Delachaux & Niestlé (Collection Textes de Base en Psychologie).

Wertsch, J. (1985). Vygotsky: The man and his theory. In J. V. Wertsch (Ed.), *Vygotsky and the social formation of mind* (pp. 1-

16). Harvard University Press.

Wertsch, J. (1985). *Vygotsky and the social formation of mind.* Harvard University Press.

Wertsch, J. (1987). *Voices of mind.* Inaugural lecture, Oct.27, 1987, Department of Development and Socialism, Faculty of Social Sciences, University of Utrecht, The Netherlands), 10-11.

Wertsch, J. (1987). Collective memory: issues from a sociohistorical perspective. *Quarterly Newsletter of the Laboratory of Comparative Human Cognition, 9*(1), 19-22.

Wertsch, J. (1987). Modes of discourse in the nuclear arms debate. *Current Research on Peace and Violence, 10*(2-3), 102-112.

Wertsch, J. (1987). Vygotsky's classic. *Comtemporary Psychology, 32* (11), 932-934.

Wertsch, J. (1988). Vygotsky's "new theory of mind". *American Scholar. 57,* 81-89.

Wertsch, J. (1988). The fragmentation of discourse in the nuclear arms debate. *Multilingua, 7*(1-2), 11-33.

Wertsch, J. (1988). Précurseurs sociaux du fonctionnement cognitif individuel: Le problème des unités d'analyse. In R. A. Hinde, A. N. Perret-Clermont & J. Stevenson-Hinde (Eds.), *Relations interperson-nelles et développement des savoirs* (pp.395-418). Cousset, Delval.

Wertsch, J. (1989). Semiotic mechanisms in joint cognitive activity. *Infancia y Aprendizaje, (47),* 3-36.

Wertsch, J. (1989). Introduction to a special issue of cultural dynamics devoted to "sociocultural approaches to mind". *Cultural Dynamics, 2*(2), 137-139.

Wertsch, J. (1989). A sociocultural approach to mind: Some theoretical considerations. *Cultural Dynamics, 2*(2), 140-161.

Wertsch, J. (1989). A sociocultural approach to mind. In W. Damon (Ed.), *Child development today and tomorrow* (pp. 14-33). San Francisco: Jossey-Bass Inc.

Wertsch, J. (1990). A meeting paradigms: Vygotsky and psychanalysis. *Contemporary Psychoanalysis, 26*(1), 53-73.

Wertsch, J. (1990). Dialogue and dialogism in sociohistorical approach to mind. In I. Markova & R. Foppa (Eds.), *The dynamic of dialogue.* UK: Harvester Wheatsheaf.

Wertsch, J. (1990). The voice of rationality in a sociohistorical approach to mind. In L. L. Moll (Ed.), *Vygotsky and education.* Cambridge University Press.

Wertsch, J. (1991). *Voices of the mind: A sociohistorical approach to mediated action.* Cambridge, MA: Cambridge University Press.

Wertsch, J. (1991). A sociocultural approach to Socially shared cognition. In L. Resnick, J. M. Leviner & S. D. Teasley (Eds.), *Perspectives on socially shared cognition* (pp. 85-100). Washington DC: American Psychological Association.

Wertsch, J. (1991). Sociocultural setting and zone of proximal development: The problem of text-based realities. In L. T. Landsmann (Ed.), *Culture, schooling, and psychological development* (Vol. 4, 71-86). New Jersey: Ablex.

Wertsch, J. (1992). Keys to cultural psychology. *Culture, Medicine and Psychiatry, 16*(3), 273-280.

Wertsch, J. (1992). The developmental line of Sylvia Scribner. *Quarterly Newsletter of the Laboratory of Comparative Human Cognition, 14*(4), 143-145.

Wertsch, J. (1993). Foreword. In L. S. Vygotsky & A. R. Luria, Studies on the history of behavior: Ape, premitive and child (ix-xii). NJ: Lawrence Erlbaum Associates.

Wertsch, J. (1993). Commentary on Valsiner's & Lawrence's article, Conceptual roots of internalization: From transmission to transformation. *Human Development, 36*, 168-171.

Wertsch, J. (1994). Commentary on Moll's article: Reclaiming the natural line in Vygotsky's theory of cognitive development. *Human Development, 37*(6), 343-345.

Wertsch, J. (1994). The primacy of mediated action. *Mind, Culture, and Activity: An International Journal, 1*(4), 202-208.

Wertsch, J. (1995). E-mail Message, XLCHC, January 28.

Wertsch, J. (1995). Commentary on Van Der Veer's & Arievitch's article, Furthering the internalization debate: Gal'prin's contribution. *Human Development, 38*, 127-130.

Wertsch, J. (1995). The need for action in sociocultural research. In J. Wertsch, P. del Rio & A. Alvarez (Eds.), *Sociocultural studies of mind* (pp. 56-74). New York: Cambridge University Press.

Wertsch, J. (1995). Sociocultural research in the copyright age. *Culture & Psychology.*

Wertsch, J. (1996). The world on paper: The conceptual and cognitive implications of reading and writing. *Language in Society, 25*(1), 125-128.

Wertsch, J. (1996). The role of abstract rationality in Vygotsky's image of mind. In A. Tryphon & J. Vonèche (Eds.). (1994). *Piaget-Vygotsky: The social genesis of thought.* England, Hove: Erlbaum.

Wertsch, J., & Stone, C. A. (1978). Microgenesis as a tool for developmental analysis. *Quarterly Newsletter of the Laboratory of Comparative Human Cognition, 1,* 8-10.

Wertsch, J., & Lee, B. (1984). The multiple levels of analysis in a theory of action. *Human Development, 27,* 193-196.

Wertsch, J., Minick, N., & Arns, F. (1984). The creation of context in joint problem solving. In B. Rogoff & J. Lave (Eds.), *Everyday cognition* (pp. 151-171). Cambridge, MA: Harvard University Press.

Wertsch, J., & Stone, C. A. (1985). The concept of internalization in Vygotsky's account of the genesis of higher mental functions, In J. Wertsch (Ed.), *Culture, communication and cognition* (pp. 162-179). Cambridge: Cambridge University Press.

Wertsch, J., Hickmann, M., & McLane, G. C. (1978). A microgenetic analysis of strategy formation. Unpublished manuscript.

Wertsch, J., & Hickmann, M. (1987). Problem solving in social interaction: a microgenetic analysis. In M. Hickmann (Ed.), *Social and functional approaches to language and thought* (pp. 251-266). New York: Academic Press.

Wertsch, J., & Hagstrom, F. W. (1990). Vygotskian reformulation of Whitman's thesis on self-regulation. *American Journal of Mental Redardation, 94*(4), 371-372.

Wertsch, J., & Minick, N. J. (1990). Negotiating sense in the zone of proximal development. In M. Schwebel, C. A. Maher, & N. S. Fagler (Eds.), *Promoting cognitive growth over the life span.* New York : Cambridge University Press.

Wertsch, J., & Kannor, B. (1992). A sociocultural approach to intellectual development. In R. S. Sternberg & C. A Berg (Eds.), *Intellectual development* (pp.328-349). Cambridge University Press.

Wertsch, J., McNamee G. D., McLane, J. B., & Budwig, N. A. (1980). The adult-child dyad as a problem-solving system. *Child Develo-pment, 51*), 1215-1221.

Wertsch, J., & Bivens, J. A. (1992). The social origins of individual mental functioning: Alterantives and perspectives. *Quarterly Newsletter of the Laboratory of Comparative Human Cognition, 14*(2), 35-44. This chapter is to appear in the forthcoming book. In R. R. Cocking & K. A. Renninger (Eds.), *The development and meaning of psychological distance.* Hillsdale, NJ: Lawrence Erlbaum Associates

Wertsch, J., & Tulviste, P. (1992). L. S. Vygotsky and the contemporary developmental. psychology. *Developmental Psychology, 28*(4), 548-557. Also reprinted in R. D. Parke, P. A. Ornstein, J. J. Rieser J. & C. Zahn-Waxler (Eds.), *A century of developmental psycholo-*

gy 1884-1994. Washington, DC: American Psychological Association. 1994.

Wertsch, J., & Rupert, L. J. (1993). The authority of cultural tools in a sociohistorical approach to mediated agency. *Cognition & Instruction, 11*(3-4), 227-239.

Wertsch, J., & Smolka, A. L. (1993). Continuing the dialogue: Vygotsky, Bakhtin, and Lotman. In H. Daniels (Ed.), *Charting the agenda: Educational activity after Vygotsky* (pp. 69-92). London: Routledge.

Wertsch, J., Tulviste, P., & Hagstrom, F. (1993). A sociocultural approach to agency. In E. Forman, N. J. Minick, & C. A. Stone (Eds.), *Contexts for learning: Sociocultural dynamics in children's development* (pp. 336-356). New York: Oxford University Press.

Wertsch, J., Hagstrom, F., & Kikas, E. (1995). Voices of thinking and speaking. In L. Martin, K. Nelson & E. Tobach (Eds.), *Sociocultural psychology: Theory and practice of doing and knowning* (pp. 276-290). New York: Cambridge University Press.

Wertsch, J., & Chikako, T. (1995). Discourse and learning in the classroom: A sociocultural approach. In L. P. Steffe & J. E. Gale (Eds.), *Constructivism in education* (pp. 159-174). Hillsdale, NJ: Lawrence Erlbaum Associates

Wertsch, J., del Rio, P., & Alvarez, A. (1995). Sociocultural studies: History, action, and mediation. In J. Wertsch, P. del Rio & A. Alvarez (Eds.), *Sociocultural studies of mind* (pp. 1-34). New York: Cambridge University Press.

Wertsch, J., del Rio, P., & Alvarez, A. (Eds.). (1995). *Sociocultural studies of mind.* New York: Cambridge University Press.

Wertsch, J., Sohmer, R. (1995). Vygotsky on learning and development. *Human Development, 38*(6), 332-337.

Weybright, L. (1976). The development of play and logical thinking. *Urban Review, 9*(2), 133-140.

Whang, W. H. (1993). *The impact of mathematics word problem solving by language facility.* Unpublished doctoral dissertation, University of Georgia, USA.

Whelan, T. M. (1993). *Scientific and eveyday concept formation: An application of L. S. Vygotsky's work to the speech theory of human communication.* Unpublished doctoral dissertation. Denver, Colorado: University of Denver, USA.

White, S. (1987). Lost for words: A Vygotskian perspective on the developing use of words by hearing-impaired children. *Quarterly Newsletter of the Laboratory of Comparative Human Cognition, 9*

(3), 111-115.

Wiggins, A. U. (1992). *Role functions of primary caregavers in community-based group home for deaf/hard of hearing youth with behavior deficits: A model (hard of hearing).* Unpublished doctoral dissertation, Michigan State University, USA.

Wiggins, R. A. (1993). *An alternate view of staff development: Personal professional growth within a single school setting.* Unpublished doctoral dissertation, University of Illinois at Urbana-Champaign, USA.

Williams, C. (1980). The theories of Piaget and Vygotsky concerning the relationship between thought and language. (ERIC Document ED 238592).

Williams, M. (1989). Vygotsky's social theory of mind. *Harvard Educational Review, 59*(1), 108-126.

Williams, R. (1986). The uses of cultural theory. *New Left Review, (158)*, 19-31.

Willis, P. (1977). *Learning to labor.* New York: Columbia University Press.

Wilson, A & Weinstein, L. (1990). Language, thought and internalization: A Vygotskian and psychoanalytic perspective. *Contemporary Psychoanalysis, 26*(1), 24-40.

Wilson, A., & Weinstein, L. (1992). An investigation into some implications of a Vygotskian perspective on the origins of mind: Psychoanalysis and Vygotskian psychology: part I. *Journal of the American Psychoanalytic Association, 40*(2), 349-379

Wilson, A., & Weinstein, L. (1992). Language and the psychoanalytic process: Psychoanalysis and Vygotskian psychology: part II. *Journal of the American Psychoanalytic Association, 40*(3), 725-759.

Wilson, A., Fel, D., & Greenstein, M. (1992). The self-regulating child: Converging evidence from psychoanalysis, infant research, and sociolinguistics. *Applied & Preventive Psychology, 1*(3), 165-175.

Wilson, B. G., & al. (1993). Instructional design perspectives on mathematics education with referene to Vygotsky's theory of social cognitin. *Focus on Learning Problems in Mathematics, 15*(2-3), 65-86.

Windholz, G. (1984). Pavlov and the demise of the influence of Gestalt psychology in the Soviet Union. *Psychological Research, 46*, 187-206.

Winegar, L. (1988). Child as cultural apprentice: an alternative perspective for understanding zone of proximal development. *Genetic Epistemologist, 16*(3, 31-38.

Winegar, L., & Valsiner, J. (Eds). (1992). Children's development within social context: Methodology and Theory (Vol. 1). Lawrence Erlbaum Asssociates.

Winegar, L., & Valsiner, J. (Eds). (1992). *Children's development within social context: Research and Methodology* (Vol. 2) Lawrence Erlbaum Asssociates.

Winn, R. B. (1961). *Soviet psychology*. London: Vision Press.

Winter, A., al. (1991). Caregiver-child interaction in the development of the self: The contributions of Vygotsky, Bruner and Kaye to Mead's theory. *Symbolic Interaction, 14*(4), 433-448.

Wittfogel, K. (1963). Some remarks on Mao's handling of concepts and problems of dialectics. *Studies in Soviet Thought, 3*(4), 251-269.

Wolff, R. (1993). Consciousness and revolution in Soviet philosophy. *Rethinking Marxism, 6*(3), 135-137.

Wolman, B. B. (Ed.). (1968). *Historical roots of contemporary psychology*. New York: Harper & Row.

Wood, D. (1980). Teaching the young child: some relationships between social interaction, language, and thought. In D. Olson (Ed.), *The social foundations of language and thought* (pp. 280-298). New York: Norton.

Wood, D. (1988). *How children think and learn.* Oxford: Basil Blackwell.

Wood, D., & al. (1996). Vygotsky, tutoring and learning. *Oxford Review of Education, 21*(1), 5-16.

Wood, D., Bruner, J., & Ross, S. (1976). The role of tutoring in problem solving. *Journal of Child Psychology & Psychiatry, 17*, 89-100.

Wood, D., & Middleton, D. (1975). A study of assisted problem solving. *British Journal of Psychology, 66*, 181-191.

Wood, S. B. (1983). *L. S. Vygotsky's theory of the reader's response to literature as found in "the psychology of art": A comparison to the esthetic theories of Kant, Coleridge, Richards, Dewey and Rosenblatt.* Unpublished doctoral dissertation, New Brunswick, Rutgers University, The State Univesity of New Jersey, USA.

Wortis, J. (1950). *Soviet psychiatry.* Baltimore: Williams & Wilkins

Wozniak, R. H. (1972). Verbal regulation of motor behavior-Soviet research and non-Soviet replications. *Human Development., 13*, 13-53.

Wozniak, R. H. (1975). Psychology and education of the learning-disabled child in the USSR. In W. M. Gruikshank, & D. P. Hallihan (Eds.) *Research and theory in minimal cerebral dysfunction and learning disability.* NY: Syracuse University Press.

Wozniak, R. H. (1975). Dialecticism and structuralism: The philosophical foundation of Soviet psychology and Piagetian cognitive developmental theory. In K. F. Riegel & G. C. Rosenwald (Eds.), *Structure and transformation: Developmental and historical aspects* (pp. 25-45). New York: John Wiley.

Wozniak, R. H. (1975). A dialectical paradigm for psychological research: Implications drawn from the history of psychology in the Soviet Union. *Human Development, 18,* 18-34.

Wozniak, R. H. (1976). Speech-for-self as a multiply reafferent human action system. In K. Riegel & J. A. Meacham (Eds.), *The developing individual in a changing world* (Vol. 1). The Hague: Mouton.

Wozniak, R. H. (1976). Intelligence, soviet dialectics, and american psychometrics: Implications for the evaluation of learning disabilities. In S. A. Corson and E. C. Corson (Eds.), *Psychiatry and psychology in USSR* (pp. 121-132). New York: Plenum Press.

Wozniak, R. H. (1980). Theory, practice, and the " Zone of proximal development" in Soviet psychoeducational research. *Contemporary Educational Psychology, 5,* 175-183.

Wozniak, R. H. (1981). The future of constructivist psychology: Reflections on Piaget. *Teachers College Record, 83,* 197-199.

Wozniak, R. H. (1983). Lev Semenovich Vygotsky (1896-1934). *History of Psychology Newsletter, 15*(3), 49-55.

Wozniak, R. H. (1983). Is a genetic epistemology of psychology possible? *Cahiers de la Fondation Archives Jean Piaget, 4,* 323-347.

Wozniak, R. H. (1987). Developmental method, zone of development, and theories of the environment. In L. S. Liben (Ed.), *Development and learning: Conflict or congruence* (pp. 225-235). Lawrence Erlbaum Associates.

Wozniak, R. H. (1992). Co-constructive, intersubjective realism: Metatheory in developmental psychology. In W. A. Kurtines, M. Azmitia, & J. L. Gewirtz (Eds.), *The role of values in psychology and human development* (pp. 89-104). New York: John Wiley & Sons.

Yaden, D. B. (1984). Inner speech, oral language, and reading: Huey and Vygotsky revisited. *Reading Psychology: An International Quarterly, 5,* 155-166.

Yingling, J. (1994). Childhood: Talking the mind into existence. In D. R. Vocate (Ed.), *Intrapersonal communication: Different voices, different minds* (pp. 121-143). New Jersey: Lawrence Erlbaum Associates.

You, L. C. (1992). *A Vygotskian microgenetic analysis of the effect of classroom dialogues on students' internalization process.* Unpublished doctoral dissertation, The University of Texas at Austin, USA.

Youniss, J. (1984). Discussion: Single mind and social mind. *Human Development, 27*), 134-135.

Youniss, J. (1994). Vygotsky's fragile genius in time and place. *Human Development, 37*, 119-124.

Zazanis, E. (1992). Reflections on an evolvingpsychology. *Quarterly Newsletter of the Laboratory of Comparative Human Cognition, 14*(4), 145-147.

Zebroski, J. T. (1982). *Writing as "activity": Composition development from the perspective of the Vygotskian school.* Unpublished doctoral dissertation, The Ohio Sate University, USA.

Zebroski, J. T. (1982). Soviet psycholinguistics: implications for teaching writing. In W. Frawley (Ed.), *Linguistics and literacy* (pp. 51-63). NY: Plenum Press

Zebroski, J. (1983). Writing as "activity": Composition development from the perspective of the Vygotskian school. *Dissertation Abstracts International*ₐ (44), 94.

Zebroski, J. T. (1986). *Tropes and zones.* Correspondences: Four.

Zebroski, J. T. (1986). The uses of theory: A Vygotskian approch to composition. *Writing Instructor, 5*(2), 57-67

Zebroski, J. T. (1989). The social construction of self in the work of Lev Vygotsky. *Writing Instructor, 8*(4), 149-156.

Zebroski, J. T. (1992). Mikhail Bakhtin and the question of rhetoric. *Rhetoric Society Quarterly, 22*(4), 22-28.

Zebroski, J. T. (1994). *Thinking through theory: Vygotskian perspectives on the teaching of writing.* Postmouth, NH: Boynton/Cook Publishers.

Zebroski, J. T. (1994). A Vygotsky theory of writing. In *Thinking through theory: Vygotskian perspectives on the teaching of writing* (pp. 154-178). Postmouth, NH: Boynton/Cook Publishers.

Zebroski, J. T. (1994). Vygotsky on composing: Theoretical implications. In *Thinking through theory: Vygotskian perspectives on the teaching of writing* (pp. 194-202). Postmouth, NH: Boynton/Cook Publishers.

Zebroski, J. T. (1994). The stuggle for voice. In *Thinking through theory:Vygotskian perspectives on the teaching of writing* (pp. 225-237). Postmouth, NH: Boynton/Cook Publishers.

Zebroski, J. T. (1994). Vygotsky's theory of self. In *Thinking through theory: Vygotskian perspectives on the teaching of writing* (pp. 238-

45). Postmouth, NH: Boynton/Cook Publishers.

Zebroski, J. T. (1994). Vygotsky and composition: Influences on an emerging field. In *Thinking through theory: Vygotskian perspectives on the teaching of writing* (pp. 272-314). Postmouth, NH: Boynton/Cook Publishers.

Zender, M. A., & Zender, B. F. (1974). Vygotsky's view about the age periodization of child development. *Human Development, 17*, 24-26.

Zevin, R. N. (1984). More than a musical error. *American Psychologist, 39*(8), 917

Zimmerman, B. J. (1993). Commentary on Tudge's & Winterhoff's article: Vygotsky, Piaget and Bandura: Perspectives on the relations between the social world and cognitive development. *Human Development, 36*, 82-86

Zivin, G. (1979). Removing common confusions about egocentric speech, private speech, and self regulation. In G. Zevin (Ed.), *The development of self-regulation through private speech* (pp. 13-49). New York: Wiley.

Zivin, G. (Ed.). (1979). *The development of self-regulation through private speech.* New York: Wiley.

Zukow, P. G. (1980). *A microanalytic study of the role of the caregiver in the relationship between symbolic play and language acquisition during the one-word period.* Unpublished doctoral dissertation, University of California, Los Angeles, USA.

Discussion of the works of L. S. Vygotsky in Netherlands

Carpay, J. (1993). In the footsteps of Lev S. Vygotsky. Amsterdam: Free University Press.

de Graaf, W. (1994). Sociogenesis: Subject-forms between inertia and innovation. In W. de Graaf & R. Maier (Eds.), *Sociogenesis reexamined* (pp. 185-201). New York: Springer-Verlag.

de Graaf, W., & Maier, R. (1994). Sociogenesis reexamined: An introduction. In W. de Graaf & R. Maier (Eds.), *Sociogenesis reexamined* (pp. 1-16). New York: Springer-Verlag.

Elbers, E. (1986). Interaction and instruction in the conservation experiment. *European Journal of Psychology of Education, 1*(1), 77-89.

Elbers, E. (1987). Critical psychology and the development of motivation as historical process. In J. M. Broughton (Ed.), *Critical theories of psychological development* (pp. 149-175). New York: Plenum Press.

Elbers, E. (1988). Social context and the child's construction of knowledge. Utrecht: Elinkwijk.

Elbers, E. (1989). *Internalization and the study of adult-child interaction*. Paper presented at the First European Congress of Psychology, Amsterdam.

Elbers, E. (1991). The development of competence and its social context. *Educational Psychology Review, 3*(2), 73-94.

Elbers, E. (1991). Context, culture and competence. Answers to criticism. *Educational Psychology Review, 3*(2), 137-148.

Elbers, E. (1994). Sociogenesis and children's pretended play: A variation on Vygotskian themes. In W. de Graaf & R. Maier (Eds.), *Sociogenesis reexamined* (pp. 219-241. New York: Springer-Verlag.

Elbers, E., Maier, R., Hoekstra, T., & Hoogsteder, M. (1990). *How can we analyze adult-child interaction?* Poster presented at the 9th European Conference on Developmental Psychology, Stirling, England.

Elbers, E., Maier, R., Hoekstra, T., & Hoogsteder, M. (1992). Internalization and adult-child interaction. *Learning & Instruction, 2*, 101-118.

Goudena, P. (1983). *Private speech: An analysis of its social and self-regulatory functions*. PhD thesis. University of Utrecht.

Goudena, P. (1987). The social nature of private speech of preschoolers during problem solving.
International journal of Behavioral Development, 10, 187-206.

Goudena, P. (1992). The problem of abbreviation and private speech. In

R. M. Diaz & L. E. Berk (Eds.), *Private speech: From social interaction to self-regulation* (pp. 215-224). Lawrence Erlbaum Associates.

Goudena, P. (in press). *Four issues concerning private speech.*

Haenen, J. (1995). *Piotr Gal'perin: Psychologist in Vygotsky's footsteps.* Commack, NY: Nova Science Publishers.

Haenen, J. (1995). Report of the Vygotsky conference. *Educational Psychologist, 30*(2), 103-104.

Haenen, J. (1995). The legacy of A. N. Leontiev. *Journal of Russian & East European Psychology, 33*(6), 6-11.

Hickmann, M. (Ed.). (1980). *Proceeding from a working conference on the social foundations of language and thought.* Chicago: Center for Psychological Studies.

Hickmann, M. (1982). *The development of narrative skills: Pragmatic and metapragmatic aspects of discourse cohesion.* Unpublished doctoral dissertation, University of Chicago, USA.

Hickmann, M. (1984). Contexte et fonction dans le développement du langage. In M. Delau (Ed.), *Langage et communication à l'âge préscolaire.* France, Rennes: Presses Universitaires de Rennes.

Hickmann, M. (1985). Metapragmatics in child language. In E. Mertz & R. J. Parmentier (Eds.), *Semiotic mediation: Sociocultural and psychological perspective.* New York: Academic Press

Hickmann, M. (1987). Introduction: Language and thought revisited. In M. Hickmann (Ed.), *Social and functional approaches to language and thought* (pp. 1-13). New York: Academic Press.

Hickmann, M. (1987). Pragmatics in child language: Some issues in developmental theory. In M. Hickmann (Ed.), *Social and functional approaches to language and thought.* New York: Academic Press.

Hickmann, M. (Ed.). (1987). *Social and functional approaches to language and thought.* New York: Academic Press.

Hickmann, M. (1991). Le discours rapporté: Aspects métapragmatiques du langage et de son développement. *Bulletin de Psychologie, Tome XLIV*(399), 121-137.

Hoogsteder, M. (1991). *Internalization and instruction: Vygotskian nterpretations of internalization.* Unpublished manuscript, University of Utrecht, Department of General Social Sciences, Utrecht. The Netherlands.

Maier, R. (1992). Internalization in cognitive development: An examination of Piaget's theory. In R. Maier (Ed.), *Internalization: Conceptual issues and methodological problems.* Utrecht: ISOR.

Maier, R. (Ed.). (1992). *Internalization: Conceptual issues and methodological problems.* Utrecht: ISOR.

Maier, R. (1994). Questioning the mechanism of sociogenesis. In R.

Maier & W. de Graaf (Eds.), *Sociogenesis reexamined* (pp. 133-145). New York: Springer-Verlag.

Maier, R., Elbers, E., Hoekstra, T., & Hoogsteder, M. (1992). The puzzle of Wertsch. *Cultural Dynamics, 5,* 25-42.

Van Beek, Y., & Geerdink, J. (1989). Intervention with preterms: Is it educational enough? Special Issue: Infancy and education: Psychological considerations. *European Journal of Psychology of Education, 4*(2), 251-265

Van Der Veer, R. (1983). *Vygotsky as a critical methodologist: The analytical bias.* Leiden: Department of Pedagogics.

Van Der Veer, R. (1984). *Cultuur en cognitie.* Groningen: Wolters-Noordhoff.

Van Der Veer, R. (1984). Early period in the works of L. S. Vygotsky: The influence of Spinoza. In M. Hedegaard, P. Hakkarinen, & Engestrom (Eds.), *Learning and teaching on a scientific bases* (pp. 87-98). Aarhus: Psychologisch Instituut.

Van Der Veer, R. (1985). The cultural-historical approach in psychology: A research program? *Quarterly Newsletter of the Laboratory of Comparative Human Cognition, 7*(4), 108-113.

Van Der Veer, R. (1985). Similarities between the theories of G. H. Mead and L. S. Vygotsky: An explanation?. In S. Bem, H. Rappard & Hoorn, W. Van (Eds.), *Studies in the history of the social sciences* (Vol. 3, 1-11). Leiden: Psychologisch Instituut.

Van Der Veer, R. (1985). In defense of Vygotsky. In S. Bem, H. Rappard & W. Van. Hoorn (Eds.), *Proceedings of the 1983 CHEIRON Europe Conference.* Leiden: Psychologisch Instituut.

Van Der Veer, R. (1987). A review of thought and language. Lev Vygotsky (Newly revised, translated and edited by A. Kozulin, MA: MIT Press, 1986). *Journal of Mind and Behavior, 8*(1), 175-177.

Van Der Veer, R. (1986). Vygotsky's developmental psychology. *Psychological Reports. 59,* 527-536.

Van Der Veer, R. (1987). El dualismo en psicologia: Un analisis Vygotskiano. In M. Siguan (Ed.), *Actualidad de Lev S. Vigotski* (Actuality de Lev S. Vygotsky). Barcelona: Anthropos.

Van Der Veer, R. (1987). The relationship between Vygotsky and Mead reconsidered. A comment on Hans-Johann Glock. *Studies in Soviet Thought, 34,* 91-93.

Van Der Veer, R. (1988). The concept of culture in Vygotsky's cultural-historical theory. *Proceedings of the 7th European CHEIRON Conference,* Budapest, 4-8 septembre. Hungarian Psychological Association.

Van Der Veer, R. (1989). Overcoming dualism in psychology:

Vygotsky's analysis of theories of emotion. *Quarterly Newsletter of the Laboratory of Comparative Human Cognition, 11,* 124-131.

Van Der Veer, R. (1990). The reform of Soviet psychology: A historical perspective. *Studies in Soviet Thought, 40,* 205-221.

Van Der Veer, R. (1991). The anthropological underpinning of Vygotsky's thinking. *Studies in Soviet Thought, 42*(2), 73-91.

Van Der Veer, R. (1994). The forbidden colors game: An argument in favor of internalization? In R. Van Der Veer., M. H. Van Ijzendoorn., & J. Valsiner (Eds.), *Reconstructing the mind: Replicability in research on human development* (pp. 233-254). New Jersey: Ablex Publishing Company.

Van Der Veer, R. (1992, December). *The concept of development and the development of concepts.* Paper presented at the Workshop: Learning, development and zone of proximal development, Bordeaux, France.

Van Der Veer, R. (1994). Pierre Janet's relevance for a socio-cultural approach. In R. A. Rosa & J. Valsiner (Eds.), *Historical and theoretical discourse in socio-cultural studies.* Madrid: Fundacion Infancia y Apprendizaje.

Van Der Veer, R. (1994). The concept of sociogenesis in cultural-historical theory. In W. de Graaf & R. Maier (Eds.), *Sociogenesis reexamined* (pp. 117-131). New York: Springer-Verlag.

Van Der Veer, R. (1994). The concept of development and the development of concepts: Education and development in Vygotsky's thinking. *European Journal of Psychology of Education, 9*(4), 293-300.

Van Der Veer, R., & Valsiner, J. (1987). Dualisme in de psychologie van de emotie: Een analyse van Vygotskij. [Dualism in the psychology of e motion: An analysis of Vygotsky]. *Nederlands Tijdschrift voor de Psychologie en haar Grensgebieden, 42*(8), 405-413.

Van Der Veer, R., & Arievitch, I. (1994). Reception of Piotr Ya Gal'prin's ideas in the west. *Perceptual & Motor Skills, 78* (1), 177-178.

Van Der Veer, R., & Arievitch, I. (1995). Furthering the internalization debate: Gal'prin's contribution. *Human Development, 38,* 113-126.

Van Der Veer, R., & Valsiner, J. (1988). Lev Vygotsky and Pierre Janet: On the origin of the concept of sociogenesis. *Developmental Review, 8,* 52-65.

Van Der Veer, R., & Valsiner, J. (1992). Voices at play: Understanding Van Der Veer and Valsiner. *Comenius, 12*(4), 423-429.

Van Der Veer, R., & Van IJzendoorn, M. H. (1983). Vygotsky's cultural historical theory: Critique of the distinction between lower and higher psychological processes. *Gedrag, Tijdschrift Voor Psychologie, 114,* 155-168.

Van Der Veer, R., & Van IJzendoorn, M. H. (1985). Vygotsky's theory of the higher psychological processes: some criticisms. *Human Development, 28,* 1-9.

Van Der Veer, R., & Van IJzendoorn, M. H. (1988). Early childhood attachment and later problem solving: A Vygotskian perspective. In J. Valsiner (Ed.), *Child development within culturally structured environments* (Vol. 1, pp. 215-246). Norwood, N.J: Ablex.

Van Der Veer, R., Van Ijzendoorn, M. H., & Valsiner, J. (Eds.). (1994). *Reconstructing the mind. Replicability in research on human development.* New Jersey: Ablex Publishing Company.

Van Der Veer, R., & Valsiner, J. (1991). *Understanding Vygotsky: A quest for synthesis.* Oxford: Basil Blackwell.

Van Der Veer, R., & Valsiner, J. (1991). Sociogenetic perspectives in the work of Pierre Janet. *Storia della Psicologia, 3,* 6-23.

Van Der Veer, R., & Valsiner, J. (Eds.). (1994). *The Vygotsky reader.* Oxford: Basil Blackwell.

Van Der Veer, R., & Valsiner, J. (1994). Preface. In R. Van Der Veer & J. Valsiner (Eds.), *The Vygotsky reader.* Oxford: Basil Blackwell.

Van Der Veer, R., & Valsiner, J. (1994). Reading Vygotsky: From fascination to construction. In R. Van Der Veer & J. Valsiner (Eds.), *The Vygotsky reader* (pp. 1-9). Oxford: Basil Blackwell.

Van Geert, P. (1991). A dynamic systems model of cognitive and language growth. *Psychological Review, 98,* 3-53.

Van Geert, P. (1992). Vygotsky's dynamic systems. *Comenius, 12*(4), 383-401.

Van Geert, P. (1994). A dynamics of development. In R. Port & T. van Gelder (Eds.), *Mind as motion.* Cambridge, MA: MIT Press.

Van Geert, P. (1994). *Dynamic systems of development: Change between complexity and chaos.* New York: Harvester-Wheatsheaf.

Van Geert, P. (1994). Vygotskian dynamics of development. *Human Development, 37*(6), 346-365.

Van Ijzendoorn, M. H. (1986). The cross-cultural validity of the strange situation from a vygotskian perspective. *Behavioral & Brain Sciences, 9*(3), 558-559.

Van Ijzendoorn, M. H., & Van Der Veer, R. (1983). Holzkamp's critical psychology and the functional-historical method: A critical apprairsal. *Storia e Critica della Psicologia, 4,* 5-26.

Van Ijzendoorn, M. H., & Van Der Veer, R. (1984). *Main currents of critical psychology. Vygotsky, Holzkamp, and Riegel.* New York: Irvington Publishers.

Van Ijzendoorn, M. H., & Van Der Veer, R. (1984). Historical roots of critical psychology: The cultural-historical school. In M. H. Van Ijzendoorn & R. & Van Der Veer, *Main currents of critical psychology. Vygotsky, Holzkamp, and Riegel* (pp. 13-99). NY: Irvington Publishers.

Van Ijzendoorn, M. H., & Van Der Veer, R. (1984). Recent developments in critical psychology: The Berlin school of critical psychology. In M. H. Van Ijzendoorn & R. & Van Der Veer, *Main currents of critical psychology. Vygotsky, Holzkamp, and Riegel* (pp. 107-180). NY: Irvington Publishers.

Van Ijzendoorn, M. H., & Van Der Veer, R. (1984). Recent developments in critical psychology: Dialectical psychology. In M. H. Van Ijzendoorn & R. & Van Der Veer, *Main currents of critical psychology. Vygotsky, Holzkamp, and Riegel* (pp. 181-225). New York: Irvington Publishers.

Van Oers, B. (1988). Activity, semiotics and the development of children. *Comenius, 8,* 398-406.

Van Parreren, C. F., & Carpay, J. A. M. (1980). *Soviet psychologists on education and cognitive development.* Gromingen: Wolters-Noordhoff (in Dutch).

Van Ree, F. (1974). Vigotski versus Freud. *Tijdschrift voor Psychiatrie, 16*(5), 301-308.

Discussion of the works of L. S. Vygotsky in Switzerland

Arievitch, I., & Stetsenko, A. (1989). From Vygotsky to Gal'perin: Development of an idea of mental action's externality. *Storia e Critica della Psicologia*, (1), 111-113.

Ascher, E. (1991). La société dans l'homme. *Revue Européenne des Sciences Sociales, 19*(89), 25-41.

Barisnikov, K., & Petitpierre. G. (1994). Introduction. In L. S. Vygotsky, *Défectologie et déficience mentale* (pp. 17-30). Neuchâtel -Paris: Delachaux & Niestlé (Collection Textes de Base en Psycho.)

Bronckart, J. P. (1969). *Le rôle régulateur du langage.* Unpublished doctoral dissertation, University of Liege, Belgium.

Bronckart, J. P. (1970). Le rôle régulateur du langage: *Critique expérimentale des travaux D'A. R. Luria. Neuropsychologia, 8*, 451-463.

Bronckart, J. P. (1973). The regulating role of speech: A cognitive approach. *Human Development, 16*, 417-439.

Bronckart, J. P. (1977). *Théorie du langage: Une introduction critique.* Belgique, Bruxelles: Pierre Mardaga. (Bronckart devoted six pages to Vygotsky's work, pp. 65-70).

Bronckart, J. P. (1985). Vygotski, une oeuvre en devenir. In B. Schneuwly & J. P. Bronckart (Eds.), *Vygotski aujourd'hui* (pp. 7-21). Neuchâtel-Paris: Delachaux & Niestlé (Collection Textes de Base en Psychologie).

Bronckart, J. P. (1992, July). *Vygotsky's past and current influences.* In XXV International Congress of Psychology, Brussels.

Bronckart, J. P. (1995). Theories of action, speech, natural language, and discourse. In J. Wertsch, P. del Rio & A. Alvarez (Eds.), *Sociocultural studies of mind* (pp. 75-91). NY: Cambridge University Press.

Bronckart, J. P., & Ventouras-Spycher, M. (1979). The piagetian concept of representation and the Soviet-inspired view of self-regulation. In G. Zivin (Ed.), *The development of self-regulation through private speech* (pp. 99-131). New York: Wiley.

Brossard, A. (1990). *Regards, interactions sociales et développement cognitif chez l'enfant de 6 à10 ans dans des épreuves opératoires piagetiennes.* Thèse d'état. Université Lumière-Lyon 2. Département de psychologie.

Brossard, A. (1992). *La psychologie du regard: De la perception visuelle aux regards.* Neuchâtel-Paris: Delachaux & Niestlé

Doise, W. (1982). *L'explication en psychologie sociale.* Paris: PUF, France.

Doise, W. (1985). Psychologie sociale et constructivisme cognitif.

Archives de Psychologie, 53, 127-140.

Doise, W. (1985). Le développement social de l'intelligence: Aperçu historique. In G. Mugny (Ed.), *Psychologie sociale du développement cognitif* (pp. 39-55). Berne: Peter Lang.

Doise, W. (1990). The development of individual competencies through social interaction. In H. C. Foot, M. J. Morgan & R. H. Shute (Eds.), *Children helping children.* New York: John Wiley & Son Ltd.

Doise, W. (1990). Individual cognitive functioning: societal aspect. In H. T. Himmenlweit & G. Gaskell (Eds.), *Societal psychology* (pp. 92-111). London: Sage

Doise, W. (1991). Coopération et conflit dans une perspective Piagetienne. *Revue Européenne des Sciences Sociales, 19*(89), 13-23.

Doise, W. (1992, July). *Social mediation in knowledge acquisition.* In XXV International Congress of Psychology, Brussels.

Doise, W. (1993). La double dynamique sociale dans le développement cognitif. *International Journal of Psychology, 28*(5), 611-626.

Doise, W., & Mugny, G. (1984). *The social development of the intellect.* Oxford: Pergamon Press.

Doise, W., Mugny, G., & Perret-Clermont, A. N. (1974). Ricerche preliminari sulla sociogenesi delle structure cognitive. *Lavoro Educativo, 1,* 33-50.

Doise, W., Mugny, G., & Perret-Clermont, A. N. (1975). Social interaction and the development of cognitive operations. *European Journal of Social Psychology, 5,* 367-383.

Doise, W., Mugny, G., & Perret-Clermont, A. N. (1976). Social interaction and cognitive development: Further evidence. *European Journal of Social Psychology, 6* (2), 245-247.

Doise, W., Dionnet, S., & Mugny, G. (1978). Conflit socio-cognitif, marquage social et développement cognitif. *Cahiers de Psychologie, 21,* 231-243.

Doise, W., & Mugny, G. (1979). Individual and collective conflicts of centrations in cognitive development.
European Journal of Social Psychology, 9, 105-108.

Doise, W., & Mugny, G. (1981). *Le développement social de l'intelligence.* Paris, Inter Editions.

Doise, W., & Mackie, D. (1981). On the social nature of cognition. In J. Forgas (Ed.), *Social cognition* (Chapter 5). New York: Academic Press

Doise, W., & Hanselmann, C. (1990). Interaction sociale et acquisition de la conservation du volume. *European Journal of Psychology of Education, 5*(1), 21-31.

Doise, W., & Hanselmann, C. (1991). Conflict and social marking in the acquisition of operational thinking. *Learning and Instruction, 1,* 119-127.

Flammer, A., & Avramakis, J. (1992). Developmental tasks-where do they come from? In von M. Cranach, W. Doise, & G. Mugny (Eds.), *Social representations and the social bases of knowledge* (pp. 56-63). Bern: Hogrefe & Huber Publishers.

Grossen, M. (1986). Interaction adulte-enfant en situation de test. *Cahiers de Psychologie, Université de Neuchâtel,* (24), 15-22.

Grossen, M. (1988). L'Intersubjectivité en situation de test. *Dossiers de Psychologie(* 36, Université de Neuchâtel, Cousset, Delval.

Grossen, M. (1988). *La construction sociale de l'Intersubjectivité entre adulte et enfant en situation de test.* Fribourg: Editions Delval, Cousset.

Grossen, M. (1991). Comment on Elbers's article: Which competence? for whom? for what?. *Educational Psychology Review, 3*(2), 95-102.

Grossen, M., & Perret-Clermont, A. N. (1984). Some elements of a social psychology of operational development of the child. *Quarterly Newsletter of the Laboratory of Comparative Human Cognition, 6*(3), 51-57.

Grossen, M., & Perret-Clermont, A. N. (1994). Psycho-social perspective on cognitive development: Construction of adult-child intersubjectivity in logic tasks. In W. de Graaf & R. Maier (Eds.), *Sociogenesis reexamined* (pp. 243-260). New York: Springer-Verlag.

Lambert, J. L. (1994). La défectologie et la déficience mentale: Lapproche de Vygotsky. In L. S. Vygotsky, Défectologie et déficience mentale (pp.7-16). Neuchâtel-Paris: Delachaux & Niestlé (Collection Textes de Base en Psychologie).

Mugny, G., & Doise, W. (1978). Socio-cognitive conflict and structure of individual and collective performances. *European Journal of Social Psychology, 8,* 181-182.

Mugny, G., Doise, W., & Perret-Clermont, A. N. (1976). Conflit de centrations et progrès cognitif. *Bulletin de Psychologie, 29*(321), 199-204.

Mugny, G. (Ed.). (1985). *Psychologie sociale du développpement cognitif.* Berne: Peter Lang.

Mugny, G., & al. (1988). Saillance du marquage social et progrès cognitifs: Influence de l'explication des régles sociales. *Revue Suisse de Psychologie, 47* (4), 261-266.

Mugny, G., Doise, W., & Levy, M. (1978). Conflit socio-cognitif et développement cognitif. *Revue Suisse de Psychologie, 37,* 22-43.

Mugny, G., & Carugati, F. (1985). *L'intelligence au pluriel: Les représentations sociales de l'intelligence et de son développement.* Editions DelVal.

Palmonari, A., & Doise, W. (1984). *Social interaction in individual development.* Cambridge, Cambridge University Press.

Paola De Paolis., Doise, W., & Mugny, G. (1987). Social markings in cognitive operations. In W. Doise & S. Moscovici (Eds.), *Current issues in European social psychology* (Vol. 2, pp. 1-45). Cambridge: Cambridge University Press.

Payne, T. R. (1966). On the theoretical foundations of Soviet psychology. *Studies in Soviet Thought, 6(2)*, 124-134. Also in E. Laszlo (Ed.), *Philosophy in the Soviet Union* (pp. 104-114). Dortrecht: D. Reidel. 1967

Payne, T. R. (1969). *S. L. Rubinstein and the philosophical foundations of Soviet psychology.* Dortrecht: D. Reidel

Perret-Clermont, A. N. (1976). *L'interaction sociale comme facteur du développement cognitif.* Thèse de Doctorat, Genève: Université de Genève.

Perret-Clermont, A. N. (1980). Interactions sociales et représentations symboliques dans le cadre du problème additifs. *Recherches en Didactique des Mathématiques,1(3)*, 297-350.

Perret-Clermont, A. N. (1980). Social interaction and cognitive development in children. London: Academic Press. (Translated into Arabic by Mohamed ELhammoumi).

Perret-Clermont, A. N. (1981). *La construction de l'intelligence dans l'interaction sociale.* Berne, Peter Lang, 1979, (2ème éd.)

Perret-Clermont, A. N. (1987). Les interactions sociales ont une histoire. In CRESAS, *On n'apprend pas tout seul: Interactions sociales et construction des savoirs* (pp.132-134). Paris: ESF. Institut National de Recherche Pédagogique.

Perret-Clermont, A. N. (1993). What is it that develops? *Cognition & Instruction, 11(3-4)*, 197-205.

Perret-Clermont, A. N., Mugny, G., & Doise, W. (1976). Une approche psychosociologique du développement cognitif. *Archives de Psychologie, 44(171)*, 135-144.

Perret-Clermont, A. N., & Schubauer-Leoni, M. L. (1980). Conflict and cooperation as opportunities for learning. In P. Robinson (Ed.), *communication in development.* London: Academic Press.

Perret-Clermont, A. N., Brun, J., Saada, E. H., & Schubauer-Leoni, M. L. (1984). Psychological processes, operatory level and the acquisition of knowledge. *Interactions Didactiques(2*, University of Geneva & Neuchâtel.

Perret-Clermont, A. N., Nicolet, M., & Grossen, M. (1988). Testonsnous des compétences cognitives. *Revue Internationale de Psychologie Sociale, 1(*1), 71-9.

Perret-Clermont, A. N., & Nicolet, M. (Eds.). (1988). *Intéragir et connaître*. Cousset, Delval.

Perret-Clermont, A. N., & Schubauer-Leoni, M. L. (1989). Social factors in learning and teaching: towards an integrative perspective. *International Journal of Educational Research, 13*(6), 575-580.

Perret-Clermont, A. N., Perret, J. F., & Bell, N. (1991). The social construction of meaning and cognitive activity in elementary school children. In L. Resnick, J. M. Leviner & S. D. Teasley (Eds.), *Perspectives on socially shared cognition* (pp. 41-62). Washington DC: American Psychological Association.

Perret-Clermont, A. N., Schubauer-Leoni, M., & Grossen, M. (1991). Interactions sociales dans le développemnet cognitif: Nouvelles directions de recherche. *Cahiers de Psychologie de l'Université de Neuchâtel, (*29), 17-39.

Perret-Clermont, A. N., Pontecorvo, C., & Trognon, A. (1992). Adult-child conversation (special issue). *Verbum, (*1 & 2), 3-102.

Perret-Clermont, A. N., Schubauer-Leoni, M., & Trognon, A. (1992). L'extorsion des réponses en situation asymétrique [The extortion of responses in asymmetrical situation. *Verbum, (*1 & 2), 3-32.

Piaget, J. (1962). Comments on Vygotsky's critical remarks concerning the Language and thought of the child, and Judgment and reasoning in the child. In L. S. Vygotsky, *Thought and language* (pp. 1-14). Cambridge, MA.: The MIT. Press.

Piaget, J. (1979). Comments on Vygotsky's critical remarks concerning the Language and thought of the child, and Judgment and reasoning in the child. *Archives de Psychologie, 47*(183), 237-249.

Piaget, J. (1985). Commentaires sur les remarques critiques de Vygotsky. In B. Schneuwly, & J. P. Bronckart (Eds.), *Vygotski aujourd'hui* (pp. 120-137). Neuchâtel-Paris: Delachaux & Niestlé (Collection Textes de base en psychologie).

Piaget, J. (1985). Commentaire sur les remarques critiques de Vygotski concernant le langage et la pensée chez l'enfant et le jugement et le raisonnement chez l'enfant. In L. Vygotsky, *Pensée et langage* (pp.387-399). Paris: Messidor/ Editions Sociales

Piaget, J. (1995). Commentary on Vygotsky's criticisms of language and thought of the child and judgment and reasoning in the child. *New Ideas in Psychology, 13*(3), 325-340.

Piaget, J. (1995). Commentary on Vygotsky's criticisms of language and thought of the child and judgment and reasoning in the child. In Arabic, Translated by Mohamed Elhammoumi.

Reusser, K. (1993). Tutoring systems and pedagogical theory:

Representational tools for understanding, planning, and reflection in problem solving. In S. Derry & S. Lajoie (Eds.), *Computers as cognitive tools* (pp. 143-177). Hillsdale, NJ: Erlbaum.

Schneuwly, B. (1984). *Le texte discursif écrit à l'école.* Thèse de Doctorat, Genève: Université de Genève.

Schneuwly, B. (1985). La construction sociale du langage écrit chez l'enfant. In B. Schneuwly, & J. P. Bronckart (Eds.), *Vygotski aujourd'hui* (pp. 169-201). Neuchâtel-Paris: Delachaux & Niestlé (Collection Textes de Base en Psychologie).

Schneuwly, B. (1987). Les capacités humaines sont des constructions sociales. Essai sur la théorie de Vygotski. *European Journal of Psychology of Education, 2(4),* 5-16.

Schneuwly, B. (1988). Le langage écrit chez l'enfant: La production des textes informatifs et argumentatifs. Neuchâtel-Paris: Delachaux & Niestlé

Schneuwly, B. (1988). Vygotsky and Spinoza. *Proceedings of the 7th Proceedings of the 7th European CHEIRON Conference,* Budapest, 4-8 septembre. Hungarian Psychological Association.

Schneuwly, B. (1989). Le 7e chapitre de pensée et langage de Vygotski: Esquisse d'un *modèle psychologique de la production langagière. Enfance, 42(1-2),* 23-30.

Schneuwly, B. (1989). La conception Vygotskienne du langage écrit. *Etudes de Linguistique Appliquée, 73),* 107-1170.

Schneuwly, B. (1994). Contradiction and development: Vygotsky and paedology. *European Journal of Psychology of Education, 9(4),* 281-291.

Schneuwly, B., & Bronckart, J. P. (Eds.). (1985). *Vygotski aujourd'hui.* Neuchâtel-Paris: Delachaux & Niestlé (Collection Textes de Base en Psychologie).

Schubauer-Leoni, M. (1986). Le contrat didactique: Un cadre interprétatif pour comprendre les savoirs manifestés par les élèves en mathématiques. *European Journal of Psychology of Education,, 1(2),* 139-153.

Schubauer-Leoni, M. L., Perret-Clermont., & Grossen, M. (1992). The construction of adult-child intersubjectivity in psychological research and in school. In von M. Cranach, W. Doise, & G. Mugny (Eds.), *Social representations and the social bases of knowledge* (pp. 69-77). Bern: Hogrefe & Huber Publishers.

Schubauer-Leoni, M. L., & Grossen, M. (1993). Negotiating the meaning of questions in didactic and experimental contracts. *European Journal of Psychology of Education, 8(4),* 51-471.

Sinclair, H. (1972). Some notes comments on Fodor's 'Reflections on L. S. Vygotsky's thought and language'. *Cognition, 1,* 317-318.

Tryphon, A., & Vonèche, J. (Eds.). (1994). *Piaget-Vygotsky: The social genesis of thought*. England, Hove: Erlbaum.

Von Cranach, M., Doise, W., & Mugny, G. (Eds.). (1992). *Social representations and the social bases of knowledge*. Levinson, NY: Hogrefe & Huber.

Discussion of the works of L. S. Vygotsky in France

Beaudichon, J. (1990). En quoi les recherches sur le développement des compétences sociales questionnent-elles lles théories générales du développement cognitifs? In: Gaby Netchine-Grynberg (Ed.), *Développement et fonctionnement cognitifs chez l'enfant* (pp. 185-199). Paris: PUF.

Beaudichon, J., Legros, S., & Oléron, P. (1973). Les débuts de l'autorégulation verbale du compotement: Nouveau contrôle expérimental des thèses D'A. R. Luria. *Neuropsychologia, 11*, 337-341.

Beaudichon, J., Legros, S., & Vandromme, L. (1989). La prise en charge du contrôle de la communication à visée instrumentale: Aspects interpersonnels et intrapersonnels. *Enfance, 42*(1-2), 57-65.

Beaudichon, J., Vandenplas-Holper, C. & Ducroux, N. (1985). Analyse des interactions et de leurs effets dans la communication référentielle et la maîtrise de notions. In: G. Mugny (Ed.), *Psychologie sociale du développement cognitif* (pp. 125-149). Berne: Peter Lang.

Beaudichon, J., Vebra, M & Winnykamen, F. (1988). Interactions sociales et acquisition de connaissances chez l'enfant: une approche pluridimensionnelle. *Revue Internationale de Psychologie Sociale, 1*, 129-141.

Bernicot, J. (1994). Speech acts in young children: Vygotsky's contribution. *European Journal of Psychology of Education, 9*(4), 311-319.

Blaye, A. (1992). Collaborative learning at the computer: How social processes "intreface" with human computer relation. *European Journal of Psychology of Education, 7*(4), 257-267.

Blicharski, T., Gravel, F., & Trudel, M. (1994). Represenational and communicative processes in the social construction of early temperament. In A. Vyt, H. Bloch & M. H. Bornstein (Eds.), *Early childhood development in the French tradition: contribution from current research* (pp. 315-331). New Jersey: Lawrence Erlbuam.

Brossard, M. (1989). Espace discursif et activités cognitives: Un apport de la théorie vygotskienne. *Enfance, 42*(1-2), 49-56.

CRESAS. (1987). On n'apprend pas tout seul: Interactions sociales et construction des savoirs. Paris: ESF.

Codol, J. P. (1989). Vingt ans de cognition sociale. *Bulletin de Psychologie, 42*(390), 472-491.

Deconchy, J. P. (1990). Sociocultural contexts and psychological mechanisms. In H. T. Himmenlweit & G. Gaskell (Eds.), *Societal psychology* (pp. 177-192). London: Sage.

Delau, M. (1986). the ontogenesis of semiotic processes in early infancy. In M. Hildebrand-Nelshon & G. Rückriem (Eds.), *Proceedings of the First Congress on Activity Theory, 2,* 263-272).

Delau, M. (1989). Actualité de la notion de médiation sémiotique de la vie mentale. *Enfance, 42*(1-2), 31-38.

Delau, M. (1990). *Les origines sociales du développement mental.* Paris: Armand Colin.

Delau, M. (1993). Communication and the development of symbolic play: The need for a pragmatic perspective. In J. Nadel & L. Camaioni (Eds.), *New perspectives in early communicative development* (pp. 97-115). London: Routledge.

Fijalkow, J. (1989). Auto-langage et apprentissage de la lecture. *Enfance, 42*(1-2), 83-90

Fraisse, P. (1977). Introduction. In A. Massucco, *Psychologie soviétique.* Paris: Payot.

François, J. (1989). Langage et pensée: Dialogue et mouvement discursif chez Vygotski et Bakhtine. *Enfance, Tome 42*(1-2), 39-47.

Gaonach, D. (1989). Apport de concepts vygotskiens à l'analyse de productions en langues étrangère. *Enfance, 42*(1-2), 91-100.

Gilly, M. (1988). Interaction entre pairs et constructions cognitives: modèles explicatifs. In A. N. Perret-Clermont & M. Nicolet (Eds.), *Intéragir et connaître* (pp. 19-28). Cousset, Delval.

Gilly, M. (1994). Psychologie sociale des constructions cognitives: Perspectives européennes. *Bulletin de Psychologie, XLVI*(412), 671-683

Gilly, M., & Roux, J. P. (1984). Efficacité comparée du travail individuel et du travail en interaction socio-cognitive dans l'appropriation et la mise en œuvre de règles de résolution chez des enfants de 11-12 ans. *Cahiers de Psychologie Cognitive, 4,* 171-189.

Gilly, M, Fraisse, J., & Roux, J. P. (1988). Résolution de problèmes en dyades et progrès cognitifs chez des enfants de 11 à 13 ans: dynamiques interactives et mécanismes socio-cognitifs. In A. N. Perret-Clermont & M. Nicolet (Eds.), *Intéragir et connaître* (pp. 73-92). Cousset, Delval.

Goldman, L. (1959). *Recherches dialectiques.* Paris: Editions Gallimard.

Moal, A. (1992). Le développement de l'éducabilité en psychologie de la formation: Vers une médiation des apprentissage. *Orientation Scolaire et Professionnelle, 21*(1), 107-123.

Nadel, J. (1994). The development of communication: Wallon's framework and influence. In A. Vyt, H. Bloch & M. H. Bornstein (Eds.), *Early childhood development in the French tradition: contribution from current research* (pp. 177-189). New Jersey: Lawrence Erlbuam Associates.

Nadel, J., & Camaioni, L. (Eds.). (1993). *New perspectives in early communicative development*. London: Routledge.

Nadel, J., & Camaioni, L. (Eds.). (1993). Introduction. In J. Nadel & L. Camaioni (Eds.), *New perspectives in early communicative development* (pp. 1-5). London: Routledge.

Naville, P. (1946). *Psychologie, marxisme et materialisme*. Paris: Marcel Rivière.

Netchine-Grynberg, G., & Netchine, S. (1989). Instrument psychologique et formation de l'espace graphique. *Enfance, 42*(1-2), 101-109.

Netchine-Grynberg, G. (1990). Toward a psychological theory of the objects of knowledge. *Multidisciplinary Newsletter for Activity Theory*. (5-6), 10-15.

Netchine-Grynberg. (1991). The theories of Henri Wallon: From act to thought. *Huam Development, 34*, 363-379.

Oléron, P. (1972). Langage et développement mental. Bruxelles: Charles Dessart. (Oléron devoted seven pages to Vygotsky's work, pp. 62-68).

Pagès, R. (1986). L'emprise: concepts et chantiers. *Bulletin de Psychologie, 39*(374), 101-127.

Pagès, R. (1987). L'intelligence entre le conflit et l'aménité: A propos du conflit socio-cognitif. In J. L. Beauvois, R. V. Joule & J. M. Monteil (Eds.), *Perspectives cognitives et conduites sociales.: Théories implicites et conflits cognitifs* (Vol. 1, pp. 249-303). Editions Del Val.

Pagès, R., & Trognon, A. (1988). Interaction et distance sociale: un titre solliciteur. *Revue Internationale de Psychologie Sociale, 1*(1), 7-9.

Recherches sur la psychologie de l'enfant d'âge scolaire en USSR. (1972). Aspects de l'Ecole Soviétique. Paris: Recherches Internationales à la Lumière du Marxisme.

Roelens, R. (1962). "Une recherche psychologique méconnue: Le courant "dramatique" de Georges Politzer à aujourd'hui. *La Pensée*, (103), 76-101.

Roussey, J. Y., & al. (1992). Effects of social regulations and computer assiatance on the monitoring of writing. *European Journal of Psychology of Education, 7*(4), 295-309.

Savoyant, A. (1979). Eléments d'un cadre d'analyse de l'activité: Quelques conceptions essentielles de la psychologie Soviétique. *Cahiers de Psychologie, 22*, 17-28.

Sève, L. (1978). *Man in marxist theory and the psychology of personality*. NJ: Harvester Press.

Sève, L. (1985). Découverte de Vygotski. *La Pensée*(247), 110-115. Also in L. S. Vygotsky, *Pensée et langage* (pp.7-19). Paris:

Messidor Editions Sociales. 1985

Sève, L. (1989). Dialectique et psychologie chez Vygotski. *Enfance,* *42*(1&2), 11-16.

Tabouret-Keller, A. (1989). De quoi parle Vygotski quand il parle de langue. *Enfance, 42*(1-2), 17-22.

Trognon, A. (1993). How does the process of interaction work when two interlocutors try to resolve a logical problem? *Cognition & Instruction, 11*(3-4), 325-345.

Verba, M. (1993). Cooperative formats in pretend play among young children. *Cognition & Instruction, 11*(3-4), 265-280.

Verba, M. (1994). The beginnings of collaboration in peer interaction. *Human Development, 37,* 125-139.

Vergnaud, G. (1989). La formation des concepts scientifiques : Relire Vygotski et débattre avec lui aujourd'hui. *Enfance, 42*(1-2), 11-118.

Voutsinas, D. (1992). En relisant Georges Politzer. *Bulletin de Psychologie, XLV*(408), 725-735.

Vygotski: Colloque sur la pensée Vygotskienne. France: Paris, décembre, 1987.

Zapata, R. (Ed.). (1982). *Luttes philosophiques en USSR 1922-1931.* Paris: Presses Universitaires de France.

Zapata, R. (Ed.). (1982). La formation de la philosophie soviétique. In R. Zapata (Ed.), *Luttes philosophiques en USSR 1922-1931* (pp. 25-44). Paris: Presses Universitaires de France.

Zazzo, R. (1960). *Les jumeaux, le couple et la personne.* Paris: Presses Universitaires de France.

Zazzo, R. (1975). *Psychologie et marxisme: La vie et l'oeuvre d'Henri Wallon* [Psychology and marxism: The life and the work of Henri Wallon]. Paris: Denoël/Gonthier.

Zazzo, R. (1989). L. Vygotski (1896-1934). *Enfance, 42*(1&2), 3-9.

Zazzo, R. (Ed.). (1989). L. Vygotski. No. Spécial, *Enfance, 42*(1&2. No. Spécial, 125 pages.

Zazzo, R. (1995). Psychologie and marxisme. *Bulletin de Psychologie, XLVIII*(421), 592-611.

Discussion of the works of L. S. Vygotsky in Italy

Baldo, M. (1988). Discourse patterns in first and second language: An ethnographic approach. *Ressegna Italiana di Linguistica Applicata, 20*(1), 61-80.

Camaioni, L. (1993). The social construction of meaning in early infant-parent and infant-peer relations. In J. Nadel & L. Camaioni (Eds.), *New perspectives in early communicative development* (pp. 159-170). London: Routledge.

Carugati, F., De Poalis, P., & Mugny, G. (1979). A paradigm for the study of social interactions in cognitive development. *Italian Journal of Psychology, 6*, 147-155.

Carugati, F., De Poalis, P., & Mugny, G. (1981). Conflit de centration et progrès cognitif. III: régulations cognitives et relationnelles du conflit socio-cognitif. *Bulletin de Psychologie, 34*(352), 843-852.

Carugati, F., & Gilly, M. (1993). The multiple sides of the same tool: Cognitive development as a matter of social constructions and meanings. *European J. of Psychology of Education, 8*(4), 345-354.

deRosa, A. S. (1992). Thematic perspectives and epistemic principles in developmental social cognitionand social representation: The meaning of a developmental approach to the investigation of social representations. In von M. Cranach, W. Doise, & G. Mugny (Eds.), *Social representations and the social bases of knowledge* (pp. 120-143). Bern: Hogrefe & Huber Publishers.

Faenzi, A. (1984). Attualita e produttivita di Vygotskij per l'indagine semiotica. *Storia e Critica della Psicologia, 5*, 389-407.

Faenzi, A. (1986). La genesi dei comportamenti cooperativi e competitivi nello sviluppo. Un approccio integrato. [The beginning of cooperative and competitive behavior in development: An integrated approach]. *Eta evolutiva, (23)*, 5-14.

Iannaccone, A., & Perret-Clermont, A. N. (1993). Qu'est-ce qui s'apprend? Qu'est-ce qui se développe? [What is learned? What is developing?]. In J. Wassmann & P. R. Dasen (Eds.), *Les savoirs quotidiens* (pp. 235-258). Fribourg, Suisse: Editions Universi-taires.

Laschi, T. (1975). Il linguaggio del bambino: Le ipotesi di Piaget e Vygotskij. *Vita dell'Infanzia, 12*, 29-35.

Manacorda, M. A. (1979). La pedagogia di Vygotsi. *Riforma della Scuola, 26*), 31-39.

Massucco, A. (1977). *Psychologie soviétique.* Paris: Payot.

Mecacci, L. (Ed.). (1976). *La psicologia Sovietica 1917-1936.* Roma: Editori Riuniti.

Mecacci, L. (1979). Vygotskij: per una psicologia dell'uomo. *Riforma della Scuola, 26*, 24-30.

Mecacci, L. (1979). *Brain and history: The relationship between neurophysiology and psychology in soviet research.* New York: Brunner Mazel.

Mecacci, L. (1981). Introduzione: Koffka e la psicologia Sovietica. *Storia e Critica della Psicologia, 2*, 95-98.

Mecacci, L. (1981). Brain and socio-cultural environment. *Journal of Social Biology and Structure, 4*, 319-327.

Mecacci, L. (1983). *Vygotskij: Antologia di scritti.* Bologne: Il Mulino.

Moroni, A. (1988). Il metodo storico in psicologia e pedagogia. [The historical method in psychology and education]. *Studi di Psicologia dell'Educazione, 7*(2-3), 7-22

Mussatti, T. (1979, June). Vygotski et la psychologie de l'enfance. In *Congrès "Vygotski et les sciences de l'homme".* Italy: Rome.

Mussatti, T. (1986). Early peer relations: The perspectives of Piaget and Vygotsky. In E. Mueller & C. Cooper (Eds.), *Process and outcome in peer relationship* (pp. 25-53). Academic Press.

Mussatti, T. (1993). Meaning between peers: The meaning of the peer. *Cognition & Instruction, 11*(3-4), 241-250.

Orgolini, M. (1979). La formazione dei concetti in Piaget, Bruner e Vygotsky. *Scula e Citta,* (6-7), 261-270.

Palmonari, A., & Doise, W. (1984). *Social interaction in individual development.* Cambridge: Cambridge University Press.

Pontecorvo, C. (1990). Social context, semiotic mediation, and forms of discourse in constructing knowledge. In H. Mandl, E. De Corte, N. Bennett, & H. F. Friedrich (Eds.), *Learning and instruction* (pp. 1-26) Oxford: Pergamon Press.

Pontecorvo, C. (1993). Social interaction and knowledge acquisition. *Educational Psychology Review, 5*, 293-310.

Pontecorvo, C. (Ed.). (1993). *La condivisione della conoscenza* (Shared knowledge). Florence: La Nuova Italia.

Pontecorvo, C. (1993). Forms of discourse and shared thinking. *Cognition & Instruction, 11*(3-4), 189-196.

Pontecorvo, C., & Girardet, H. (1993). Arguing and reasoning in understanding historical topics. *Cognition & Instruction, 11*(3-4), 365-395.

Tornatore, L. (1980). Vygotskij e l'educazione linguistica. *Scula e Citta, 21*, 251-256.

Veggetti, M. S. (1986). Lev Semenovic Vygotskij: La sociogenesi della conoscenza e il modello del processo cognitivo. Un superamento delle prospettive descrittive nella psicologia dello sviluppo mentale? [Lev Semenovic Vygotsky: The sociogenesis of knowledge and the model of the cognitive process: Overcoming the descriptive views of mental development in psychology?] *Studi di Psicologia dell'Educazione, 5*(3), 7-28

"Vygotski et les sciences de l'homme". Colloquium on Vygotsky's thought. Italy: Rome, June 1979.

Zanocco, G., Proli, F., & Secchi, C. (1974). Contribution to the study of the structure of dream narrative. *Rivista Sperimentale di Freniatria e Medicina Legale delle Alienazioni Mentali, 98*(5), 825-847

Discussion of the works of L. S. Vygotsky in Canada

Bain, B. (1974). *Toward an integration of Piaget and Vygotsky: Bilingual considerations.* Paper presented at 18th International Congress of Applied Psychology, Italy.

Bain, B. (1975). Toward an integration of Piaget and Vygotsky: Bilingual considerations. *Linguistics,* 5-20.

Bain, B. (Ed.). (1983). *The sociogenesis of language and human conduct.* New York: Plenum Press.

Bain, B., & Yu, A. (1978). Toward an integration of Piaget and Vygotsky: A cross-cultural replication (France, Germany, Canada) concerning cognitive consequences of bilinguality. In M. Paradis (Ed.), *Aspects of bilinguism.* Columbia, SC: Hornbeam.

Bain, B., & Yu, A. (1980). Cognitive consequences of raising children bilingually: One parent/one language. *Canadian Journal of Psychology, 34,* 304-313.

Bain, B., & Yu, A. (1980). Raising children bilingually in Alsace, Alberta and Hong Kong: One parent/one language. *New Horizons, 21,* 80-106.

Bain, B., & Yu, A. (1982). The cognitive style of bilingual children. *Acta Psychologica Sinita, 14,* 351-357.

Bain, B., Panarin, A. Iu., & Panarin, I. A. (1995). Rearing children bilingually (With yet again reference to Vygotsky and Luria). *Journal of Russian & East European Psychology, 33*(3), 35-55.

Bakhurst, D. J. (1986). Thought, speech and the genesis of meaning: On the 50th anniversary of Vygotsky's Myslenie I Rec. *Studies in Soviet Thought, 31,* 103-129.

Bakhurst, D. J. (1988). Activity, consciousness, and communication. *Quarterly Newsletter of the Laboratory of Comparative Human Cognition, 10,* 31-39.

Bakhurst, D. J. (1988). *E. V. Ilyenkov and contemporary Soviet philosophy.* Unpublished doctoral dissertation. Oxford: Exeter College, England.

Bakhurst, D. J. (1990). Social memory in Soviet thought. In D. Middleton & D. Edwards (Eds.), *Collective remembering* (pp. 203-226). Sage Publications.

Bakhurst, D. J. (1991). *Consciousness and revolution in Soviet philosophy.* Cambridge: Cambridge University Press.

Bakhurst, D. J. (1991). Vygotsky. In D. J. Bakhurst, *Consciousness and revolution in Soviet philosophy* (pp. 59-90). Cambridge: Cambridge University Press.

Bakhurst, D. J. (1991). The socially constitued individual: Rethinking thought. In D. J. Bakhurst, *Consciousness and revolution in Soviet philosophy* (pp. 217-258). Cambridge: Cambridge University Press.

Bakhurst, D. J. (1992). J. M. Moravcsik, Thought and language. *Canadian Philosophical Review, 12(6)*, 409-411.

Bakhurst, D. J. (1995). On the social constitution of mind: Bruner, Ilyenkov, and the defence of cultural psychology. *Mind, Culture, & Activity, 2(3)*, 158-171.

Bakhurst, D. J. (in press). Lessons from Ilyenkov. *Communication Review.*

Bakhurst, D. J. (1996). Wittgenstein and social being. In D. J. Bakhurst & C. Cypnowich (Eds.), *The social self* (pp. 30-46). London: Sage.

Bakhurst, D. J. & Padden, C. (1991). The Meshcheryakov experiment: Soviet work on the education of the blind-deaf. *Learning & Instruction, 1,* 201-215.

Bednarz, N., & Garnier, C. (Eds.). (1989). *Construction des savoirs: Obstacles et conflits.* Canada, Montréal: Agence d'Arc.

Bekkari, M. (1991). *Theoretical and clinical integration of Luria's thesis of cognitive development and Erikson's psychosocial stages (cognitive development, psychosocial stages).* Unpublished doctoral dissertation, Canada: University of Alberta, Canada.

Bishop, J. (1986). Change lives in the poetry of its meaning. *Canadian Journal of Counseling, Vol 20(1)*, 21-32

Bountrogianni, M., & Pratt, M. (1990). Dynamic assessment implications for classroom consultation, peer tutoring and parent education. In E. Cole & J. A. Siegel (Eds.), *Effective consultation in school psychology* (pp. 129-140). New York: Hogrefe & Huber Publishers.

Braun, C., Rennie, B. J., & Gordon, C, J. (1987). An examination of contexts for reading assessment. *Journal of Educational Research, 80(5)*, 383-389.

Cameron, C. A., & Davidson, M. L. (1981). Development of sorting skills in elementary school children. *Social Behavior and Personality, 9(1)*, 1-7.

Chang, G. L., & Wells, G. (1988). The literate potential of collaborative talk. In M. MacLure, T. Phillips, & A. Wilkinson (Eds.), *Oracy matters.* Milton Keynes, Engalnd: Open University Press.

Chang-Wells, G. L. M., & Wells, G. (1993). Dynamics of discourse: Literacy and the construction of knowledge. In E. Forman, N. J. Minick, & C. A. Stone (Eds.), *Contexts for learning: Sociocultural dynamics in children's development* (pp. 58-90). New York: Oxford University Press.

Colvert, D. J. (1990). *The nature of parent-child interaction during preschool children's early writing activities.* Unpublished doctoral dissertation: University of Toronto, Canada.

Coughlan, P., & Duff, P. A. (1994). Same task, different activities: Analysis of SLA task from an activity theory perspective. In J. P. Lantolf & G. Appel (Eds.), *Vygotskian approaches to second language research* (pp. 173-193). New Jersey: Ablex.

Cowper-Smith, N. A. (1991). *A study of adolescent coping.* Unpublished doctoral dissertation: University of Alberta, Canada.

Das, J. P. (1988). Coding, attention, and planning: A cap for every head. In J. W. Berry, S. H. Irvine, & E. B. Hunt (Eds.), *Indigenous cognition: Functioning in cultural context.* NATO ASI series D: Behavioural and social sciences (Vol. 4, pp. 39-56). Netherlands, Dordrecht: Martinus Nijhoff Publishing.

Das, J. P. (1995). Some thoughts on wo aspects of Vygotsky's work. *Educational Psychologist, 30*(2), 93-98.

Das, J. P., & Conway, R. N. F. (1992). 'Reflections on remediations and transfer: A Vygotskian perspective. In. H. C. Haywood & D. Tzuriel (Eds.), *Interactive assessment* (pp. 94-115). New York: Springer-Verlag.

Das, J. P., & Naglieri, J. (1992). Assessment of attention, simultaneous-successive coding and planning. In. H. C. Haywood & D. Tzuriel (Eds.), *Interactive assessment* (pp. 207-232). New York: Springer-Verlag.

Desjarlais, L. (1985). Vygotsky: Une alternative psychotechnique. *Journal of Educational Thought, 19*(2), 117-133.

Desjarlais, L. (1985). Adolescence, crissance et développement. Toronto: Ministère de l'Education. (Desjarlais devoted one chapter to Vygotsky's work).

Downing, J. (Ed.), *Cognitive psychology and reading in the USSR.* Amsterdam: North-Holand.

Downing, J. (1988). Comparative perspectives on the developments of the cognitive psychology of reading in the USSR. In J. Downing (Ed.), *Cognitive psychology and reading in the USSR* (pp. 1-27). Amsterdam: North-Holand.

Downing, J. (1988). Central cognitive themes in Soviet theory and practice in reading instruction. In J. Downing (Ed.), *Cognitive psychology and reading in the USSR* (pp. 427-448). Amsterdam: North-Holand

Duncan, R. M. (1991). An examination on Vygotsky's theory of children's private speech. *Resources in Education,* Dec.), 128.

Duncan, R. M. (1991). *Microgenetic development in preschoolers' private speech.* Unpublished doctoral dissertation, Wilfrid Laurier University, Canada.

Duncan, R. M. (1995). Piaget and Vygotsky revisited: Dialogue or assimilation? *Developmental Review, 15*(4), 458-472.

Fry, P. (1992). Assessment of private and inner speech of older adults in relation to depression. In R. M. Diaz & L. E. Berk (Eds.), *Private speech: From social interaction to self-regulation* (pp. 267-284). Lawrence Erlbaum Associates.

Groenwold, W. (1990). *Distancing strategiess in block play and their role in the development of representational competence: A case study.* Unpublished doctoral dissertation: University of Alberta, Canada.

Gulutsan, M. (1967). Jean Piaget in Soviet psychology. *Alberta Journal of Educational Research, 13,* 239-247.

Gulutsan, M. (1973). Psychological orientation of Soviet teachers. *Alberta Journal of Educational Research, 19*(4), 284-   294.

Ilott, H. G. (1987). *Communicative competence in kindergarten.* Unpublished doctoral dissertation, University of Alberta, Canada.

Isaak, J. A. L. (1982). *Avant-garde art and the avant-garde texts of James Joyce, Gertrude Stein and the english vorticists.* Unpublished doctoral dissertation, University of Toronto, Canada.

Jamieson, J. R., Pedersen, E. (1993). Deafness and mother-child interaction: Scaffolded instruction and the learning of problem-solving skill. *Early Development & Parenting, 2,* 229-242.

Jamieson, J. R. (1994). Teaching as transaction: Vygotskian perspectives on deafness and mother-child interaction. *Exceptional Children, 60*(5), 434-449.

Jamieson, J. R. (1995). Visible thought: Deaf children's use of signed and spoken private speech. *Sign Language Studies, (*86), 63-80.

Johnson, J. (1991). Constructive processes in bilingualism and their cognitive growth effects. In E. Bialystok (Ed.), *Language processing in bilingual children* (pp. 193-221). Cambridge University Press.

Kelner, L. (1992). *The relation between teacher behaviour and children's play in traditional preschools.* Unpublished doctoral dissertation, York University, Canada.

Lajoie, S. (1993). Computer environments as cognitive tools for enhancing learning. In S. Derry & S. Lajoie (Eds.), *Computers as cognitive tools* (pp. 261-288). Hillsdale, NJ: Erlbaum.

Lajoie, S., & Derry, S. (Eds.). (1993). *Computers as cognitive tools.* Hillsdale, NJ: Erlbaum.

Latshaw, J. L. (1985). *An anti-depth examination of four preadolescents responses to fantasy literature.* Unpublished doctoral dissertation: University of Saskatchewan, Canada.

Lefrancois, R. R. (1988). Psychology for teaching (6th ed.). Wadsworth Publishing Co. (Lefrancois devoted three pages to Vygotsky's work, pp. 198-200).

Martin, J. (1973). *A comparison of the developmental stages proposed by L. S Vygotsky and J. Piaget.* Unpublished doctoral dissertation, University of Alberta, Canada.

McCabe, A. (1979). A paradox of self-regulation in speech motor-interaction: Semantic degradation and impulse segmentation. In G. Zevin (Ed.), *The development of self-regulation through private speech.* New York: Wiley.

McCleland, R. J. (1989). *Profiles of underachieving gifted students.* Unpublished doctoral dissertation, University of Alberta, Canada.

McLeish, J. (1950). Aspects of Soviet and American psychology. *Soviet Studies, 1*), 243-246.

McLeish, J. (1951). Psychology in the Soviet Union, *Quarterly Bulletin British Psychological Society, 12,* 47-52.

McLeish, J. (1972). The Soviet conquest of illiteracy. *Alberta Journal of Educational Research, 18,* 307-326.

McLeish, J. (1975). Soviet psychology: History, theory and content. London: Methuen.

McLeish, J. (1975). Thought and speech: The central problem of Soviet psychology. In J. McLeish, *Soviet psychology: History, theory, and content* (pp. 247-250). London: Methuen.

McLeish, J. (1975). Vygotsky's 'cultural-historical' school. In J. McLeish, *Soviet psychology: History, theory, and content* (pp. 121-124). London: Methuen.

Meichenbaum, D. (1974). Self-instructional strategy training: A cognitive prothesis for the aged. *Human Development, 17*(4), 273-280

Meichenbaum, D. (1975). Theoretical and treatment implications of developmental research on verbal control of behavior. *Canadian Psychological Review, 16*(1), 22-27

Meichenbaum, D., & Goodman, S. (1979). Clinical use of private speech and critical questions about its study in natural settings. In G. Zevin (Ed.), *The development of self-regulation through private speech* (pp. 265-294). New York: Wiley.

Miller, J. L. (1994). Linguistic tools for intellectual work: A review of Voices of the mind by James Wertsch. *New Ideas in Psychology, 12*(1), 61-72.

Missiuna, C., & Samuels, M. (1988). Dynamic assessment: Review andcritique. *Special Services in the Schools, 5*(1-2), 1-22

Moran, L. (1977). Personal and common components of cognitive dictionaries. *Psychological Reports, 40*(3, Pt 1), 795-806

Moss, E. (1992). The socioaffective context of joint cognitive activity. In T. L. Winegar, J. Valsiner (Eds.), *Children's development within social context* (Vol. 1 pp. 117-154). NJ: Lawrence Erlbaum.

Mullett, J. (1992). *Ecological view of four social contexts investigated with a Lewinian methodology.* Unpublished doctoral dissertation: University of Victoria, Canada.

Olson, D. (1992). Scribner on writing. *Quarterly Newsletter of the Laboratory of Comparative Human Cognition, 14*(4), 138.

Olson, D. (1994). Theories of literacy and mind from Levy-Bruhl to Scribner and Cole. In *The world on paper: The coneptual and cognitive implications of writing and reading* (pp.20-44). Cambridge: Cambridge University Press.

Olson, D. (1994). *The world on paper: The coneptual and cognitive implications of writing and reading. Cambridge*: Cambridge University Press.

Olson, D. (1995). Writing and the mind. In J. Wertsch, P. del Rio & A. Alvarez (Eds.), *Sociocultural studies of mind* (pp. 95-123). NY: Cambridge University Press.

Palacio-Quintin, E. (1990). L'éducation cognitive à l'école. *European Journal of Psychology of Education, 5*(2), 213-242.

Parrila, R. K. (1995). Vygotskian views on language and planning in children. *School Psychology International, 16*(2), 167-183.

Pascual-Leone, J. (1991). Commentary. *Human Development, 35*(5), 288-293.

Patterson, D. L. (1989). *Talking about my body: Being and language.* Unpublished doctoral dissertation, University of Alberta, Canada.

Peterson, C., & McCabe, A. (1994). A social interactionist account fo developing decontextualized narrative skill. *Developmental Psychology, 30*(6), 937-948.

Rubin, K. H. (1979). The impact of natural setting on private speech. In G. Zevin (Ed.), *The development of self-regulation through private speech.* New York: Wiley.

Sierpinska, A. (1993). The development of concepts according to Vygotski. *Focus on Learning Problems in Mathematics, 15*(2-3), 87-107.

Stewin, L. L, & Martin, J. (1974). The developmental stages of L. S Vygotsky and J. Piaget: A comparison. *Alberta Journal of Educational Research, 20*(4), 348-   362.

Tarr, P. R. (1993). *Two-year-old children's artistic expression in a group setting: Interaction and the construction of meaning.* Unpublished doctoral dissertation, The University of British Columbia, Canada.

Tolman, C. (1981). The metaphysic of relations in Klaus Riegel's "dialectic" of human development. *Human Development, 24,* 33-51.

Tolman, C. (1983). Further comments on the meaning of "dialectic"

Human Development, 26), 320-324.

Tolman, C. (1988). Theoretical unification in psychology: A materialistic perspective. In W. J. Baker, L. P. Mos, H. V. Rappard & H. J. Stam (Eds.), *Recent trends in theoretical psychology*. New York: Springer-Verlag.

Tolman, C. (1989). What's critical about Kritische Psychologie? *Canadian Psychology, 30*(4), 628-635.

Tolman, C. (1991). Theoretical indeterminacy, pluralism, and the conceptual concrete. *Theory & Psychology, 1*, 147-162.

Tolman, C. (1994). *Psychology, society and subjectivity: An introduction to German critical psychology*. London: Routledge.

Tolman, C. (1994). From phylogenesis to the dominance of sociogenesis. In *Psychology, society and subjectivity: An introduction to German critical psychology* (pp.86-104). London: Routledge.

Tolman, C., & Maiers, W. (1991). *Critical psychology: Contributions to an historical science of the subject*. Cambridge: Cambridge University Press.

Trigger, G. B. (1966). Engels on the part played by labor in the transition from ape to man: An anticipation of contemporary anthropological theory. *Canadian Review of Sociology & Anthropology, 4*(3), 165-176.

Wells, G. (1993). Working with a teacher in the zone of proximal development: Action research on the learning and teaching of science. *Journal of the Society of Accelerative Learning & Teaching, 18*(1-2),

Wells, G. (1993). Reevaluating the IRF sequence: A proposal for the articulation of theories of activity and discourse for the analysis of teaching and learning in the classroom. *Linguistics & Education, 5*, 1-398.

Wells, G. (1994). The complimentary contribution of Halliday and Vygotsky to a "language-based theory of learning". *Linguistics & Education, 6*(1), 41-90.

Wells, G., & Chang, G. L. (1989). Intersubjectivity in the construction of knowledge. Presented at the Biennial Conference of the Society for Research in Child Development, Kansas City, April 1989.

Zelazo P. D., Pinon, D. E., & Reznick, J. S. (1995). Response control and execution of verbal rules. *Developmental Psychology, 31*(3), 508-517.

Discussion of the works of L. S. Vygotsky in Norway

Bråten, Ivar. (1984). Verbal mediation and literacy problems: Verbal self-instructions as a mediating strategy when learning irregular words. Part I. *Scandinavian Journal of Special Education,62*, 211-235. [in Norwegian].

Bråten, Ivar. (1984). Verbal mediation and literacy problems: Verbal self-instructions as a mediating strategy when learning irregular words. Part II. *Scandinavian Journal of Special Education,62*, 290-316. [in Norwegian].

Bråten, Ivar. (1991). Vygotsky as precursor to metacognition: I. The concept of metacognition and its roots. *Scandinavian Journal of Educational Research,35(3)*, 179-192.

Bråten, Ivar. (1991). Vygotsky as precursor to metacognition: II. Vygotsky as metacognitivist. *Scandinavian Journal of Educational Research, 35(4)*, 305-320.

Bråten, Ivar. (1992). Vygotsky as precursor to metacognition: III. Recent metacognitive research with a Vygotskian framework. *Scandinavian Journal of Educational Research, 36(1)*, 3-19.

Hundeide, K. (1980). The origin of the child's replies in experimental situaltions. *Quarterly Newsletter of the Laboratory of Comparative Human Cognition, 2(1)*, 15-18.

Hundeide, K. (1981). Contractual congruence and logical consistency. *Quarterly Newsletter of the Laboratory of Comparative Human Cognition, 3(4)*, 77-79.

Hundeide, K. (1985). The Tacit backgound of children's judgments. In J. Wertsch (Ed.), *Culture, communication and cognition: Vygotskian perspectives.* Cambridge University Press.

Hundeide, K. (1988). Metacontracts for situational definitions and for presentation of cognitive skills. *Quarterly Newsletter of the Laboratory of Comparative Human Cognition, 10(3)*, 85-91.

Hundeide, K. (1993). Intersubjectivity and inter-pretive background in children's development and interaction. *European Journal of Psychology of Education, 8(4*, 439-450.

Hundeide, K. (in press). *Cultural constraints on cognitive enrichment.*

Junefelt, K. (1990). The zone of proximal development and communicative development, *Nordic Journal of Linguistics, 13(2)*, 135-148.

Discussion of the works of L. S. Vygotsky in Sweden

Adelswärd, V., & Säljö, R. (1994). Becoming a conscientious objector: The use of arms and institutional accounting practices. In R. Maier & W. de Graaf (Eds.), *Sociogenesis reexamined* (pp. 205-217). New York: Springer-Verlag.

Hjorland, B. (1993). *Subject representation and information seeking: Contribution to a theory based on the theory of knowledge.* Unpublished doctoral dissertation. Goteborgs University. Sweden (In Danish)

Hydén, L. C. (1983). Vygotskij: Psykologi mellan kris och enhet. [Vygotskij: Psychology between crisis and unity]. *Nordisk Psykologi, 35*(4), 243-254.

Hydén, L. C. (1984). Three interpretations of the acti-vity concept: Leont'ev, Rubinshein and critical psychology. In M. Hedegaard, P. Hakkarainen, & Y. E. Engeström (Eds.), *Learning and teaching on a scientific basis* (pp. 33-41). Arhus: Psykologisk Institut.

Kavathatzopoulos, I. (1988). *Instruction and the development of moral judgment (Piaget, Vygotsky, Kohlberg).* Unpublished doctoral dissertation, Uppsala University, Sweden.

Säljö, R. (1991). Introduction: Culture and learning. *Learning & Instruction, 1,* 179-185.

Säljö, R. (1991). Learning and mediation: Fitting reality into a table. *Learning & Instruction, 1,* 261-272.

Säljö, R. (1991). Vygotskian lessons. *Quarterly Newsletter of the Laboratory of Comparative Human Cognition, 13*(1), 71-73.

Säljö, R. (1992). Putting mind back into action. *Quarterly Newsletter of the Laboratory of Comparative Human Cognition, 14*(4), 140-141.

Säljö, R., & Wyndhamn, J. (1988). A week has seven days. Or does it? *For the Learning of Mathematics, 8,* 16-19

Säljö, R., & Wyndhamn, J. (1990). Problem solving, academic performance, and situated reasoning: A study of joint activity in formal setting. *British Journal of Educational Psychology, 60,* 245-254.

Sundelin-W. V. (1986). Normal autism och symbios: En kritisk granskning. [Normal autism and symbiosis: A critical examination]. *Psykisk Halsa, 27*(2), 140-146.

Discussion of the works of L. S. Vygotsky in Spain

Alvarez, A., & Rio, del. P. (1984). El momento de Vygotski: El porqué de un homenaje. *Infancia y Aprendizaje,* (27-28), 1-6.

Alvarez, A., & Rio, del. P. (Eds.). (1994). *Perspectives in socio-cultural research: Education as cultural construction* (Vol. 4). Madrid: Fundacion Infancia y Aprendizaje

Anuario de Psicologia. (1985). Special issue: Vygotsky's thought. *33*(2).

Aznar, A. E. (1985). La Psicologia del Arte de Vigotski. [Vygotsky's Psychology of Art.]. Special Issue: About Vygotsky's thought. *Anuario de Psicologia, 33*(2), 129-138.

Belinchon, M., Rivière, A., & Igoa, J. M. (1992). *Psicologia del lenguaje: Investigacion y teoria.* Madrid: Trotta.

Coll, C. (1984). Estructura grupal, nteraccion entre alumnos y aprendizaje escolar. *Infancia y Aprendizaje,* (27-28), 119-138.

Coll, C. (Ed.). (1988). *Psicologia de la educacion* [psychology of education]. Madrid: Alianza.

Coll, C., & Mercer, N. (Eds.). (1994). *Perspectives in socio-cultural research: Interaction* (Vol. 3). Madrid: Fundacion Infancia y Aprendizaje

Coll Salvador, C. (1985). Accion, interaccion y construccion del conocimiento en situaciones educativas. [Action, interaction, and knowledge building in educational situations]. Special Issue: About Vygotsky's thought. *Anuario de Psicologia, 33*(2), 59-70

Del Rio, P., & Alvarez, A. (1985). La influencia del entorno en la educacion: La apotacion de los modelos ecologicos. *Infancia y Aprendizaje,* (29), 3-32.

Del Rio, P., & Alvarez, A. (1988). Aprendizaje y desarollo: La teoria actividad y la zona de desarollo proximo [Lerarning and development: Acitivity theory and zone of proximal development] (pp.1-34). In C. Coll (Ed.), *Psicologia de la educacion* . Madrid: Alianza.

Del Rio, P., & Alvarez, A. (1995). Tossing, praying, and reasoning: The changing architectures of mind and agency. In J. Wertsch, P. del Rio & A. Alvarez (Eds.), *Sociocultural studies of mind* (pp. 215-247). New York: Cambridge University Press.

Del Rio, P., & Alvarez, A. (1995). Directivity: The cultural and educational construction of morality and agency. Some questions arising from the legacy of Vygotsky. *Anthropology & Education Quarterly, 26*(4), 384-409.

Forns, S. M., & Boada, C. H. (1985). Consideraciones sobre la zona de desarrollo potencial desde la evaluacion psicologica. [Estimating the

zone of potential development via psychological evaluation].
Special Issue: About Vygotsky's thought. *Anuario de Psicologia,*
33(2), 71-79.

Lalueza Sazatornil, J. L. (1991). *Development of symbols in*
interactive play in children with down syndrome and non-
handicapped children. Unpublished doctoral dissertation, Universitat
Autonoma de Barcelona, Spain. (in Spanish)

Mata de la, M. L., & Ramirez, J. D. (1989). Cultura y procesos
cognitivos: hacia una psicologia cultural. [Culture and cognitive
processes: Toward a cross-cultural psychology]. *Infancia y Aprendi-*
zaje, (46), 49-70

Moro, C., & Rodriguez, C. (1988). A propos de la divergence Piaget-
Vygotsky, une suggestion pour une approche du développement au
premier âge. Proceeding of the *7th European CHEIRON Conference,*
Budapest, 4-8 septembre), 451-464. Hungarian Psychological
Association.

Moro, C., & Rodriguez, C. (1989). L'interaction triadique bébé-objet-
adulte durant la première annéee de la vie de l'enfant. *Enfance, 42*(1-
2), 75-82.

Moro, C., & Rodriguez, C. (1994). Prelinguistic sign mixity and
flexibility in interaction.
European Journal of Psychology of Education, 9(4), 301-310.

Moro, C., & Rodriguez, C. (in press). *How children learn to give*
meaning to things: Suggestions for a semiological analysis of the
zone of proximal development.

Moro, C., Rodriguez, C., & Schneuwly, B. (1990). Présentation. In A.
Rivière, La psychologie de Vygotsky (pp.5-24). Belgique: Pierre
Mardaga.

Palacios, J. (1987). Reflexiones en torno a als implicaciones educativas
se la obra de Vygotski [Reflections in terms of the educational
implications of Vygotsky's work]. In M. Siguan (Ed.), *Actualidad*
de Lev S. Vigotski (Actuality de Lev S. Vygotsky) (pp. 176-188).
Barcelona: Anthropos.

Palacios, J. (1987). Las ideas de los padres sobre sus hijos en la
investigacion evolutiva. [The role of parents' ideas about their
children in the study of development]. *Infancia y Aprendizaje, (39-*
40), 97-111

Pena, C. J., & Perez, P. M. (1985). La neuropsicologia de Vigotski y
Luria: El cerebro lesionado. [The neuropsychology of Vygotsky and
Luria: The injured brain]. Special Issue: About Vygotsky's thought.
Anuario de Psicologia, 33(2), 29-42

Perez, P. M. (1985). Bibliografia de Lev S. Vigotski. (Bibliography of
Lev S. Vygotsky.) Special Issue: About Vygotsky's thought.

Anuario de Psicologia, 33(2), 151-163

Ramirez, J. D. (1987). Desarrollo del lenguaje y control de las acciones: En torno a la regulacion verbal. [Language development and control of actions: Concerning verbal regulation]. *Infancia y Aprendizaje, 37*(1), 71-89

Ramirez, J. D. (1992). The functional differentiation and private speech: A dialogic approach. In R. M. Diaz & L. E. Berk (Eds.), *Private speech: From social interaction to self-regulation* (pp. 199-214). Lawrence Erlbaum Associates.

Ramirez, J. D. (1994). Adults learning literacy: The role of private speech inreading comprehension. In V. John-Steiner, C. P. Panofsky & L. W. Smith (Eds.), *Sociocultural approaches to language and literacy: An interactionist perspective* (pp. 305-330). NY: Cambridge University Press.

Ramirez, J. D. (in press). The role of extralinguistic context in egocentric speech production. *Quarterly Newsletter of the Laboratory of Comparative Human Cognition.*

Rivière, A. (1983). Interaciocion y simbolo en autstas. *Infancia y Aprendizaje,* (22), 3-26.

Rivière, A. (1984). La psicologia de Vygotski (The psychology of Vygotsky). *Infancia y Aprendizaje,* (27-28), 7-86.

Rivière, A. (1985). *La psicologia de Vygotski* [The psychology of Vygotsky]. Madrid: Visor

Rivière, A. (1987). *El sujeto de la psicologia cognitiva.* Madrid: Alianza Psicologia.

Rivière, A. (1990). La psychologie de Vygotsky. Belgique: Pierre Mardaga.

Rivière, A. (1990). Notes biographiques: La période de formation. In A. Rivière, *La psychologie de Vygotsky* (pp. 29-41). Belgique: Pierre Mardaga.

Rivière, A. (1990). La psychologie Soviétique des années vingt: Ses antécédants et sa situation. In A. Rivière, *La psychologie de Vygotsky* (pp. 43-48). Belgique: Pierre Mardaga.

Rivière, A. (1990). Réflexes et conscience: Apports critique de Vygotsky à la recherche d'une psychologie dialectique. In A. Rivière, *La psychologie de Vygotsky* (pp. 49-55). Belgique: Pierre Mardaga.

Rivière, A. (1990). La crise de la psychologie et l'apport métathéorique de Vygotsky. In A. Rivière, *La psychologie de Vygotsky* (pp. 57-67). Belgique: Pierre Mardaga.

Rivière, A. (1990). L'activité instrumentale et l'interaction comme unité d'analyse de la psychologie des fonctions supérieures. In A. Rivière, *La psychologie de Vygotsky* (pp. 69-77). Belgique: Pierre Mardaga.

Rivière, A. (1990). Les études expérimentales sur la genèse et la variabilité culturelle des fonctions supérieures: La méthode génétique expérimentale. In A. Rivière, *La psychologie de Vygotsky* (pp. 79-88). Belgique: Pierre Mardaga.

Rivière, A. (1990). Les relations entre apprentissage et développement: La "zone proximale du développement". In A. Rivière, *La psychologie de Vygotsky* (pp. 89-95). Belgique: Pierre Mardaga.

Rivière, A. (1990). Les conceptions éducatives de Vygotsky et ses apports à la pédologie et à la défectologie. In A. Rivière, *La psychologie de Vygotsky* (pp. 97-104). Belgique: Pierre Mardaga.

Rivière, A. (1990). L'Union Soviétique au début des années trente et quelques-unes des critiques faites à Vygotsky. In A. Rivière, *La psychologie de Vygotsky* (pp. 105-108). Belgique: Pierre Mardaga.

Rivière, A. (1990). Le développement en tant que processus historique: Les apports de Vygotsky à une théorie générale du développement. In A. Rivière, *La psychologie de Vygotsky* (pp. 109-114). Belgique: Pierre Mardaga.

Rivière, A. (1990). L'ébauche d'une théorie de l'organisation neuro-physiologique des fonctions supérieures et les intérêts neuropsychologique de Vygotsky. In A. Rivière, *La psychologie de Vygotsky* (pp. 115-120). Belgique: Pierre Mardaga.

Rivière, A. (1990). La pensée et la parole: La conception sémiotique de la conscience, la genèse, la structure et la fonction du langage intérieur. In A. Rivière, *La psychologie de Vygotsky* (pp. 121-134). Belgique: Pierre Mardaga.

Rivière, A. (1990). Quelques hypothèses Vygotskiennes au-delà de Vygotsky. In A. Rivière, *La psychologie de Vygotsky* (pp. 135-141). Belgique: Pierre Mardaga.

Rivière, A. (1990). Les critiques faites à Vygotsky et la période de long silence de la psychologie Soviétique. In A. Rivière, *La psychologie de Vygotsky* (pp. 143-145). Belgique: Pierre Mardaga.

Rivière, A. (1990). Language and theory of mind: Vygotsky, Skinner and beyond. In D. E. Blackman, & H. Lejeune (Eds.), *Behaviour analysis in theory and practice: Contributions and controversies* (pp. 199-213). Lawrence Erlbaum Associates.

Rivière, A. (1990). Origen y desarrollo de la funcion simbolica en el nino. In J. Palacios, A. Marches, & C. Coll (Eds.), *Desarrollo psicologico y educacion* (Vol. 1 pp. 113-130). Madrid: Alianza.

Rivière, A. (1991). *Objetos con menté.* Madrid: Alianza.

Rivière, A., & al. (1987). Individuation et interaction avec le sensori-moteur: Notes sur la construction génétique du sujet et de l'objet social. In M. Siguan (Ed.), *Comportement, cognition, conscience. La psychologie à la recherche de son objet.* Paris: PUF.

Rosa, A., Ochita, E., Moreno, E., Fernandez, E., Carretero, M., & al. (1984). Cognitive development in blind children: A challenge to piagetian theory. *Quarterly Newsletter of the Laboratory of Comparative Human Cognition, 6,* 75-81.

Rosa, R. A. (1985). Entrevista con Michael Cole. *Estudios de Psicologia, 21,* 3-20.

Rosa, R. A., & Moll, L. C. (1985). Computadores, comunicacion y educacion: una colaboracion internacional en la intervencion e investigacion educativa. [Computers, communication and education: An international collaboration in educational intervention and research]. *Infancia y Aprendizaje, 30*(1), 1-17

Rosa, R. A. (1994). History of psychology: A ground for reflexivity. In R. A. Rosa & J. Valsiner (Eds.), *Historical and theoretical discourse in socio-cultural studies.* Madrid: Fundacion Infancia y Apprendizaje.

Rosa, R. A., & Montero, I. (1990). The historical context of Vygotsky's work: A sociohistorical approach (pp.59-88). In L. Moll (Ed.), *Vygotsky and education.* Cambridge University Press.

Rosa, R. A., & Valsiner, J. (Eds.). (1994). *Historical and theoretical discourse in socio-cultural studies.* Madrid: Fundacion Infancia y Apprendizaje.

Rosel, J. (1984). Cognicion y representacion de la continuidad espacial en el nino. *Infancia y Aprendizaje,* (27-28), 237-252.

Serra, R. M. (1985). Estetica y Psicologia: dejando el arte en el silencio para comprender las raices de la palabra. Comentario a Vigotski. [Esthetics and psychology: Leaving art in silence to understand word roots: Commentary on Vygotsky]. Special Issue: About Vygotsky's thought. *Anuario de Psicologia, 33*(2), 140-149.

Siguan, M. (1984). Comentarios a la influencia de la obra de Vygotski en la psicologia del lenguaje. *Infancia y Aprendizaje,* (27-28), 253

Siguan, M. (Ed.). (1987). *Actualidad de Lev S. Vigotski* (Actuality de Lev Semenovich Vygotsky). Barcelona: Anthropos.

Spanish historical-cultural psychology: Language and development. Special Issue. (1991). *Infancia y Aprendizaje,* (53).

Vera F., J. A., Quinones, V. E., Garcia, S. J., & Pedraja, L. M. J. (1990). James y Vygotski: Influencia del funcionalismo en la psicologia sovietica. [James and Vygotski: Influence of functionalism in Soviet psychology]. *Revista de Historia de la Psicologia, 11*(3-4), 123-131

Vila, I. (1985). Lenguaje, pensamiento y cultura [Language, thought, and culture]. Special Issue: About Vygotsky's thought. *Anuario de Psicologia, 33*(2), 17-28.

Vila, I. (1990). Sesenta anos despues de la publicacion de El significado historico de la crisis en psicologia de Lev S. Vigotski. [Sixty years after The Historical Meaning of the Crisis in Psychology by Lev S. Vigotski]. *Anuario de Psicologia, 44*(1), 61-66.

Vila, I. (in press). *Lev Semenovitch Vygotsi: La mediacion semiotica de la mente.*

Vila, I. (in press). Aprendiendo a regular la accion conjunta: El formato de dar y tomar.

Vila, I., & Boda, H. (1989). Vygotski et l'ontogenèse du langage. *Enfance, 42*(1-2), 67-73.

Vila, I., & Boda, H. (in press). consciencia e interaccion social: Las propuestas de la psicologia Sovietica.

Villegas i Besora, M. (1989). The failure of communication in schizophrenic thought disorder. XXth Anniversary Conference of Communication and Cognition. *Communication and Cognition, 22*(2), 191-201.

Discussion of the works of L. S. Vygotsky in England

Atkinson, P. (1985). *Structure and reproduction: An introduction to the sociology of Basil Bernstein.* London: Methuen.

Arnold, P. (1985). Vygotsky and the education of the deaf child. *British Association of Teachers of the Deaf, 9*(2), 30

Arnold, P. (1985). Experimental psychology and the deaf child. *Journal of Rehabilitation of the Deaf, 19*(1-2), 4-8

Berg, L. (1968). *Risinghill: Death of a comprehensive school.* Harmondsworth: Penguin.

Bernstein, B. (1960). Aspects of language and learning in the genesis of the social process.
Journal of Child Psychology & Psychiatry, 1, 313-324.

Bernstein, B. (1961). Social class and linguistic development: A theory of social learning. In A. Halsey & al. (Eds.), *Education, economics, and society.* NY: Free Press of Glencoe.

Bernstein, B. (1981). Codes, modalities and the process of cultural reproduction: A model. *Language in Society, 10,* 327-263.

Bernstein, B. (1993). Foreword. In H. Daniels (Ed.), *Charting the agenda: Educational activity after Vygotsky* (pp. xiii-xxiii). London: Routledge.

Blackman, D. E., & Lejeune, H. (Eds.). (1990). *Behaviour analysis in theory and practice: Contributions and controversies.* NJ: Erlbaum.

Brine, J., Perrie, M., & Sutton, A. (Eds.). (1980). *Home, school, and leisure in the Soviet Union.* London: Allen & Unwin.

Bryant, P. (1987). Intelligence and children's development. In R. L. Gregory, & P. K. Marstarand (Eds.), *Creative intelligences* (pp. 9-18). Ablex Publishing Corp.

Bryant, P. (1994). The root of intellectual development. In A. Vyt, H. Bloch & M. H. Bornstein (Eds.), *Early childhood development in the French tradition: contribution from current research* (pp. 167-170). New Jersey: Lawrence Erlbuam Associates.

Burgess, T. (1993). Reading Vygotsky. In H. Daniels (Ed.), *Charting the agenda: Educational activity after Vygotsky* (pp. 1-29). London: Routledge.

Cameron, N. (1939). Deterioration and regression in schizophrenic thinking. *Journal of Abnormal & Social Psychology, 34,* 265-270.

Catan, L. (1986). The dynamic display of process: Historical development and contemporary uses of the microgenetic method. *Human Development, 29*(5), 252-263.

Daniels, H. (1988). An inquiry into different forms of special school organzation, pedagogic practice and pupil discrimination. *Collected*

Original Resources in Education, 12 (2).

Daniels, H. (1990). Number competence and communication difficulty: A Vygotskian analysis. *Educational Studies, 16*(1), 49-59.

Daniels, H. (1990). Vygotskian theory and special education practice in Russia. *Educational Studies, 19*(1), 79-89.

Daniels, H. (Ed.). (1993). *Charting the agenda: Educational activity after Vygotsky.* London: Routledge.

Daniels, H. (1993). Preface. In H. Daniels (Ed.), *Charting the agenda: Educational activity after Vygotsky* (pp.xxiv-xxix). London: Routledge.

Daniels, H. (1993). The individual and the organization. In H. Daniels (Ed.), *Charting the agenda: Educational activity after Vygotsky* (pp. 46-68). London: Routledge.

Daniels, H., & Lunt, I. (in preparation). *The theoretical basis of primary school teaching: Some comparisons.*

Douglas, J. E., & Sutton, A. (1978). The development of speech and mental processes in a pair of twins: A Case study. *Journal of Child Psychology and Psychiatry, 19*, 49-56.

Edwards, D., & Middleton, D. (1988). Conversational remembering and family relationships: How children learn to remember. *Journal of Social and Personal Relationships, 5*(1), 3-25

Evans, P. (1993). Some implications of Vygotsky's work for special education. In H. Daniels (Ed.), *Charting the agenda: Educational activity after Vygotsky* (pp. 30-45). London: Routledge.

Eysenck. H. J. (1982). The sociology of psychological knowledge, the genetic interpretation of IQ, and Marxist-Leninist ideology. *Bulletin of the British Psychological Society, 35*, 449-451.

Glachan, M., & Light, P. (1982). Peer interaction and learning: can two wrongs make a right? In G. Butterworth & P. Light (Eds.), *Social cognition.* Chicago: University of Chicago Press.

Goody, J. (1980). Thought and writing. In E. Gellener (Ed.), *Soviet and western anthropology* (pp. 119-133). New York: Columbia University Press.

Harré, R. (1983). *Personal being.* Oxford: Basil Blackwell.

Harré, R. (1992). Introduction: The second cognitive revolution. *American Behavioral Scientist, 36*, 5-7.

Harré, R. (1992). What is real in psychology. *Theory & Psychology, 2*, 153-158.

Harré, R. (1995). Discursive psychology. In J. A. Smith, R. Harré & L. Van Langenhove (Eds.), *Rethinking psychology* (pp. 143-159). London: Sage Publications.

Harré, R. (in press). *Positioning: The role of moral orders in the psychology of social action.* Oxford: Basil Blackwell.

Harré, R., & Van Langenhove, L. (1991). Varieties positioning. *Journal of the Theory of Social Behaviour, 21,* 393-408.

Henriques, J., Hollway, W., Urwin, C., Venn, C., & Walkerdine, V. (1984). Changing the subject: Psychology, social regulation, and subjectivity. London: Methuen.

Hinde, R. A., Perret-Clermont, A. N., & Stevenson-Hinde, J. (Eds.). (1988) *Relations interpersonnelles et développement des savoirs. Cousset, Delval, (trad. version anglaise: Social relationships and cognitive development.* Oxford, Clarendon Press, 1985).

Laird, A. J. (1950). *Some quantitative and qualitative aspects of Vygotsky testing.* Unpublished degree thesis. George Combe Psychological Laboratory, University of Edinburgh.

Levine, J. (1993). Learning english as an additional languagein multilingual classrooms. In H. Daniels (Ed.), *Charting the agenda: Educational activity after Vygotsky* (pp. 190-215). London: Routledge.

Light, P., & Glachan, M. (1985). Facilitation of individual problem solving through peer interaction. *Educational Psychology, 25*(3 & 4), 217-225.

Light, P., & Perret-Clermont, A. N. (1986). Social construction of logical structures or social construction of meaning? *Dossiers de Psychologie, Université de Neuchâtel,* (27).

Light, P., & Perret-Clermont, A. N. (1989). Social context effects in learning and testing. In A. Gellatly, D. Rogers & J. A. Sloboda (Eds.), *Cognition and social worlds* (pp. 99-112). Oxford Science Publications, University Press.

Light, P., Sheldon, S., & Woodhead, M. (Eds.). (1991). *Learning to think.* London: Routledge.

Light, P., & Butterworth, G. (Eds.), (1993). *Context and cognition: Ways of learning and knowing.* Hillsdale, NJ: Erlbaum.

Lock, A., Service, V., Brito, A., & Chandler, P. (1989). The social structuring of infant cognition. In A. Slater, & G. Bremner (Eds.), *Infant development* (pp. 243-271). Lawrence Erlbaum Associates.

Lunt, I. (1993). The practice of assessment. In H. Daniels (Ed.), *Charting the agenda: Educational activity after Vygotsky* (pp. 145-170). London: Routledge.

M'Comisky, J. G., & Worsley, A. R. (1970). A modified form of the Vigotsky test. *British Journal of Medical Psychology, 43),* 193-196.

Meadows, S. (1993). *The child as thinker: The development and acquisition of cognition in childhood.* London: Routledge.

Mercer, N. (1991). An accounting for what goes in classroom: What have neo-Vygotskian got to offer? *BPS Education Section Review, 15,* 61-67.

Mercer, N. (1993). Culture, context and the construction of knowledge in the classroom. In P. Light & G. Butterworth (Eds.), *Context and cognition: Ways of learning and knowing* (pp. 28-46). Hillsdale, NJ: Lawrence Erlbaum Associates.

Middleton, D. (1987). Some issues and approaches. *Quarterly Newsletter of the Laboratory of Comparative Human Cognition, 9*(1), 2-5.

Middleton, D. (1992). Counter currents in Sylvia Scribner's work. *Quarterly Newsletter of the Laboratory of Comparative Human Cognition, 14*(4), 131-132.

Middleton, D., & Edwards, D. (1987). Facing the future in developmental reflections on the zone of proximal development. *Quarterly Newsletter of the Laboratory of Comparative Human Cognition, 9*(3), 117-1119.

Middleton, D., & Edwards. D. (Eds.). (1990). *Collective remembering.* Sage Publications.

Middleton, D., & Edwards. D. (1990). Introduction. In D. Middleton & D. Edwards (Eds.), *Collective remembering* (pp. 1-22). Sage Publications.

Middleton, D., & Edwards. D. (1990). Conversational remembering: A social psychological approach. In D. Middleton & D. Edwards (Eds.), *Collective remembering* (pp. 23-45). Sage Publications.

Newson, J., & Newson, E. (1975). Intersubjectivity and the transmission of culture: On the social origins of symbolic functioning. *Bulletin of the British Psychological Society, 28,* 437-446.

Papadopoulou, K. (1990). *Acquisition and development of reflexive social emotions.* Unpublished doctoral dissertation, University of Sussex, England.

Pickering, J., & Skinner, M. (Eds.). (1991). *From sentience to symbols: Readings on consciousness.* University of Toronto Press.

Pollard, A. (1993). Learning in primary schools. In H. Daniels (Ed.), *Charting the agenda: Educational activity after Vygotsky* (pp. 171-189). London: Routledge.

Ryle, A. (1991). Object relations theory and activity theory: A proposed link by way of the procedural sequence model. *British Journal of Medical Psychology, 64*(4), 307-316.

Semeonoff, B., & Laird, A. J. (1952). The Vygotsky test as a measure of intelligence. *British Journal of Psychology, 43,* 94-103.

Semeonoff, B & Trist, E. (1958). Diagnostic performance tests. London: Tavistock Publications.

Semin, G. (1989). On genetic social psychology: A rejoinder to Doise. *European Journal of Social Psychology, 19,* 402-405.

Semin, G., & Papadopoulou, R. (1989). The acquisition of reflexive social emotions: The transmission and reproduction of social control through joint action. In G. Duveen, & B. B. Lloyd (Eds.), *Social representation and development of knowledge* (pp. 107-125). Cambridge: Cambridge University Press.

Shiach, G. M. (1972). *Teach them to speak.* London: Ward Lock.

Short, M. P. (1977). *The adaptation of a Soviet teaching experiment based on the Vygotskii Blocks, and its application to an English ESN population.* Unpublished doctoral dissertation, Faculty of Education, University of Birmingham, England.

Simon, J. (1966). *Education and society in Tudor.* England. Cambridge Univesrsity Press.

Simon, J. (1987). Vygotsky and Vygotskians. *American Journal of Education, 95*(4), 609-613.

Smith, L. (1993). Alternatives to constructivism. In L. Smith, *Necessary knowledge: Piagetian perspectives on constructivism* (pp. 123-143). NJ: Lawrence Erlbaum Associates.

Smith, L. (1994). The social construction of rational understanding. In A Tryphon & J. Vonèche (Eds.), *Piaget-Vygotsky: The social genesis of thought.* England, Hove: Erlbaum.

Smith, L. (1995). Introduction to sociological studies. In J. Piaget, Sociological studies (pp.1-22). London: Routledge

Spencer, I. (1995). Lev Vygotsky: A neo-Stalinist myth. *Critique, 27,* 201-208.

Subbostsky, E. (1996). *Vygotsky's distinction between lower and higher mental functions and recent studies on infant cognitive development.* E-mail Message, XLCHC, Vygotsky Project Page.

Sutton, A. (1975). *An annotated translation of L. S. Vygotskii.* Working paper.

Sutton, A. (1977). Acupuncture and deaf-muteism: An essay in cross-cultural defectology. *Educational Studies, 3,* 1-10.

Sutton, A. (1978). *One intervention's aftermath.* Paper read at the Annual Conference of the Developmental Section of the British Psychological Society, Nottingham, September.

Sutton, A. (1978). A dialectical psychology of child development: Some aspects and implications of Vygotskian psychology. In P. Barnett (Ed.), *Education papers* (pp. 26-39). London: CUL.

Sutton, A. (1979). Models and measures in development psychology. In R. Woods *(Ed.), Rehabilitating psychometrics. London: Social Science Research Council.* Repulished in *Educational Studies. 1980, 6*(2), 111-126.

Sutton, A. (1979). *Vygotskii and the dialectical method.* Paper read at the Annual Conference of the Developmental Section of the British Psychological Society, September.

Sutton, A. (1980). Measures and models in developmental psychology.

Educational Studies, 6(2), 111-126.

Sutton, A. (1980). Cultural disadvantage and Vygotskii's stages of development. *Educational Studies, 6*(3), 199-209.

Sutton, A. (1980). Backward children in the USSR: An unfamiliar view of a familiar problem. In J. Brine., M. Perrie., & A. Sutton (Eds.), *Home, school, and leisure in the USSR.* London: Allen & Unwin.

Sutton, A. (1980). A dialectical psychology of child development: Some aspects and implications of Vygotskian psychology. *Communist University of London: Collected Papers on Education),* 26-39.

Sutton, A. (1983). An introduction to Soviet developmental psychology. In S. Meadows (Ed.), *Developing thinking: Approaches to children's cognitive development.* NY: Metheun

Sutton, A. (1984). Conductive education in the midlands, summer 1982: Progress and problems in the importation of an educational method. *Educational Studies, 10*(2), 121-130.

Sutton, A. (1986). Conductive education: A challenge to integration. *Educational & Child Psychology, 3*(2), 5-12.

Sutton, A. (1988). L. S. Vygotsky: The cultural-historical theory-national minorities and the ZPD. In R. M. Gupta & P. Coxhead (Eds.), *Cultural diversity and learning efficiency* (pp. 89-116). New York: St. Martin's.

Sutton, A. (1989). Conductive education and child psychology. *Educational & Child Psychology, 9*(4), 339-345.

Sutton, A. (1991). An introduction to Soviet developmental psychology. In S. Meadows (Ed.), *Developing thinking.* London: Methuen.

Sutton, A. (1992). Conductive education: A complex question for psychology. *Educational Psychology, 9*(1), 49-56.

Sutton, A. (in press). *Dialectics, catastrophe, and revolution.*

Sutton, A., & Nash, S. (in press). *Verbal regulation by stages: Easy experiments for the non-normative evaluation of young children.*

Tough, J. (1976). *Listening to children talking: A guide to appraisal of children's use of language.* London: Ward Lock.

Williams, W. H. (1991). *Transfer of self-instructional and metacognitive training of communication skills for people who have learning difficulties.* Unpublished doctoral dissertation, University of Wales, England.

Wood, D. (1988). *How children think and learn.* Basil Blackwell.

Wood, D. (1991). Aspects of teaching and learning. In P. Light, S. Sheldon, & M. Woodhead (Eds.), *Learning to think. Child development in social context* (Vol. 2 pp. 97-120). London: Routledge.

Woolfson, C. (1977). Culture, language and the human personality. *Marxism Today, 21*(8), 229-240.

Woolfson, C. (1982). *The labour theory of culture: A reexamination of Engels' theory of human origins*. London: Routledge & Kegan Paul.
Woolfson, C. (1982). Labour and culture. In C. Woolfson, *The labour theory of culture: A reexamination of Engels' theory of human origins* (pp. 67-78). London: Routledge & Kegan Paul.

Discussion of the works of L. S. Vygotsky in Germany

Bauersfeld, H. (1995). The structuring of the structures: Development and function of mathematizing as a social practice. In L. P. Steffe & J. E. Gale (Eds.), *Constructivism in education* (pp. 137-158). Hillsdale, NJ: Lawrence Erlbaum Associates.

Boesch, E. (1980). *Kultur und handlung* [Culture and action]. Bern: Huber

Boesch, E. (1984). Handlungstheorie und kulturpsychologie [Action theory and cultural psychol.]. *Psychologische Beiträge, 30*, 233-247.

Boesch, E. (1991). *Symbolic action theory and cultural psychology.* Heidelberg/New York: Springer.

Boesch, E. (1992). Culture-individual-culture: The cycle of knowledge. In von M. Cranach, W. Doise, & G. Mugny (Eds.), *Social representations and the social bases of knowledge* (pp. 89-95). Bern: Hogrefe & Huber Publishers.

Braun, K. H. (1979). *Kritik des Freudo-Marxismus.* Köln: Pahl-Rugenstein.

Braun, K. H. (1991). Play and ontogenesis. In C. Tolman & W. Maiers (Eds.), *Critical psychology: Contributions to an historical science of the subject* (pp. 212-233). Cambridge: Cambridge University Press.

Braun, K. H., & Holzkamp, K. (Eds.). (1977). *Kritische psychologie.* Köln: Pahl-Rugenstein.

Brenner, H., & Gallas, H. (1970). Wygotski und die grundlegung einer materialistischen sprachtheorie. *Alternative, 74*, 205-209.

Duit, R. (1995). The constructivist view: A fashionable and fruiful paradigm for science education research and practice. In L. P. Steffe & J. E. Gale (Eds.), *Constructivism in education* (pp. 271-285). Hillsdale, NJ: Lawrence Erlbaum Associates.

Glock, Hans-johann. (1986). Vygotsky and Mead on the self, meaning and interpretation. *Studies in Soviet Thought, 31*, 131-148.

Gössmann, W. (1979). Wygotskis begriff der inneren sprache und seine bedeitung für den schreibprozess. *Wirkendes Wort, 29*, 13-28.

Guthke, J. (1982). The learning test concept--an alternative to the traditional static intelligence test. *German Journal of Psychology, 6*(4), 306-324.

Guthke, J., & Wingenfeld, S. (1992). The learning test concept: Origins, state of the art, and trends. In. H. C. Haywood & D. Tzuriel (Eds.), *Interactive assessment* (pp. 64-93). NY: Springer-Verlag.

Hildebrand-Nilshon, M., & Ruckriem, G. (Eds.). (1988). *Proceedings of the first annual international congress on activity theory.* West

Berlin.

Holzkamp, K. (1972). *Kritische psychologie: Vorbereitende arbeiten.* Frankfurt Main: Fischer-Verlag.

Holzkamp, K. (1973). *Sinnliche erkenntnishistorischer ursprang and gesellsschaftliche function der wahrnehmung.* Frankfurt: Athenäum-Verlag.

Holzkamp, K. (1977). Die überwindung der wissenschflichen beliebigkeit psychologischer theorien durch die kritische psychologie. *Zeitschrift für Sozialpsychologie, 8,* 1-22 & 78-79. Trans. into English in R. Hogan & W. Jones (Eds.), *Perspectives in personality* (2), 93-123). Greenwich, CT: JAI Press.

Holzkamp, K. (1983). *Grundlegung der psychologie.* Frankfurt: Campus-Verlag.

Holzkamp, K. (1991). Experience of self and scientific objectivity. In C. Tolman & W. Maiers (Eds.), *Critical psychology: Contributions to an historical science of the subject.* Cambridge: Cambridge University Press.

Holzkamp, K. (1991). Psychoanalysis and Marxist psychology. In C. Tolman & W. Maiers (Eds.), *Critical psychology: Contributions to an historical science of the subject.* Cambridge: Cambridge University Press.

Holzkamp, K. (1992). On doing psychology critically. *Theory & Psychology, 2,* 193-204.

Holzkamp, K. (1993). *Lernen: Subjecktwissenschaftliche grundlegung.* Frankfurt: Campus-Verlag.

Keseling, G. (1979). *Sprache als abbild und werkzeug. Ansätze zu einer sprachtheorie auf der grundlage der kulturhistorischen psychologie der Wygotskischule.* Köln.

Luckmann, T. C. (1977). *Einfüehrung. In L. Vygotski, Denken und sprechen.* Frankfurt/Main: Fischer.

Papousek, H., & Papousek, M. (1994). Language and thought in children: A look behind curtains. In A. Vyt, H. Bloch & M. H. Bornstein (Eds.), *Early childhood development in the French tradition: contribution from current research* (pp. 241-243). New Jersey: Lawrence Erlbuam Associates.

Raeithel, A. (1994). The look back into history prolongs the stretches of travel still lying before us. *Mind, Culture, and Activity: An International Journal, 1(1&2),* 89-101.

Richard, J. (1973). Ein neuer text Wygotskjs und wie man ihn lesen könnte. *Asthetik und Kommunikation, 1,* 10-14.

Rissom, I. (1979). Zum begrif des zeichens in den arbeiten Vygotskijs. In M. Geier & al. (Eds.), *Sprachbewubtsein. Elf untersuchungen zum zusammenhang von sprachwissenschaft und kulturhistorische psychologie* (pp. 9-32). Stuttgart.

Rissom, I. (1985). *Der beigriff des zeichens in den arbeiten lev Semenovic Vygotskijs* [The concept of sign in the works of Lev Semenovich Vygotsky]. Goppingen Arbeiten Zur Germanistik. Nr.426.

Scheerer, E. (1980). Gestalt psychology in the Soviet Union: I. The period of enthusism. *Psychological Research, 41*, 113-132.

Scheerer, E. (Ed.). (1980). Luria memorial issue. *Psychological Research, 41.*

Staeuble, L. (1968). Faschistoide und kritischautonome haltung. Versuch über die rolle des konzepts "Einstelliung zu kritischer vernunft" in der vorurteilsforschung. *Zeitschrift für Soziologie und Sozialpsychologie, 20*, 38-61.

Stroebe, W. (1980). The critical school in German social psychology. *Personality & Social Psychology Bulletin, 6*, 105-112.

Wild, E. (1980). Inneres sprechenaeussere sprache. Klett, Stuttgart.

Wittig, H. E. (1959). Marx and education: Philosophical origins of communist pedagogy. *Soviet Survey, (*30), 77-81.

Discussion of the works of L. S. Vygotsky in Japan

Ahmed, M. K. (1988). *Speaking as cognitive regulation: A study of L1 and L2 dyadic problemsolving activity.* Unpublished doctoral dissertation, University of Delaware, Newark, USA.

Ahmed, M. K. (1994). Speaking as cognitive regulation: A Vygotskian perspective on dialogic communication. In J. P. Lantolf & G. Appel (Eds.), *Vygotskian approaches to second language research* (pp. 157-171). New Jersey: Ablex.

Fujinaga, Tamotsu, Kasuga, Takashi, Uchida, Nobuko, Saiga, Hisataka. (1990). Long term follow up study of children developmentally retarded by early environmental deprivation. *Genetic, Social, and General Psychology Monographs, 116*(1), 37-104.

Hatano, G. (1982). Cognitive consequences of practice in culture specific procedural skills. *Quarterly Newsletter of the Laboratory of Comparative Human Cognition, 4* (1), 15-18.

Hatano, G. (1992). Comments on "the cognitive consequences of literacy". *Quarterly Newsletter of the Laboratory of Comparative Human Cognition, 14*(4), 120-122.

Hatano, G. (1993). Commentary: Time to merge Vygotskian and constructivist conceptions of knowledge acquisition. In E. Forman, N. J. Minick, & C. A. Stone (Eds.), *Contexts for learning: Sociocultural dynamics in children's development* (pp. 153-166). New York: Oxford University Press.

Hatano, G., & Inagaki, K. (1991). Sharing cognition through collective comprehension activity. In L. Resnick, J. M. Leviner., & S. D. Teasley (Eds.), *Perspectives on socially shared cognition* (pp. 331-348). Washington DC: American Psychological Association.

Inagaki, K. (1981). Facilitation of knowledge integration through classroom discussion. *Quarterly Newsletter of the Laboratory of Comparative Human Cognition, (3),* 26-28.

Inagaki, K. (1983). Collective scientific discovery by young children. *Quarterly Newsletter of the Laboratory of Comparative Human Cognition, (5),* 13-18.

Sayeki, Y. (1992). Comments on Sylvia Scribner's "The cognitive consequences of literacy" and "Mind in action: A functional approach to thinking". *Quarterly Newsletter of the Laboratory of Comparative Human Cognition, 14*(4), 141-143.

Tsunola, T. (1995). An approach to an integrated sensorimotor system in the human central brain and a subconscious computer. In J.

Wertsch, P. del Rio & A. Alvarez (Eds.), *Sociocultural studies of mind* (pp. 124-135). NY: Cambridge University Press.

Discussion of the works of L. S. Vygotsky in Hungary

Arievitch, I. M., & Stetsenko, A. P. (1988). From Vygotsky to Galperin: Development of an idea of mental act's 'outsidedness. *Proceedings of the 7th European CHEIRON Conference*, Budapest, Hungary, 4-8 Sept), 16-21.

Garai, L. (1983). Marxian personality psychology. In R. Harré & Lamb (Eds.), *The encyclopedic dictionary of psychology* (pp. 364-366). London: Basil Blackwell.

Garai, L. (1985). Thesis on the brain, meaning, and dualism. *Studia Psychologica, 27*(2), 157-168.

Garai, L. (1993). *A psychosocial essay on identity* (in Hungarian). Budapest: T-Twins.

Garai, L., & Köcski, M. (1989). The principle of social relations and the principle of activity. *Soviet Psychology, 27*, 50-69.

Garai, L., & Köcski, M. (1990). The psychological status of activity and social relationship: On the continuity of the theories of Lev Vygotsky and Alexei Leontyev. *Soviet Journal of Psychology, 11*(5), 3-14.

Garai, L., & Kocski, M. (1991). Positivist and hermeneutic principles in psychology: Activity and social categorisation. *Studies in Soviet Thought, 42*(2), 123-135.

Garai, L., & Kocski, M. (1995). On the mental status of activity and social relation: The question of continuity between the theories of Vygotsky and Leontiev. *Psikhol. Zh., 11*(5), 17-26. (in Hungarian).

Garai, L., & Kocski, M. (1995). An other crisis in psychology: A possible motive for the Vygotsky boom. *Journal of Russian & East European Psychology, 33*(1), 82-94.

Vari-Szilagyi, I. (1988). G. H. Mead and L. S. Vygotsky: A comparative analysis. *Proceedings of the 7th European CHEIRON Conference*, Budapest, Hungary, 4-8 September), 690-698.

Vari-Szilagyi, Ibolya. (1991). G. H. Mead and L. S. Vygotsky on action. *Studies in Soviet Thought, 42*(2), 93-121.

Discussion of the works of L. S. Vygotsky in Yugoslavia

Bubelini, J. (1979). Questions of periodicity of mental development in D. B. Elkonin's conception. *Psychologia a Patopsychologia Dietata, 14*(5), 387-394

Ignjatovic-Savic, Nada, Kovac-Cerovic, Tunde, Plut, Dijana., & Pesikan, Ana. (1988). Social interaction in early childhood and its developmental effects. In J. Valsiner (Ed.), *Child development within culturally structured environments* (Vol. 1, pp. 89-158). Norwood, NJ: Ablex.

Ivic, I. (1986). Deux types de la communication préverbale et le developpement du langage chez l'enfant. *Zbornik Filozofskog Fakulteka, Serija B, XIV*), 69-73.

Ivic, I. (1987). Le social au coeur de l'individuel. In CRESAS, On n'apprend pas tout seul: Interactions sociales et construction des savoirs. Paris: ESF. Institut National de Recherche Pédagogique.

Ivic, I. (1989). Profiles of educators: Lev S. Vygotsky (1896-1934). *Prospects, 19*(3), 427-436.

Ivic, I. (1995). Lev S. Vygotsky. *Prospects, 25*(4), 761-786.

Discussion of the works of L. S. Vygotsky in Argentina

Azcoaga, J. E. (1984). Comment. In G. Blanck (Ed.), *Vigotski: Memoria y vigencia* [Vygotsky: Memory and actuality] (pp.206). Buenos Aires: Cultura y Cognicion.

Azcoaga, J. E. (1984). Vigotski y la psicolinguistica actual [Vygotsky and current psycholinguistics]. In G. Blanck (Ed.), *Vigotski: Memoria y vigencia* [Vygotsky: Memory and actuality] (pp. 139-145). Buenos Aires: Cultura y Cognicion.

Blanck, G. (1977, June, 25). *Social determination of specifically human mental activity.* Booklet. Buenos Aires: Stokoe.

Blanck, G. (1983). Carlos Marx y la psicologia. *Contexto.*

Blanck, G. (Ed.). (1984). *Vigotski: Memoria y vigencia* [Vygotsky: Memory and actuality]. Buenos Aires: Cultura y Cognicion.

Blanck, G. (1984). Vida y obra de Vigotski [The life and the work of Vygotsky]. In G. Blanck (Ed.), *Vigotski: Memoria y vigencia* [Vygotsky: Memory and actuality]. Buenos Aires: Cultura y Cognicion.

Blanck, G., & Ardila, R. (Eds.). (1984). *Crisis e integracion de la psicologia como ciencia.* Buenos Aires: Cultura y Cognicion.

Blanck, G. (1987). Teoria y metodo para una ciencia psicologia unificada [Theory and method for a unified psychological science].In M. Siguan (Ed.), *Actualidad de Lev S. Vigotski* (Actuality de Lev S. Vygotsky) (pp. 102-127). Barcelona: Anthropos.

Blanck, G. (1989, Sept., 8). La neuropsicologia de Vigotski a Luria [Neuropsychology from Vygotsky to Luria]. *Perspectivas Sistematicas.*

Blanck, G. (1990). Vygotsky: the man and his cause. In L. Moll (Ed.), *Vygotsky and education* (pp. 31-58). Cambridge University Press.

Blanck, G., & Van Der Veer, R. (1990, January 9). Vigotski y Mead: Una psicologia social de los procesos cognitivos [Vygotsky and Mead: A social psychology of cognitive processes]. *Boletin Argentino de Psicoogia.*

Blanck, G., & Van Der Veer, R. (1991). *Vigotski: Una introducion critica* [Vygotsky: A critical introduction]. Buenos Aires: Dialectica.

Golder, M. (Ed.). (1986). *Reportajes contemporaneos a la psicologia sovietica* [Contemporary reports on Soviet psychology]. Buenos Aires: Cartago.

Silvestri, A., & Blanck, G. (1990). *Bajtiny Vigotski: La organizacion semiotica de la concienci*a [Bakhtin and Vygotsky: The semiotic organization of mind]. Barcelona: Anthropos.

Smolka, A. L., De Goes, M. C. R., & Pino, A. (1995). The

constitution of the subject: A president question. In J. Wertsch, P. del Rio & A. Alvarez (Eds.), *Sociocultural studies of mind* (pp. 165-184). New York: Cambridge University Press.

"Vygotsky and cultural anthropology". *Colloquium on Vygotsky's thought*. Argentina: Buenos Aires, 1984.

Discussion of the works of L. S. Vygotsky in New Zealand

Clay, M., & Cazden, C. B. (1990). A Vygotskian interpretation of reading recovery. In L. Moll (Ed.), *Vygotsky and education* (pp. 206-222). Cambridge University Press.

McMillan, B. W. (1991). All in the mind: Human learning and development from an ecological perspective. In J. R. Morss, & T. Linzey (Eds.), *Growing up: The politics of human learning* (pp. 30-45). Longman.

McNaughton, S. (1991). The faces of instruction: Models of how children learn from tutors.In J. R. Morss, & T. Linzey (Eds.), *Growing up: The politics of human learning* (pp. 135-150). Longman.

McNaughton, S., & Leyland, J. (1990). The shifting focus of maternal tutoring across different difficulty levels on a problem solving task. *British Journal of Developmental Psychology, 8*(2), 147-155.

Discussion of the works of L. S. Vygotsky in Northern Ireland

Morss, J. R. (1985). Old Mead in new battles: The impersonal and interpersonal in infant knowledge. *New Ideas in Psychology, 3*(2), 165-176.

Morss, J. R. (1986). Old Mead in new battles: A reply to Shotter. *New Ideas in Psychology, 4*(1), 85-88.

Morss, J. R. (1988). The public world of childhood. *Journal for the Theory of Social Behaviour, 18*(3), 323-343.

Morss, J. R. (1990). The biologising of childhood: Developmental psychology and the Darwinian myth. Lawrence Erlbaum Associates.

Morss, J. R. (1994). Stepping forward, stepping backward: Review of developmental psychology in the Soviet Union by Jaan Valsiner. *New Ideas in Psychology, 12*(1), 99-102.

Morss, J. R., & Linzey, T. (Eds.). (1991). *Growing up: The politics of human learning.* Longman

Discussion of the works of L. S. Vygotsky in Finland

Engeström, Yrjö. (1986). The zone of proximal development as the basis category of educational psychology. *Quarterly Newsletter of the Laboratory of Comparative Human Cognition, 8* (1), 23-42.

Engeström, Yrjö. (1987). *Learning by expanding: An activitytheoretical approach to developmental research.* Helsinki: Orienta-Konsultit.

Engeström, Yrjö. (1988). Introduction: How to do research activity? *Quarterly Newsletter of the Laboratory of Comparative Human Cognition, 10* (2), 30-31.

Engeström, Yrjö. (1988). Reconstructing work as an object of research. *Quarterly Newsletter of the Laboratory of Comparative Human Cognition, 10* (1), 21-27.

Engeström, Yrjö. (1989). The cultural-historical theory of activity and the study of political repression. *International Journal of Mental Health, 17*(4), 29-41.

Engeström, Yrjö. (1990). *Learning, working, and imagining: Twelve studies in activitytheory.* Helsinki: Orienta-Konsultit.

Engeström, Yrjö. (1990). Activity theory and individual and social transformation. Presidential address at the second international congress for research on activity theory, In Lahti, Finland, May 21-25,1990. (22 pages).

Engeström, Yrjö. (1990). Toward an activity-based methodology for studying cognition at work. *Quarterly Newsletter of the Laboratory of Comparative Human Cognition, 12*(4), 116-117.

Engeström, Yrjö. (1991). Activity theory and individual and social transformation. *Activity Theory, 7/8)*, 6-17.

Engeström, Yrjö. (1991). A legacy in transition. *Quarterly Newsletter of the Laboratory of Comparative Human Cognition, 13*(1), 66-68.

Engeström, Yrjö. (1991). Developmental work research: Reconstructing expertise through expansive learning. In M, I. Nurminen & G. R. S. Weir (Eds.), *Human jobs and computer interfaces.* Amsterdam: Elsevier.

Engeström, Yrjö. (1992). *Interactive expertise: Studies in distributed working intelligence. University of Helsinki.* Department of Education, Research Bulletin #83.

Engeström, Yrjö. (1992). *Artifacts and talk as mediators of medical teamwork.* Paper presented at the Conference Discourse and the Professions, Upsala, Sweden.

Engeström, Yrjö. (1993). The working health center project: Materializing zones of proximal development in a network of organizational innovation. In T. Kaupoinen & M. Lahtonen (Eds.), *Action research in Finland.* Helsinki: Ministry of Labor.

Engeström, Yrjö. (1995). Innovative organizational learning in medical and legal settings. In L. Martin, K. Nelson & E. Tobach (Eds.), *Sociocultural psychology: Theory and practice of doing and knowning* (pp. 326-356). New York: Cambridge University Press.

Engeström, Yrjö, Brown, K., Engeström, R., & Koistinen, K. (1990). Organizational forgetting: An activity-theoretical perspective. In D. Middleton & D. Edwards (Eds.), *Collective remembering* (pp. 139-168). Sage Publications.

Engeström, Yrjö., Miettinen, R. (in press). *Perspectives on activity theory.* Cambridge: Cambridge University Press.

Engeström, Yrjö., & Middleton. D. (Eds.). (in press). *Cognition and communication at work.* Cambridge: Cambridge University Press.

Hautamaki, A. (1981). Activity, environment, social class and voluntary learning. *Acta Psychologica Fennica, 8,* 21-32

Hautamaki, A. (1981). Tahdonalaisen oppimisen omaksuminen: "Olen mita opin." [The mastery of voluntary learning: "I am what I learn."] *Psykologia, 16*(4), 205-215

Hautamaki, J., & Hautamaki, A. (1981). Pajakt efter en metodden kulturhistoriska skolan och ett konkret studium av psyket. [The search for a method: The social historical school and a concrete study of the psyche]. *Nordisk Psykologi, 33*(1), 1-10

Leiman, M. (1992). The concept of sign in the work ofVygotsky, Winnicott and Bakhtin: Further integration of object relations theory and activity theory. *Brittish Journal of Medical Psychology, 65*(3), 209-221.

Sariola, E. (1982). L. S. Vygotskin anti skitsofrenian ajatushairioiden tutkimukselle. [L. S. Vygotsky's contribution to the study of schizophrenic thought disorders]. *Psykologia, 17*(3), 171-179

Discussion of the works of L. S. Vygotsky in Denmark

Axel, E. (1992). One developmental line in European activity theories. *Quarterly Newsletter of the Laboratory of Comparative Human Cognition, 14*(1), 8-17.

Brostrom, S. (1992). Quick response: An ethnographic analysis of dramagame in a Danish preschool. *Quarterly Newsletter of the Laboratory of Comparative Human Cognition, 14*(1), 17-22.

Engelsted, N. (1994). Sense and significance in phylogenetic reconstruction: A commentary on Arne Raeithel's "Symbolic production of social coherence". *Mind, Culture, and Activity: An International Journal, 1*(1&2), 107-118.

Engelsted, N., Hedegaard, M., Karpatscholf, B., & Mortensen, A. (Eds.). (1993). *The societal subject.* Aarhus: Aarhus University Press.

Hedegaard, M. (1986). Two approaches to thinking and knowledge acquisition. *Quarterly Newsletter of the Laboratory of Comparative Human Cognition, 8*(2), 58-63.

Hedegaard, M. (1989). Motivational development in schoolchildren. *Multidisciplinary Newsletter for Activity Theory, 1*, 30-38.

Hedegaard, M. (1990). The zone of proximal development as basis for instruction. In L. Moll (Ed.), *Vygotsky and education* (pp. 349-371). Cambridge University Press.

Hedegaard, M. (1992). Reflection in honor of Sylvia Scribner's socio-cultural approach. *Quarterly Newsletter of the Laboratory of Comparative Human Cognition, 14*(4), 122-123.

Hedegaard, M. (1995). The qualitative analysis of the development of a child's theoretical knowledge and thinking. In L. Martin, K. Nelson & E. Tobach (Eds.), *Sociocultural psychology: Theory and practice of doing and knowning* (pp. 293-325). New York: Cambridge University Press.

Hedegaard, M., Hakkarainen, P., & Engeström, Yrjö. (Eds.). (1984). *Learning and teaching on a scientific basis: Methodological and epistemological aspects of the activity theory of learning and teaching.* Aarhus: Aarhus Universitet, Psykologisk institut.

Mortensen, A. (1990). Culture and microcosmos of indivuals: The idiosyncratic room of the person. *Quarterly Newsletter of the Laboratory of Comparative Human Cognition, 12*(4), 146-153.

Sinha, C. (1988). *Language and representation: A socio-naturalistic approach to human development.* Hemel Hempstead: Harvester

Wheatsheaf. (For a discussion of the Vygotsky's writings in relation to Darwin, and Vygotsky critique of Piaget's explanation of egocentric speech: pp. 92-98)

Sinha, C. (1989). Evolution, development and social production of mind. *Cultural Dynamics, 2*(2), 188-207.

Sinha, C. (1989). Reading Vygotsky. *History of Human Sciences, 2*(3), 309-331.

Sinha, C. (1994). Iconology and imagination: Explorations in socio-genetic economies. In W. de Graaf & R. Maier (Eds.), *Sociogenesis reexamined* (pp. 93-116). New York: Springer-Verlag.

Uhrenholdt, G. (1982). Elementer til en special-paedagogik for smaborn. [Elements of special education for infants]. *Skolepsykologi, 19*(5), 362-373.

Discussion of the works of L. S. Vygotsky in Vietnam

Hac, Pham-Minh., & Ardila, A. (1977). Vygotsky's system of psychological ideas and its place in the development of psychology. *Revista Latinoamericana de Psicologia, 9*(2), 283-299.

Discussion of the works of L. S. Vygotsky in Puerto Rico

de Guerrero, M. C. M. (1990). *Nature of inner speech in mental rehearsal of the second language.* Unpublished doctoral dissertation, Inter American University of Puerto Rico, San German, Puerto Rico.

de Guerrero, M. C. M. (1994). Form and functions of inner speech in adult second language learning. In J. P. Lantolf & G. Appel (Eds.), *Vygotskian approaches to second language research* (pp. 83-115). New Jersey: Ablex.

de Guerrero, M. C. M., & Villamil, O. S. (1994). Social-cognitive dimension in L2 peer revision.
Modern Language Journal, 78(4), 484-496.

Discussion of the works of L. Vygotsky in Czechoslovakia

Kosco, J., & Marsalova, L. (1979). K. F. Riegel's attempt at a "dialectic" conception of lifelong developmental psychology. *Psychologia a Patopsychologia Dietata, 14*(5), 395-409

Zelman, J. (1988). Tvorba L. S. Vygotskeho. [Works of L. S. Vygotskij]. *Psychologia a Patopsychologia Dietat, 23*(2), 123-130

Discussion of the works of L. S. Vygotsky in South Africa

Gilbert, A. J. (1987). *Psychology and social change in the third world: A cognitive perspective.* Unpublished doctoral dissertation, University of South Africa, South Africa.

Malan, J. N. (1992). *Optimising the achievement potential of the preschool child through a nonformal introduction to literacy: A nonformal parent programme (Afrikaans text).* Unpublished doctoral dissertation, University of Pretoria, South Africa.

Moll, I. (1993, April). The material and the social in Vygotsky's theory of cognitive development. *Resources in Education,* 127.

Moll, I. (1994). Reclaiming the natural line in Vygotsky's theory of cognitive development. *Human Development, 37*(6), 333-342.

Nel, A. D. (1990). *An aid programme in addition for pupils with mathematical problems: A cognitive-theoretical perspective.* Unpublished doctoral dissertation, University of Pretoria, South Africa.

Turnbull, O., & Bagus, R. (1991). The translation of the Luria Neuropsychological investigation into Zulu: Its relationship to the work of A. R. Luria and L. S. Vygotsky. *South African Journal of Psychology, 21*(1), 61-63.

Tolman, S. G. (1991). The translation of the Luria Neuropsychological investigation into Zulu: Its relationship to the work of A. R. Luria and L. S. Vygotsky: A reply. *South African Journal of Psychology, 21*(1), 63-66.

Tolman, S. G., & Msengana, N. B. (1990). Neuropsychological assessment: Problems in evaluating the higher mental functioning of Zulu-speaking people using traditional western-techniques. *South African Journal of Psychology, 20*(1), 20-24.

Discussion of the works of L. S. Vygotsky in Israel

Ben-Hur, M. (Ed.). (1994). *On Feuerstein's instrumental enrichment: A collection.* Palatine, IL: IRI/SkyLight.

Feuerstein, R. (1980). *Instrumental enrichment: An intervention program for cognitive modificability.* Baltimore, MD: University Park Press.

Feuerstein, R. (1994). The making of man learning to learn: An interview with Reuven Feuerstein (30 min. videotape) by James Bellanca, producer. Palatine, IL: IRI/SkyLight.

Feuerstein, R., & Feuerstein, S. (1991). Mediating learning experience: A theoretical review. In R. Feuerstein, P.S. Klein & A. J. Tannenbaum (Eds.), *Mediated learning experience (MLE): Theoretical, psychological and learning implications.* London: Freund Publishing House.

Landsmann, L. T. (Ed.) (1991). The conceptualization of writing in the confluence of interactive models of development. In L. T. Landsmann (Ed.), *Culture, schooling, and psychological development* (Vol. 4, pp. 87-111). New Jersey: Ablex.

Mevarech, Z. R., & Kramarski, B. (1993). Vygotsky and Papert: Social-cognitive interactions within Logo environments. *British Journal of Educational Psychology, 63,* 96-109.

Tzuriel, D., & Haywood, C. (1992). The learning of interactive-dynamic approaches to assessment of learning potential. In. H. C. Haywood & D. Tzuriel (Eds.), *Interactive assessment* (pp. 3-37). New York: Springer-Verlag.

Discussion of the works of L. S. Vygotsky in Mexico

Candela, A. (1995). Consensus construction as a collective task in Mexican science classes. *Anthropology & Education Quarterly,* *26*(4), 458-474.

Ribes, E. (1982). Los eventos privados: Un problema para la teoria de la conducta? [Private events: A problem for behavior theory?] *Revista Mexicana de Analisis de la Conducta, 8*(1), 11-29

Discussion of the works of L. S. Vygotsky in Australia

Garton, A. F. (1992). Social interaction and the development of language and cognition. Lawrence Erlbaum Associates.

Goodnow, J. (1987). Cultural conditions and individual behaviors: Conceptual and methodological links. *Australian Journal of Psychology, 38*, 231-244.

Goodnow, J. (1990). Using sociology to extend psychological accounts of cognition.
Human Development, 33, 81-107.

Goodnow, J. (1993). Afterword: Direction of post Vygotskian research. In E. Forman, N. J. Minick, & C. A. Stone (Eds.), *Contexts for learning: Sociocultural dynamics in children's development* (pp. 369-381). New York: Oxford University Press.

Goodnow, J., Miller, P., & Kessel, F. (Eds.) (1995). *Cultural practices as contexts for development.* San Francisco: Jossey-Bass.

Phillips, S. (1977). The contributions of L. S. Vygotsky to cognitive psychology. *Alberta Journal of Educational Research, 23*(1), 31-42

Discussion of the works of L. S. Vygotsky in Brazil

Bacalarski, M. C. (1996). *Vygotsky's developmental theories and the adulthood of computer mediated communication: A comparison and an illumination.* E-mail Message, XLCHC, Vygotsky Project Page.

Emihovich, C., & Lima, E. S. (1995). The many facets of Vygotsky: A cultural-historical voice from the future. *Anthropology & Education Quarterly, 26*(4), 375-383.

Lampreia, C., Nicolaci, da. C., & Ana, M. (1986). O papel da linguagem no desenvolvimento cognitivo [The role of language in cognitive development]. *Psicologia Teoria e Pesquisa, 2*(2), 101-115.

Lima, E. S. (1995). Culture revisited: Vygotsky's ideas in Brazil. *Anthropology & Education Quarterly, 26*(4), 443-457.

Lima, E. S. (1995).Vygotsky in the international scene: A brief overview. *Anthropology & Education Quarterly, 26*(4), 490-499.

Penna, A. G. (1987). Acao e razao. [Action and reason.) *Arquivos Brasileiros de Psicologia, 39*(1), 18-28.

Discussion of the works of L. S. Vygotsky in Poland

Kolakowski, L. (1978). Main currents of Marxism: Its origin, growth, and dissolution. Vol.1: The founder, Vol.2: The golden age, Vol.3: The breakdown. Oxford: Oxford University Press (Translated from Polish by P. S. Falla).

Raszkiewicz, H. (1986). Aspekt semiotyczny rozwoju i funkcjonowania intelektualnego. [The semiotic aspect of intellectual development and functioning]. *Przeglad Psychologiczny, 29*(2), 305-320

Shugar, G. W. (1993). The structures of peer participation in shared activity: Frameworks for acquiring communicative knowledge. In J. Nadel & L. Camaioni (Eds.), *New perspectives in early communicativedevelopment* (pp. 171-189). London: Routledge.

Discussion of the works of L. S. Vygotsky in Belgium

Day, J. D. (1983). The zone of proximal development. In M. Pressley & J. R. Levin (Eds.), *Cognitive strategy research* (pp. 155-175). NY: Springer.

Day, J. D., & Tappan, M. B. (1996). The narrative approach to moral development from the epistemic subject to dialogical selves. *Human Development, 39,* 67-82.

Goossens, L. G. (1989). *Elicitation of scientific reasoning in 11 to 17 yearolds by means of pairchoice and single evaluation tasks.* Unpublished doctoral dissertation, Université Catholique de Louvain, Belgium.

Vyt, A. (1989). The second year of life as a developmental turning point: Implications for "sensitive" caretaking. Special Issue: Infancy and education: Psychological considerations. *European Journal of Psychology of Education, 4*(2), 145-158.

Discussion of the works of L. S. Vygotsky in India

Kapur, D., & Chadha, N. K. (1986). Thinking and language: A theoretical review. *Psycho-Lingua, 16*(1), 1-8.

Discussion of the works of L. S. Vygotsky in Scotland

Butterworth, G., & Grover, L. (1988). The origins of referential communication in human infancy. In L. Weiskrantz (Ed.), *Thought without language. A Fyssen Foundation symposium* (pp. 5-24). Clarendon Press / Oxford University Press.

Butterworth, G., & Harris, M. (1994). *Principles of developmental psychology. Principles of psychology.* New Jersey: Lawrence Erlbaum Associates.

Markova, I. (1987). *Human awareness, its social development.* London: Hutchinson Education.

Markova, I. (1987). On the interaction of opposites in psychological processes. *Journal for the Theory of Social Behavior, 17,* 279-299.

Markova, I. (Ed.). (1978). *Language and the social context.* London: Wiley.

Markova, I. (1990). The development of self-consciousness: Baldwin, Mead, and Vygotsky. In J. E. Faulconer & R. Williams (Eds.), *Reconsidering psychology.* PA: Duquesne University Press.

Markova, I. (1990). On three principles of human social development. In G. Butterworth & P. Bryant (Eds.), *Causes of development* (pp. 151-174). Hillsdale, NJ: Erlbaum.

Markova, I. (1992). On solos, duets, quartets, and quintets: A response to Gardner. *New Ideas in Psychology, 10*(2), 215-221.

Markova, I. (1994). Sociogenesis of language: Perspectives on dialogism and on activity theory. In W. de Graaf & R. Maier (Eds.), *Sociogenesis reexamined* (pp. 27-46). New York: Springer-Verlag.

Markova, I., & Foppa, R. (Eds.). (1990). *The dynamic of dialogue.* London: Harvester Wheatsheaf.

Markova, I., & Foppa, R. (Eds.). (1991). *Asymmetries in dialogue.* Hemel Hempstead: Harvester Wheatsheaf.

Soden, R. (1993). Vocational education for a thinking workforce: Vygotskian perspective. *International Journal of Vocational Education & Training, 1*(1), 39-47.

Discussion of the works of L. S. Vygotsky in Egypt

Mansour, T. (1976). Introduction to Soviet psychology: Its development and directions. In Vygotsky, L. S. *Tafkir wa lugha* (pp. 3-43). Egypt, Cairo: Anglo-Egyptian Press. (in Arabic).

Discussion of the works of L. S. Vygotsky in Portugal

Jesuno, J. G. (1982). Réflexions sur la contreverse Wallon-Piaget. *Bulletin de Psychologie, 35*(355), 401-406.

The intellectual roots of Lev Vygotsky

Adler, A. (1917). *Study of organ inferiority and its psychical compensation.* New York: NMDP.

Agassiz, L. (1850). The diversity of origin of human races. *Christian Examiner, 49,* 110-145.

Agassiz, L. (1859). *An essay on classification.* London

Agassiz, E. C. (1895). *Lois Agassiz: His life and Correspondence.* Boston, Houghton: Miffilin.

Akselrod, L. (1909, July). Review of Lenin's materialism and empirocriticism. *Sovremennny Mir,* (7). Reprinted in J. M. Edie, J. P. Scanlan & M. Zeldin (Eds.), *Russian philosophy* (pp. 457-463). Chicago: Quadrangle Books, 1965.

Astle, T. (1784). *The origin and progress of writing.* London: Author.

Audermars, M., & Lafendel, L. (1923). *La maison des petits de l'institut J. J. Rousseau.* Neuchâtel and Paris: Delachaux & Niestlé.

Bachelard, G. (1927). *Essai sur la connaissance approchée.* Paris: Vrin.

Bacon, F. (1960). *The new organon and related writings.* New York: Macmillan. (Original work published in 1620).

Bakhtin, M. (1984). *Problems of Dostoevsky's poetics.* Minneapolis: Univesrsity of Minnesota Press. (Original work published in 1929).

Baldwin, J. M. (1889). *Handbook of psychology: Senses and intellect.* New York: Holt.

Baldwin, J. M. (1893). New method in child psychology. *Science, 21,* 213-214.

Baldwin, J. M. (1895). *Mental development in the child and race.* New York: Macmillan.

Baldwin, J. M. (1896). Consciousness and evolution. *Psychological Review, 3,* 300-309.

Baldwin, J. M. (1897). *Social and ethical interpretations in mental development: A study in social psychology.* New York: Macmillan.

Baldwin, J. M. (1898). On selective thinking. *Psychological Review, 6,* 1-24.

Baldwin, J. M. (1902). *Development and evolution.* NY: Macmillan.

Baldwin, J. M. (1906). *Thoughts and things, or genetic logic: Functional logic, or genetic theory of knowledge* (Vol. 1). New York: Macmillan.

Baldwin, J. M. (1908). *Thoughts and things, or genetic logic: Experimental logic, or genetic theory of thought* (Vol. 2). New York: Macmillan.

Baldwin, J. M. (1911). *Thoughts and things, or genetic logic: Interest and art* (Vol. 3). New York: Macmillan.

Baldwin, J. M. (1974). *The individual and society.* New York: Arno Press. (Original work published in 1911).

Bartlett, F. C. (1923). *Psychology and primitive culture.* Cambridge: Cambridge University Press.

Bartlett, F. C. (1932). *Remembering: A study of experimental and psychology.* Cambridge University Press.

Basov, M, Ia. (1926). *Methods for psychological observations of children.* Moscow: State Publishing House.

Bayes, T. (1763). An essay towards solving a problem in doctrine of chances. *Philosophical Transactions of the Royal Society, 53,* 370-418. Reprinted in *Biometrika, 45,* Parts 3 & 4, 293-315, 1958.

Bekhterev, V. M. (1928). *The board bases of human reflexology.* Moscow: State Publishing House.

Bentham, J. (1962). Introduction to the principles of morals and legislation. In M. Warnock (Ed.), *John Stuart Mill: Utilitarianism, on liberty, essay on Bentham, together with selected writings of Jemery Bentham and John Austin* (pp. 33-77). Cleveland: World Publishing. (Original work published in 1789).

Bergson, H. (1889). *Essai sur les données immédiades de la conscience.* Paris: Felix Alcan. Trans. as: Time and free will: An essay on the immediate data of consciousness. London: Geo. Allen & Unwin, 1910

Bergson, H. (1897). *Matière et mémoire: Essai sur la relation du corp avec l'esprit.* Paris: Felix Alcan. Trans. as: Matter and memory. London: Geo. Allen & Unwin, 1911.

Bergson, H. (1900). *Le rire: Essai sur la signification du comique.* Paris: Felix Alcan. Trans. as: Laughter: An essay on the meaning of the comic. New York: Macmillan, 1911.

Bergson, H. (1907). *L'évolution créatrice.* Paris: Felix Alcan. Trans. as: Creative evolution. New York: Henry Holt, 1911.

Bernard, C. (1960). *Introduction à la médecine expérimentale* [Introduction to the study of experimental medicine]. Paris: Flammarion. (Original work published in 1865).

Binet, A. (1894). *Psychologie des grands calculateurs et des joueurs d'échecs.* Paris: Librairie Hachette et Cie.

Binet, A. (1900). *La suggestibilté.* Paris: Schleicher.

Binet, A. (1903). *L'étude expérimentale de l'intelligence.* Paris: Schleicher.

Binet, A. (1904). La création litteraire: portrait psychologique de M. Paul Hervieu. *Année Psychologique, 10,* 1-62.

Binet, A. (1973). *Les idées modernes sur les enfants (with a preface by Jean Piaget).* Paris: Flammarion. (Original work published in 1909).

Binet, A., & Henri, V. (1894). La mémoire des phrases. *Année Psychologique, 1,* 24-59.

Binet, A., & Henri, V. (1896). La psychologie individuelle. *Année*

Psychologique, 2, 411-465.

Binet, A., & Simon, Th. (1905). Méthodes nouvelles pour le diagnostic du niveau intellectuel des anormaux. *Année Psychologique, 11*, 191-244.

Binet, A., & Simon, Th. (1908). Le développement de l'intelligence chez les enfants. *Année Psychologique, 14*, 1-94.

Binet, A., & Simon, Th. (1909). L'intelligence des imbéciles. *Année Psychologique, 15*, 1-147.

Binet, A., & Simon, Th. (1911). *A method of measuring the development of the intelligence of young children.* Lincoln, Illinois: Courier Compagny.

Binswanger, L. (1922). *Einführung in die probleme der allgemeinen psychologie.* Berlin: Sringer.

Birilev, A. V. (1901). *On touch in the deaf.* Moscow: State Publishing House.

Bleuler, E. (1912-13). Autistic thinking. *American Journal of Psychiatry, 69*, 873-886.

Bloomfield, L. (1927). Literate and illiterate speech. *American Speech, 2*, 432-439.

Bloomfield, L. (1933). *Language.* New York: Holt, Rinehart & Winston.

Blondel, Ch. (1924). *Introduction à la psychologie collective.* Paris: Alcan.

Blondel, Ch. (1924). *La psychanalyse.* Paris: Alcan.

Blondel, Ch. (1926). The morbid mind. *Psyche, 24*, 73-86.

Blondel, Ch. (1926). *La mentalité primitive.* Paris: Stock.

Blondel, Ch. (1928). *The troubled conscience and the insane mind.* London: Kegan Paul.

Blondel, Ch. (1931, February). Vie intérieure et psychologie. *Le Livre.*

Blonsky, P. P. (1911). *Studies in scientific psychology.* Moscow: State Publishing House.

Blonsky, P. P. (1926). *Pedology.* Moscow: State Publishing House.

Boas, F. (1891). Anthropological investigations in schools. *Science, 17*, 351-352.

Boas, F. (1892). The growth of children. *Science, 19*, 351-352.

Boas, F. (1892). The growth of children. *Science, 19)*, 256-257.

Boas, F. (1892). The growth of children-II. *Science, 19*, 281-282.

Boas, F. (1895). The growth of first-born children. *Science, 1* (n.s), 402-404.

Boas, F. (1897). The growth of children. *Science, 5* (n.s), 570-573.

Boas, F. (1898). A precise criterion of species. *Science, 7* (n.s), 860-861.

Boas, F. (1901). The mind of primitive man. *Science, 13* (n.s), 281-

289.

Boas, F. (1966). Intorduction. In F. Boas (Ed.), *Handbook of american indian languages* (pp. 1-79). Lincoln, NE: University of Nebraska Press. (Original work published in 1908).

Boas, F. (1910). Psychological problems in anthropology. *American Journal of Psychology, 21,* 371-384

Boas, F. (1911). *The mind of primitive man.* New York: Macmillan.

Boole, G. (1854). *An investigation of the laws of thought.* New York: Macmillan.

Boring, E. G. (1929). *A history of experimental psychology.* New York: D. Appleton & Company.

Bovet, P. (1925). *Le sentiment religieux et la psychologie de l'enfant.* Neuchâtel and Paris: Delachaux & Niestlé. [The child's religion]. New York: Dutton,1928.

Brett, G. S. (1921). *A history of psychology* (Vol. 2): *Medieval and early modern period.* London: Allen & Unwin.

Bridgman, P. W. (1928). *The logic of modern physics.* New York: Macmillan.

Brunot, F. (1927). *La pensée et la langue.* Paris: Alcan.

Brunschvicg, L. (1927). *Le progrès de la conscience dans la philosophie occidentale.* (2 vols). Paris: Alcan

Bühler, K. (1930). *The mental development of the child.* New York: Harcourt Brace. (Original work published in 1919).

Bühler, K. (1926). *Die krise der psychologie* [The crisis of psychology]. Jena: G. Fisher.

Bukharin, N. (1969). *Historical materialism: A system of sociology.* University of Michigan Press. (Original work published in 1925).

Bukharin, N. (1971). Theory and practice from the standpoint of dialectical materialism. In J. Needham (Ed.), *Science at the crossroads.* London: Cass. (Original work published in 1931).

Burt, C. (1913). *Mental tests.* Edinburgh: Brown.

Carnap, R. (1967). *The logical structure of the world: Pseudoproblems in philosophy.* New York: Macmillan. (Original work published in 1928).

Carnap, R. (1958). *Introduction to symbolic logic and its applications.* New York: Macmillan. (Original work published in 1929).

Cassirer, E. (1923, 1925, 1929). Philosophie der symbolischen formen. Bd. 1: Die sprache. Bd. 2: Das mystische denken. bd. 3: Phanomenologie der erkenntnis. Berlin: B. Cassirer. Also in English as Philosophy of symbolic forms. Vol. 1 & 2, 1957, Vol. 3, 1953. New Haven, CT: Yale University Press.

Cassirer, E. (1923). *Substance, function and Einstein's theory of relativity.* Chicago: Open Court. (Original work published in 1919).

Cattaneo, C. (1864). Dell' antitesi come metodo di psicologia sociale [Antithesis as a method for social psychology]. *Il Politecnico, 20,* 262-270.

Chukovsky, E. (1968). *From two to five.* Berkeley: University of California Press. (Original work published in 1925).

Claparède, E. (1913). *Experimental pedagogy and the psychology of the child.* London: Arnold (Original work published in1913).

Claparède, E. (1931). *L'éducation fonctionnelle.* Neuchâtel: Delachaux & Niestlé

Claparède, E. (1925). The psychology of the child at Geneva and the J. J. Rousseau Institute. *Journal of Genetic Psychology, 32,* 92-104.

Claparède, E. (1933). *La psychologie fonctionnelle. Revue de Philosophie,* (1-2)

Claparède, E. (1934). La genèse de l'hypothèse. *Archives de Psychologie, 24,* 1-154.

Clodd, E. (1905). *The story of the alphabet.* New York: D. Appleton & Company.

Comte, A. (1830-42). *Cours de philosohie positive.* Paris: Bachelier.Trans. into English, The positive philosophy. New York: AMS Press, 1974..

Cramaussel, E. (1909). *Le premier éveil intellectuel de l'enfant.* Paris: Alcan.

Cuvier, G. B. (1817). *Le règne animal distribué d'après son organisation* [The animal kingdom distributed according to its organization]

Darwin, C. (1877). Bibliographical sketch of an infant. *Mind, 2,* 285-294.

Darwin, C. (1958) *The origin of species.* New York: Mentor Book. (Original work published in 1859).

Darwin, C. (1981). *The descent of man and selection in relation to sex.* Princeton, New Jersey: Princeton University Press. (Original work published in 1871).

Darwin, C. (1965). *The expression of the emotions in man and animals.* Chicago: The Univeristy of Chicago Press. (Original work published in 1872).

Delacroix, H. (1924). *Le langage et la pensée.* Paris: Felix Alcan.

Decroly, O. (1932). Etudes de psychogenèse. Belgium: Lamertin.

Descartes, R. (1931). Discourse on method, Vol.1 Edited & Translated by: E. S. Haldane & G. R. Ross. Cambridge: CambridgeUniversity Press. (Original work published in 1637).

Descartes, R. (1931). Rules for the direction of the mind, (Vol. 1). Edited & Translated by: E. S. Haldane & G. R. Ross. Cambridge: Cambridge University Press. (Original work published in 1633).

Descartes, R. (1931). Mediations (Vol. 1). Edited & Translated by: E.

S. Haldane & G. R. Ross. Cambridge: Cambridge University Press. (Original work published in1641).

Descartes, R. (1931). Treatise on the passions of the soul, (Vol. 1) Edited & Translated by: E. S. Haldane & G. R. Ross. Cambridge: Cambridge University Press. (Original work published in 1649).

Descartes, R. (1931). Principles of philosophy, Vol.1 Edited & Translated by: E. S. Haldane & G. R. Ross. Cambridge: Cambridge University Press. (Original work published in 1644).

Descoeudres, A. (1920). Le développement de l'enfant de 2 à 7 ans. Neuchâtel and Paris: Delachaux & Niestlé

De Vries, H. (1905). Species and varieties: Their origin and mutation. Chicago: Chicago University Press.

Dewey, J. (1894). The psychology of infant language. *Psychological Review, 1,* 63-66.

Dewey, J. (1896). The reflex arc concept in psychology. *Psychological Review, 3,* 357-370.

Dewey, J. (1910). How we think. Boston, MA: Heath.

Dewey, J. (1916). The influence of Darwin on philosophy, and other essays in contemporary thought. New York: Holt & Co.

Diderot, D. (1749). Lettre sur les aveugles. Paris: Durand.

Diderot, D. (1751). Lettre sur les sourds et muets. Paris: Durand.

Dostoevsky, F. M. (1964). Crime and punishment. New York: Norton. (Original work published in 1866).

Drummon, H. (1901). The ascent of man. London: Hodder & Stoughton.

Durkheim, E. (1898). Représentations individuelles et représentations collectives. *Revue de Métaphysique et de Morale.*

Durkheim, E. (1949). The division of labor in society. Glencoe: The Free Press. (Original work published in 1893).

Durkheim, E. (1938). The rules of sociological method. New York: Free Press. (Original work published in 1895).

Durkheim, E. (1965). Suicide. New York: Free Press. (Original work published in 1897).

Durkheim, E. (1953). Sociology and philosophy. New York: Free Press. (Original work published in 1898).

Durkheim, E. (1915). The elementary forms of religious life. New York: Macmillan. (Original work published in 1912).

Durkheim, E. (1973). Moral education. New York: Free Press. (Original work published in 1925).

Durkheim, E., Mauss, M. (1963). Primitive classification. Chicago: University of Chicago Press. (Original work published in1902).

Ebbinghaus, H. (1913). Memory: A contribution to experimental psychology. Teachers College, Columbia: Columbia University

Press. (Original work published in 1885).

Elwes, R. H. M. (1901). The chief woorks of Benedict de Spinoza. (Vol. 1 & 2). London: George Bell & Sons.

Engels. F. (1978). Anti-Dühring. Moscow: Progress. (Original work published in 1878).

Engels. F. (1940). The dialectic of nature. New York: International Publishers. (Original work published in 1886).

Engels. F. (1940). Dialectics. In The dialectic of nature (pp.26-34). New York: International Publishers. (Original work published in 1886).

Engels. F. (1940). The part played by labor in the transistion from ape to man. In The dialectic of nature (pp. 279-296). New York: International Publishers. (Original work published in 1886).

Engels. F. (1942). The origin of the family, private property and the state. New York: International Publishers. (Original work published in 1884).

Engels. F. (1970). The part played by labor in the transistion from ape to man. Moscow: Progress Publishers. (Original work published in 1873-1883).

Fauconnet, P. (1920). La responsabilité. Paris: Alcan.

Fechner, G. T. (1860). Elements of psychophysics. Leipzig: Breitkopf & Härtel

Ferenczi, S. (1916). Stages in the development of sense of reality. In Sex in psychoanalysis (pp.181-203). Boston: Gorham Press. (Original work published in 1913).

Feuerbach, Anselm von. (1834). Caspar Hauser: An account of an individual kept in a dungeon, separated from all communication with the world, from early childhood to about the age of seventeen. London: Simpkin & Marshall. (Original work published in 1832).

Feuerbach, L. (1843). Principles of the philosophy of the future. New York: Bobbs-Merrill.

Fisher, R. (1925). Statistical methods for research workers. Edinburgh & London: Olivier and Boyd.

Fouillée, A. (1890). L'évolutionnisme des idées-force. Paris: Alcan.

Fouillée, A. (1893). La psychologie des idées-force. 2 vols. Paris: Alcan.

Fourier, C. (1967). Théorie des quatre mouvements et des destinées générales. Paris: Pauvert, (Original work published in 1808)

Freud, S. (1954). Project for a scientific psychology. In M. Bonaparte, A. Freud, & E. Kris (Eds.), The origins of psycho-analysis: Letters to wilhelm Fliess, drafts and notes: 1887-1902 (pp.347-445). New York: Basic Books. (Original work published in 1895).

Freud, S. (1953). The interpretation of dreams (Vol. 5). Standard edition. London: Hogarth Press. (Original work published in 1910).

Freud, S. (1960). The psychopathology of everyday life (Vol. 6). Standard edition. London: Hogarth Press. (Original work published in 1901).

Freud, S. (1957). Leonardo da Vinci and a memory of his childhood (Vol. 11). Standard edition. London: Hogarth Press. (Original work published in 1910).

Freud, S. (1957). The unconscious. Standard edition Vol. 14. London: Hogarth Press. (Original work published in 1915).

Freud, S. (1927). The future of an illusion. London: Hogarth Press.

Freud, S. (1930). Civilization and its discontents. London: Hogarth Press.

Galton, F. (1883). Inquiries into human faculty and its development. London: Macmillan

Gesell, A. (1929). Infancy and human growth. New York: Macmillan.

Guillaume, P. (1927). L'imitation chez l'enfant. Paris: Felix Alcan. Also in English: Imitation in children. Chicago: Chicago University Press, 1971.

Guillaume, P. (1927). La psychologie de la forme. Paris: Flammarion.

Guillaume, P., & Meyerson, I. (1930). Recherches sur l'usage de l'instrument chez les singes: 1-Le problème du détour. *Journal de Psychologie, 27*, 177-236.

Guillaume, P., & Meyerson, I. (1931). Recherches sur l'usage de l'instrument chez les singes: 2-L'intermédiaire lié à l'objet. *Journal de Psychologie, 28*, 481-555.

Halbwachs, M. (1952). Les cadres sociaux de la mémoire. Paris: Presses Universitaires de France. (Original work published in1925).

Hall, G. S. (1908). Adolescence (Vol.1 & 2). New York: Appleton.

Hegel., G. W. F. (1910). The phenomenology of mind. London: George Allen & Unwin. (Original work published in 1807).

Hegel., G. W. F. (1910). Freedom of self-consciousness. In The phenomenology of mind (pp.241-267. London: George Allen & Unwin. (Original work published in1807).

Hegel., G. W. F. (1912). Science of logic. London: George Allen & Unwin. (Original work published in 1812).

Hegel., G. W. F. (1967). Philosophy of the right. London: Oxford University Press. (Original work published in 1821).

Hegel., G. W. F. (1967). Philosophy of history. New York: Dover. (Original work published in 1821).

Hegel., G. W. F. (1915). The encyclopeadia of the pholosophical science. London: George Allen & Unwin. (Original work published in1817).

Heidegger, M. (1962). Being and time. New York: Harper & Row.

(Original work published in 1927).

Helmholtz, H, V. (1938). On thought in medicine (Das denken in der medizin). Baltmore: John Hopkins Press. (Original work published in 1878).

Hetzer, H., & Wolfe, K. (1928). Baby tests. *Zeitschrift Für Psychologie, 107*), 62-104

Hubert, R. (1928). La psychosociologie et le problème de la conscience. *Revue Philosophique,* 1.

Hume, D. (1964). A treatise on human nature. Aalen, Germany: Scientia Verlag. (Original work published 1739)

Hume, D. (1964). An enquiry concerning human understanding. La Salle: Open Court. (Original work published 1777)

Isaacs, S. (1930). Intellectual growth of young children. London: Routledge.

Jakobson, R. (1929). Remarques sur l'évolution phonologique du Russe. *Travaux du Circle Linguistique de Prague, 2.*

Jakobson, R. (1931). Prinzipien der historischen phonologie. *Travaux du Circle Linguistique de Prague, 4.*

James, W. (1983). Principles of psychology. Cambridge, MA: Harvard University Press. (Original work published in 1890).

James, W. (1892). Thought before language: A deaf-mute's recollections. *Philosophical Review, 1,* 613-624.

James, W. (1906). The varieties of religious experience. London: Longman.

Janet, P. (1925). Psychological healing. New York: Macmillan.

Janet, P. (1926-27). La pensée intérieure et ses troubles. Course given at the Collège de France.

Janet, P. (1889). L'automatisme psychologique. Paris: Alcan.

Janet, P. (1926). De l'angoisse à l'extase. Vol.1. Paris: Felix Alcan.

Janet, P. (1928). De l'angoisse à l'extase. Vol.2. Paris: Felix Alcan.

Janet, P. (1928). L'évolution de la mémoire et de la notion du temps. Paris: A. Chahine.

Janet, P. (1929). L'évolution psychologique de la personnalité. Paris: A. Chahine.

Johnson, E., & Charles, C. J. (1931). A note on the development of the thought forms of children as described by Piaget. *Journal of Abnormal and Social Psychology,* (26), 338-339.

Kant. I. (1964). Critique of pure reason. New York: St. Martin's Press. (Original work published in 1781).

Kant. I. (1974). Logic. Indianapolis: Bobbs-Merrill. (Original work published in 1800).

Koffka, K. (1963). The growth of the mind. Totawa, New Jersey: Littefield, Adams & Co. (Original work published in 1924).

Köhler, W. (1956). The mentality of apes. New York: Vintage. (Original work published in 1921).

Köhler, W. (1959). Gestalt psychology. New York: Mentor. (Original work published in 1929).

Kostyleff, N. (1911). La crise de la psychologie experimentale. Paris: Alcan.

Kretschmer, E. (1925). Physique and character. London: Paul Trench Traubner.

Kretschmer, E. (1926). Hysteria. New York: NMDP.

Laguna De, G. A. (1927). Speech: Its function and development. New Haven.

Lalande, A. (1925). Raison constituante et raison constituée. *Revue des Cours et des Conférences, (9 & 10)*.

Lalande, A. (1926). Vocabulaire technique et critique de la philosohie. Paris: Alcan.

Lalande, A. (1927). Qu'est-ce que la vérité? *Revue de Théologie et de Philosophie, 1-27*.

Lamarck, J. B. (1963). Zoological philosophy. New York: Hafner. (Original work published in 1802).

Landriew, M. (1908). Lamarck, le fondateur du transformisme. *Mémoires de la Société Zoologique de France, 21*.

Larsson, H. (1919). La logique de la poésie. Paris: Leroux.

Lashley, C. S. (1929). Brain mechanisms and intelligence. Chicago: Chicago University Press.

Lemaître, A. (1905). Observations sur le langage intérieur des enfants. *Archives de Psychologie, (4)*, 1-43.

Lenin, V. I. (1962). Materialism and empirico-criticism. Collected works, Vol. 14. London: Lawrence & Wishart. (Original work published in 1909).

Lenin, V. I. (1962). Philosophical notebooks. Collected works, Vol.38. London: Lawrence & Wishart.

Leroy, O. (1927). La raison primitive. Paris: Geuthner.

Lévy-Bruhl, L. (1923). Primitive mentality. New York: Macmillan. (Original work published in 1922).

Lévy-Bruhl, L. (1923). How native think. London: George Allen & Unwin LTD. (Original work published in 1910).

Lévy-Bruhl, L. (1931). La mentalité primitive (The Herbert Spencer lecture). Paris: Alcan

Lewin, K. (1926). Vorsatz, wille und bedürfnis. Berlin: Springer.

Lewin, K. (1931). The conflict between Aristotelian and Galilean modes of thought in contemporary psychology. *Journal of General Psychology, 5*, 141-177.

Locke, J. (1690). An essay concerning human understanding. London:

Dent.

Lowie, R. H. (1921). Primitive society. New York: Macmillan.

Lowie, R. H. (1925). Primitive religion. New York: Macmillan.

Lukàcs, G. (1911). History and development of modern drama (2 vols.). Budapest: Franklin.

Lukàcs, G. (1971). class and consciousness. In History and class consciousness: Studies in Marxist dialectics (pp.46-82). Cambridge, MA: Cambridge University Press. (Original work published in 1920).

Lukàcs, G. (1971). What is orthodox marxism. In History and class consciousness: Studies in Marxist dialectics (pp. 1-26). Cambridge, MA: Cambridge University Press. (Original work published in 1919).

Lukàcs, G. (1971). The changing function of historical materialism. In History and class consciousness: Studies in Marxist dialectics (pp. 223-255). Cambridge, MA: Cambridge University Press. (Lecture given at the inauguration of the Institute for Research into Historical Materialism in Budapest, June 1919).

Lukàcs, G. (1971). History and class consciousness: Studies in Marxist dialectics. Cambridge, MA: Cambridge University Press. (Original work published in 1923).

Lukàcs, G. (1971). Lenin: A study on the unity of his thought. Cambridge, MA: Cambridge University Press. (Original work published in 1924).

Lukàcs, G. (1966). Technology and social relations: Review of Bukharin. *New Left Review*(39, Sept/Oct.), 27-34. (Original work published in 1925).

Luxemburg, R. (1968). The accumulation of capital. New York: Monthly Review. (from Russian revolution of 1905 emerged   her theory of mass action).

Luxemburg, R. (1972). The accumulation of capital: An anti-critique. New York: Monthly Review.

Malinowski, B. (1922). Argonauts of the Western pacific. London.

Mandelstam, O. (1979). On the nature of the word. In The critical prose of Osip Mandelstam. Ann Arbor, MI: Ardis Press. (Original work published in 1922).

Marx, K. (1964). Economic and philosophical manuscripts 1844. New York: International Publishers. (Original work published in 1844).

Marx, K. (1967). Capital: A critique of political economy. Vol.1. New York: International Publishers. (Original work published in 1867).

Marx, K. (1904). A contribution to the critique of political economy. New York: Charles H. Kerr & Company. (Original work published in 1859).

Marx, K., & Engels, F. (1973). The German ideology. New York: International Publishers. (Original work published in 1847).

Marx, K., & Engels, F. (1968). The communist manifesto. Baltimore: Pelican-Penguin. (Original work published in 1848).

Marx, K., & Engels, F. (1975). Selected correspondence. Moscow: Progress Publishers.

Matejka, L., & Pomorska, K. (Eds.). (1978). Readings in Russian poetics: Formalist and structuralist view. Ann Arbor, MI: Ardis Press. (Original work published in 1914).

McKendrick, J. G. (1899). Hermann Ludwig Ferdinand von Helmholtz. London: Fisher Unwin.

Mead, G. H. (1903). The definition of the psychical. *Decennial Publications of the University of Chicago, 3* (Serie 1), 77-112.

Mead, G. H. (1910). What social objects must psychology presuppose? *Journal of Psychology, 7)*, 174-180.

Mead, G. H. (1910). Social consciousness and the consciousness of meaning. *Psychological Bulletin, 7*, 397-405.

Mead, G. H. (1912). The mechanism of social consciousness. *Journal of Philosophy, 9*, 401-406.

Mead, G. H. (1913). The social self. *Journal of Philosophy, 10*, 374-380.

Mead, G. H. (1925). The genesis of the self and social control. *International Journal of Ethics, 35*, 251-277.

Mead, G. H. (1974). Mind, self and society. Chicago: Chicago University Press. (Original work published in 1934).

Medvedev, P. M., & Bakhtin, M. (1985). The formal method in literary scholarship. Cambridge, MA: Harvard University Press. (Original work published in 1928).

Meillet, A. (1905/6). Comment les mots changent de sens. *Année Sociologique, 10*, 1-38.

Meillet, A. (1921). Linguistique historique et linguistique générale. Paris: La Société Liguistique de Paris.

Meyerson, E. (1931). Le cheminement de la pensée. Paris: Alcan.

Mill, J. S. (1843). Psychology and ethology. In W. Dennis (Ed.), Readings in the history of psychology (pp. 169-177). Ny: Appleton, 1948.

Mill, J. S. (1872). A system of logic ratiocinative and inductive. London: Longmans, Green.

Mill, J. S. (1962). Bentham. In M. Warnock (Ed.), John Stuart Mill: Utilitarianism, on liberty, essay on Bentham, together with selected writings of Jemery Bentham and John Austin (pp. 78-125). Cleveland: World Publishing. (Original work published in 1838).

Mill, J. S. (1962). On liberty. In M. Warnock (Ed.), John Stuart Mill: Utilitarianism, on liberty, essay on Bentham, together with selected writings of Jemery Bentham and John Austin (pp. 126-250). Cleveland: World Publishing. (Original work published in 1859).

Mill, J. S. (1962). Utilitarianism. In M. Warnock (Ed.), John Stuart Mill: Utilitarianism, on liberty, essay on Bentham, together with selected writings of Jemery Bentham and John Austin (pp.251-321). Cleveland: World Publishing. (Original work published in 1863).

Montessori, M. (1913). Pedagogical anthropology. New York: F. A. Stokes Company.

Morgan, C. L. (1896). On modification and variation. *Science, 4,* 733-740.

Müller, F. M. (1861). Lectures on the science of language. London: Longmans Green.

Müller, F. M. (1881). Selected essays on language, mythology and religion. (2 Vol.). London: Longmans Green.

Münsterberg, H. (1922). Grundzüge der psychotechink. Leipzig: Barth.

Noiré, L. (1917). The origin and the philosophy of language. Chicago: The Open Court Publishing Company.

Ogden, C. H., & Richards, I. A. (1923). The meaning of meaning. London: Kegan Paul.

Osborn, H. F. (1896). Ontogenetic and phylogenetic variation. *Science, 4,* 786-789.

Paulhan, F. (1928). Qu'est-ce que le sens des mots? *Journal de Psychologie, 25,* 289-329.

Paulhan, F. (1929). La double fonction du langage. Paris: Alcan.

Pavlov, I. P. (1928). Lectures on conditioned reflexes. Vol.1 & 2. London: Lawrence & Wishart.

Pearson, K. (1957). The grammar of science. New York: Meridian Library. (Original work published in 1892).

Piaget, J. (1915). La mission de l'idée. Lausanne: La Concorde.

Piaget, J. (1918). Recherche. Lausanne: La Concorde.

Piaget, J. (1920). La psychanalyse dans ses rapports avec la psychologie de l'enfant. *Bulletin de la Société d'Alfred Binet, 20,* 18-34.

Piaget, J. (1921). Une forme verbale de la comparaison chez l'enfant. *Archives de Psychologie, 18,* 141-172.

Piaget, J. (1971). The language and thought of the child. London: Routledge & Kegan Paul. (Original work published in 1923).

Piaget, J. (1923). La pensée symbolique et la pensée de l'enfant. *Archives de Psychologie, 18,* 273-304.

Piaget, J. (1969). Judgment and reasoning in the child. London: Routledge & Kegan Paul. (Original work published in 1924).

Piaget, J. (1924). Les traits principaux de la logique de l'enfant. *Journal de Psychologie*, (21), 48-101.

Piaget, J. (1924). L'expérience humaine et la causalité physique de L. Brunschwicg. *Journal de Psychologie, 21*, 586-607.

Piaget, J. (1925). De quelques formes primitive de causalité chez l'enfant. *Année Psychologique, 26*, 31-71.

Piaget, J. (1925). Psychologie et critique de la connaissance. *Archives de Psychologie, 19*, 193-210.

Piaget, J. (1925). Le réalisme nominal chez l'enfant. *Revue Philosophique de la France et de l'Etranger,* (99), 189-234.

Piaget, J. (1967). The child's conception of the world. London: Routledge & Kegan Paul. (Original work published in 1926).

Piaget, J. (1970). The child's conception of physiscal causality. London: Routledge & Kegan Paul. (Original work published in 1927).

Piaget, J. (1927). La première année de l'enfant. *British Journal of Psychology, 18*, 97-120.

Piaget, J. (1928). Logique génétique et sociologie [Genetic logic and sociology [*Revue Philosophique de la France et de l'Etranger, 105*, 167-205.

Piaget, J. (1928). La causalité chez l'enfant. *British Journal of Psychology, 18)*, 276-301.

Piaget, J. (1928). Psycho-pédagogie et mentalité primitive. *Journal de Psychologie, 25*, 31-60.

Piaget, J. (1928). Les trois systèmes de la penée de l'enfant. *Bulletin de la Société Française de Philosophie, 28*, 97-141.

Piaget, J. (1929). Les deux directions de la pensée scientifique. *Archives des Sciences Physiques et Naturelles, 11*, 145-162.

Piaget, J. (1929). Le parallélisme ente la logique et la morale chez l'enfant. *Proceedings of the 9th International Congress of Psychology,* (pp.3 39-340). New Jersey, Princeton: The Psychologi-cal Review Company.

Piaget, J. (1930). Moral realities in child life. *New Era in Home & School, 11)*, 112-114.

Piaget, J. (1931). Children's philosophies. In C. Murchison (Ed.), Handbook of child psychology (pp.377-391). Ma: Clark University Press.

Piaget, J. (1931). Retrospective and prospective analysis in child psychology. *British Journal of Educational Psychology*, 130-139.

Piaget, J. (1931). Le développement intellectuel chez les jeunes enfants. *Mind*, 137-160.

Piaget, J. (1962). The moral judgment of the child. London: Routledge & Kegan Paul. (Original work published in 1932).

Piaget, J. (1932). Social evolution and the new education. *Education Tomorrow*(4. London: New Education Fellowship. Also in T. Rawson (Ed.), Sixth World Conference of New Education Followship: Full Report. London: New Education Followship, 1933.

Piaget, J. (1933). Psychologie de l'enfant et l'enseignement de l'histoire. *Bulletin Trimestriel de la Conférence Internationale pour l'enseignement de l'Histoire, 2,* 8-13.

Piaget, J. (1933). L'individualité en histoire: L'individu et la formation de la raison (Individuality in history: The individual and the formation of reason). In L'individualité. 3eme Semaine Internationale de Synthèse. Paris: Alcan. Reprinted in *Cahiers Vilfredo Pareto, 1976,14,* (38-39), 81-123.

Piéron, H. (1948). Psychologie expérimentale. Paris: Armand Colin. (Original work published in 1927).

Plato. (1955). Apologia Sokratous. London: Penguin Classics Series. (Original work published in 399 BC).

Plato. (1960). Great dialogues of Plato. New York: New American Library.

Plekhanov, G. V. (1934). Essays in the history of materialism. London: Lane (Original work published in 1896).

Poincaré, H. (1952). Science and hypothesis. New York: Dover. (Original work published in 1903).

Poincaré, H. (1908). Science and method. London: Nelson.

Politzer, G. (1928). Critique des fondements de la psychologie [Critique of the foundations of psychology]. Paris: Editions Sociales.

Politzer, G. (1929). Le Bergsonisme, une mystification philosophique. Paris: Editions Sociales.

Politzer, G. (1929). Psychologie mythologique et psychologie scientifi-que. *Revue de Psychologie Concrète, 1.*

Politzer, G. (1929). Où va la psychologie concrète? *Revue de Psychologie Concrète, 2.*

Politzer, G. (1929). Note sur la psychologie individuelle *Revue de Psychologie Concrète, 2.*

Preyer, W. (1882). The mind of the child. New York: Appleton.

Quetelet, L. A. J. (1835). Sur l'homme et le développement de ses facultés, ou essai de physique sociale [Man and the developement of his faculties]. Paris: Bachelier.

Radcliffe-Brown, A. R. (1965). Structure and function in primitive society. New York: Free Pree. (Original work published in 1929).

Ratner, J. (1927). The philosophy of Spinoza: Selected from his chief works. New York: The Modern Library

Ribot, T. (1888). La psychologie de l'attention. Paris: Filex Alcan.

Ribot, T. (1926). Essai sur l'imagination créatrice. Paris: Filex Alcan.

Rivers, W. H. R. (1901). Primitive color vision.
Popular Science Monthly, 59, 44-58.

Rivers, W. H. R. (1905). Observations on the sense of the Todas. *British Journal of Psychology, 1,* 321-396.

Rivers, W. H. R. (1926). Psychology and ethnolohy. New York: Harcourt, Brace.

Romanes, G. J. (1884). Mental evolution in animals. New York: Appleton.

Romanes, G. J. (1889). Mental evolution in man. New York: Appleton.

Rousseau, J. J. (1762). Emile ou l'éducation. La Haye: Néaulme.

Rousseau, J. J. (1968). Social contract. Baltimore: Pelican-Penguin. (Original work published in 1762).

Rousseau, J. J. (1920). A discourse upon the origin and foundation of the inequality among mankind. New York: Appleton. (Original work published in 1755).

Russell, B. (1938). Principles of mathematics. New York: Norton. (Original work published in 1903).

Russell, B. (1900). A critical exposition of the philosophy of Leibniz. London: Macmillan.

Russell, B. (1910). Philosophical essays. London: Oxford University Press.

Russell, B. (1912). Problems of philosophy. London: Oxford University Press.

Russell, B. (1914). Our knowledge of the external world as a field for scientific method in philosophy. London: Allen & Unwin.

Russell, B. (1916). Principles of social reconstruction. London: Allen & Unwin.

Russell, B. (1918). Road to freedom. London: Allen & Unwin.

Russell, B. (1920). The practice and theory of Bolchevism. London: Allen & Unwin.

Russell, B. (1961). The materialistic theory of history. In R. E. Egner & L. E. Denonn (Eds.), The basic writings of Bertrand Russell 1903-1959 (pp. 528-531). New York: Simon & Schuster. (Original work published in 1920).

Russell, B. (1921). The analysis of mind. London: Allen & Unwin.

Russell, B. (1925). Materialism, past and present: Introduction to A history of materialism by F. A. Lange. London: Lund Humphries.

Russell, B. (1926). On education. London: Allen & Unwin.

Russell, B. (1927). An outline of philosophy. London: Allen & Unwin.

Russell, B. (1929). Marriage and morals. London: Allen & Unwin

Russell, B. (1930). The conquest of happiness. London: Allen & Unwin.

Russell, B. (1931). The scientific outlook. London: Allen & Unwin.

Russell, B. (1932). Education and the social order. London: Allen & Unwin.

Russell, B. (1961). Dialectical materialism. In R. E. Egner & L. E. Denonn (Eds.), The basic writings of Bertrand Russell 1903-1959 (pp.500-510). New York: Simon & Schuster. (Original work published in 1934).

Russell, B. (1961). The theory of superplus value. In R. E. Egner & L. E. Denonn (Eds.), The basic writings of Bertrand Russell 1903-1959 (pp.511-518). New York: Simon & Schuster. (Original work published in 1934).

Russell, B., & Whitehead, A. N. (1913). Principia Mathematica. London: Cambridge University Press.

Sapir, E. (1921). Language. New York: Harcourt Brace & Co.

Sapir, E. (1970). Culture, language and personality. Los Angeles: University of California Press. (Original work published in 1933).

Saussure, F. de. (1959). Course in general linguistics. New York: McGraw Hill. (Original work published in 1916).

Servaas Van Rooijen, A. J. (1888). Inventaire des livres formant la bibliothèque de Benedict de Spinoza. Netherlands: The Hague.

Shklvosky, V. (1978). The resurrection of the word. In L. Matejka & K. Pomorska (Eds.), Readings in Russian poetics: Formalist and structuralist view. Ann Arbor, MI: Ardis Press. (Original work published in 1914).

Sorch, A. (1924). The primitive archaic forms of inner experience and thought in schizophrenia. New York: NMD Press.

Spearman, C. (1923). The nature of " intelligence " and the principle of cognition. London: Macmillan.

Spearman, C. (1927). The ability of man. London: Macmillan.

Spencer, H. (1897). A system of synthetic philosophy. Volume 2: The principles of psychology. New York: Appleton. (Original work published in 1872).

Spielrein, S. (1920). *On the origin and development of speech. International Journal of Psychoanalysis, 1.*

Spielrein, S. (1923). Quelques analogies entre le pensée de l'enfant, celle de l'aphasique et la pensée subconsciente. *Archives de Psychologie, 18,* 305-322.

Spinoza, B. de. (1910). Ethics of Spinoza. New York: E. P. Dutton & Co. Inc.

Spinoza, B. de. (1909). Die ethik. Leipzig: Alfred Kront.

Spinoza, B. de. (1955). On the improvement of the understanding. The ethics. Correspondence. Mineola: Dover Publications. (Original work published in 1677).

Spinoza, B. de. (1930). Selections from the philosophy of Spinoza. Edited by J. Wild. New York: Scribner.

Stern, E. (1920). Problems of cultural psychology. *Zeitschrift für die Gesamte Staatwissenschft, 75,* 267-301. *Quarterly Newsletter of the Laboratory of Comparative Human Cognition., 12,* 12-23 (English translation).

Stern, W. (1924). Psychology of early childhood up to the sixth year of age. New York: Holt, Rinehart & Winston. (Original work published in 1914).

Stern,W. (1914). The psychological methods of testing intelligence. *Educational Psychology Monographs,* (13).

Student [W. S. Gosset]. (1908). The probable error of a mean. *Biometrika, 6,* 1-25.

Sully, J. (1896). Studies of childhood. New York: Appleton.

Sully, J. (1896). Review of "Mental development in the child and the race: Methods and processes". *Mind, 5,* 97-103.

Tarde, G. (1890). Les lois de l'imitation: Etude sociologique. Paris: Alcan. Also in English: The laws of imitation. New York: Holt, 1903.

Tarde, G. (1898). Etudes de psychologie sociale. Paris: Giare & Briere.

Terman, L. M. (1916). The measurement of intelligence. Boston: Houghton Mifflin.

Thorndike, E. L. (1898). Animal intelligence. New York: Macmillan.

Thurnwald, R. (1922). Psychologie des primitiven Menschen. In G. Kafka (Ed.), Handbuch der vergleichenden psychologie (pp.147-320). Brand 1, Munchen: Verlag von Ernest Reinhardt.

Thurnwald, R. (1929). Zauber, allgemein. *Reallexicon der Vorgeschichte.*

Thurnwald, R. (1932). Economics in primitive communities Oxford: Oxford University Press.

Titchner, E. B. (1896). An outline of psychology. New York: Macmillan.

Titchner, E. B. (1909). Lectures on the experimental psychology of the thought processes. New York: Macmillan.

Thurstone, L. L. (1924). The nature of intelligence. London: Kegan Paul.

Trotsky, L. (1970). Collected works. Moscow: Progress

Trotsky, L. (1960). The culture of the future. Moscow: Progress

Trotsky, L. (1923). Literature and revolution. Moscow: Progress

Tylor, E. B. (1870). Research into the early history of mankind. New York: Holt. (Original work published in 1865).

Tylor, E. B. (1891). Primitive culture. New York: Holt. (Original work published in 1871).

Van Der Leeuw, G. (1928). La structure de la mentalité primitive. *Revue d'Histoire et de Philosophie Religieuse.*

Voloshinov, V. N. (1976). Freudianism: A Marxist critique. New York: Academic. (Original work published in 1927).

Voltaire, F. M. A. de. (1961). Lettres philosophiques. In Mélanges. Paris: Payot. (Original work published in 1734).

Voltaire, F. M. A. de. (1970). The complete works of Voltaire. Geneva: Institut de Muse Voltaire. (Original work published in 1741).

Wagner, M. (1882). De la formation des espèces par la ségrégation. Paris: O. Dion.

Wallon, H. (1920). La conscience et la vie subconsciente. *Journal de Psychologie,* (2), 97-120.

Wallon, H. (1921). La conscience et la conscience du moi. *Journal de Psychologie,* (1), 51-64.

Wallon, H. (1921). Le problème biologique de la conscience. *Revue Philosophique,* 1, 161-185.

Wallon, H. (1923). La capacité de l'attention chez l'enfant. *Bulletin de la Société Française de Pédagogie, 12,* 361-367.

Wallon, H. (1925). Stades et troubles du développement psycho-moteur et mental chez l'enfant. Paris: Alcan.

Wallon, H. (1925). L'enfant turbulent: Recueil d'observations. Paris: Alcan.

Wallon, H. (1926). Psychologie pathologique. Paris: Alcan.

Wallon, H. (1928). L'autisme du malade et l'égocentrisme enfantin: Intervention aux discussions de la thèse de Piaget. *Bulletin de la Société Française de Philosophie, 28,* 131-136.

Wallon, H. (1928). La mentalité primitive et celle de l'enfant. *Revue Philosophique,* 7-8), 82-105.

Wallon, H. (1930). Les origines du caractères chez l'enfant:
1-L'étude du caractère. 15 January, 208-218.
2-Le comportement fonctionnel du nourrisson. 15 February, 397-412.
3-Le comportement émotionnel. 28 February, 529-546.
4-Le comportement émotionnel. 30 March, 702-712.
5-La place de l'émotion dans le comportement humain. 30 April, 124-139.
6-Les sources et les formes de l'émotion chez l'enfant. 30 May, 340-352.
7-Les sources et les formes de l'émotion chez l'enfant. 30 June, 549-560. *Revue des Cours et des Conférences.*

Wallon, H. (1929). Analyse du livre de G. Politzer: Critique des fondements de la psychologie.
Revue Philosophique, 6, 459.

Wallon, H. (1930). Principes de psychologie appliquée. Paris: Armand Colin.

Wallon, H. (1931). Science de la nature et science de l'homme: La psychologie. *Revue de Synthèse,* Oct.

Wallon, H. (1932). Sur la septième conférence internationale de psychotechinque (Moscow: Sept. 1931). *Revue de Psychologie Appliquée de l'Est,* Jan, 3-12.

Wallon, H. (1932). De l'expérience concrète à la notion de causalité et à la représentation-symbole.
Journal de Psychologie, (1-2), 112-145.

Wallon, H. (1932). La conscience de soi, ses degrés et ses mécanismes, de 3 mois à 3 ans. *Journal de Psychologie, 29*(9-10), 744-785.

Wallon, H. (1933). L'enfant et le milieu social.
Pour l'Ere Nouvelle, 91), 237-241.

Wallon, H. (1934). Les origines du caractère chez l'enfant. Paris: Bovin-
Pressses Universitaires de France.

Weber, M. (1958). The ethic protestant and the spirit of capitalism. New York: Charles Scibner's Sons. (Original work published in 1905).

Werner, H. (1900). Einführung in die entwicklungspychologie [Introduction to developmental psychology]. Leipzig, Germany: Engelmann.

Wener, H. (1940). Comparative psychology of mental development. New York: International Universities Press. (Original work published in 1926).

Weule, K. (1921). Die kultur der kulturlosen: ein blick in die anfange menschlicher geistesbetatigung. Stuttgart: Kosmos.

Wittgenstein, L. (1913, sept.). Notes on logic. Reprinted in Notebooks 1914-1916. Oxford: Basil Blackwell, 1961.

Wittgenstein, L. (1922). Tractatus logico-philosophicus. London: Kegan Paul. (Original work published in 1921).

Wittgenstein, L. (1929). Some remarks on logical form.
Proceedings of the Aristotelian Society, Suppl., (9), 162-171.

Woodworth, R. S. (1918). Dynamic psychology. New York: Columbia University Press.

Wundt, W. (1880). Logik. Stuttgart: Enke.

Wundt, W. (1910). Principles of physiological psychology. New York: Macmillan. (Original work published in 1902).

Wundt, W. (1910). Elements of folk psychology. New York: Macmillan. (Original work published in 1906).

Yerkes, R. M. (1916). The mental life of monkeys and apes. *Behavioral Monographs, 3*(1).

Yerkes, R. M. (1917). The Binet version versus the point scale method of measuring intelligence. *Journal of Applied of Psychology, 1*, 111-122.

Yerkes, R. M. (1917). How may we discover the children who need special care. *Mental Hygiene, 1*, 252-259.

Yerkes, R. M., & Yerkes, D. (1928). Concerning memory in the chimpanzee. *Journal of Comparative Psychology, 8*, 237-271.

Yerkes, R. M., & Learned, B. W. (1925). Chimpanzee intelligence and its vocal expression. Baltimore: Williams & Wilkins.

Subject index

Act, 138, 139.

Action, 14, 18, 19, 20, 27, 30, 34.

Activity, 4, 13, 16, 18, 21, 23, 24, 34, 37, 47, 72, 77, 84, 95, 96, 114, 122, 129, 144, 150, 162, 177, 178, 179.

Assisted performance, (see Zone of proximal development), 97
> of adults, 24, 32, 36, 63, 69.
>
> of children, 1, 5, 7, 14, 19, 30, 37, 39, 148, 154.
>
> frequency of peer assistance, 37, 51, 53, 58, 87, 106, 107, 140, 145, 160.
>
> in instructional conversation, 70, 93, 98, 112.
>
> reciprocities, 36.
>
> teachers, 161.
>
> varieties of peer assistance, 25, 46, 125, 139.

Auxiliary devices (tools)
> ape experiment, 10.
>
> creation of tools, 10, 164, 165.
>
> cultural tools, 150, 164, 165.
>
> functional use of objects, 164, 165.
>
> sign types, 10, 164, 165.
>
> stick, 10
>
> words, 39, 112, 130.
>
> writing, 23, 37, 118.

Child speech,
> creation of new words, 2, 5, 16.
>
> accumulation of words, 23, 25.
>
> acquisition of words, 37, 39, 41.
>
> concretization, 102, 112.
>
> effect on memory, 113, 118.
>
> egocentrism,30, 46, 48, 78, 180.
>
> emotional speech, 3, 6, 12, 42, 84, 92, 27, 162.

Co-construction, (see also Collaboration; Shared Knowledge), 109.

Cognitive development, 26, 38, 46, 49, 67, 75, 88, 94, 107, 110, 125, 131, 157, 163.

Cognitive processes, 92, 143, 154, 173.

Cognitive structuring, 143.